Beyond the
Bonus March
and GI Bill

Beyond the Bonus March and GI Bill

How Veteran Politics Shaped the New Deal Era

Stephen R. Ortiz

NEW YORK UNIVERSITY PRESS

New York and London

NEW YORK UNIVERSITY PRESS
New York and London
www.nyupress.org

Library of Congress Cataloging-in-Publication Data

Ortiz, Stephen R.
Beyond the Bonus March and GI Bill : how veteran politics shaped
the New Deal era / Stephen R. Ortiz.
p. cm.
Includes bibliographical references and index.
ISBN-13: 978-0-8147-6213-4 (cloth : alk. paper)
ISBN-10: 0-8147-6213-1 (cloth : alk. paper)
1. Veterans—United States—Political activity—History—20th century.
2. World War, 1914–1918—Veterans—United States. 3. Veterans—
Government pollicy—United States—History—20th century.
4. Veterans—United States—Economic conditions—20th century.
5. Veterans—Education—United States—History—20th century.
6. Bonus Expeditionary Forces. 7. Protest movements—Washington
(D.C.)—History—20th century. 8. New Deal, 1933–1939. 9. United
States—Politics and government—1918–1933. 10. United States—
Politics and government—1933–1945. I. Title. II. Title: Beyond the
Bonus March and G.I. Bill.
UB357.O78   2009
362.86'561097309043—dc22   2009023997

New York University Press books are printed on acid-free paper,
and their binding materials are chosen for strength and durability.
We strive to use environmentally responsible suppliers and materials
to the greatest extent possible in publishing our books.

Manufactured in the United States of America
10 9 8 7 6 5 4 3 2 1

For Renée and Bianca

Contents

Acknowledgments

As an avid, some might say obsessive, reader of Acknowledgments pages, I am daunted by the lyricism so many historians display in recognizing their debts both intellectual and personal. The lack of poetry found here, however, in no way diminishes the genuine gratitude I feel toward the people and institutions that have helped this book come to fruition.

This book is the culmination of work begun under the keen guidance of Jeff Adler, Bob Zieger, Bob McMahon, and Louise Newman. Jeff Adler offered unusually astute editorial and substantive advice, even though the topic and the approach of this project moved in directions that neither of us could have possibly guessed when I began it. Throughout, he never doubted the significance of my work or that it would be completed. For that, I am forever appreciative. Bob McMahon and Louise Newman have been constant sources of support. Bob Zieger brought his encyclopedic knowledge of the 1930s to his reading of drafts of this project at all stages. While factual errors and sloppy argumentation may remain in this book, Bob has stopped most of it in its tracks. (Of course, any such errors or sloppiness left over are my responsibility, and mine alone.) Always a cheerful supporter, Bob also has been a great mentor to me as a writer. His editorial pen is tough but nearly always right. The book is infinitely better thanks to Bob. I am proud to count him as a friend and mentor.

A wonderful group of scholars interested in veterans' issues has left its imprint on this study. Jennifer Keene played an enormous role in the development of the project. She offered to read drafts at every stage and gave very valuable suggestions along the way. What started as a "cold" e-mail to the person who wrote *Doughboys, the Great War, and the Remaking of America* has become a great personal and intellectual friendship. Her generosity to an unknown writer and her continual support throughout my career set Jennifer apart as a true role model in scholarly collegiality. G. Kurt Piehler embraced this project while directing the Center for the

Study of War and Society at the University of Tennessee. Kurt's efforts in advancing my work and career have been extraordinarily kind and supportive. Mike Neiberg, Nancy Gentile Ford, and David Gerber provided thoughtful commentary on my work in its early stages that helped shape it significantly. Bruce Vandervort and Donald Critchlow, editors of the *Journal of Military History* and the *Journal of Policy History*, respectively, and the anonymous reviewers of those journals helped refine my thinking a great deal. I am grateful for their support and encouragement.

At both the research and writing stage, numerous institutions and individuals provided financial and archival assistance. The Herbert Hoover Presidential Library Association made a research trip to the Hoover archives possible through a Robert R. McCormick Tribune Foundation travel grant. While I was there, the staff, most notably Matthew Schaefer, cheerfully led a novice through the archives. The Franklin and Eleanor Roosevelt Institute provided travel assistance to me on two separate occasions, the second time through an Albert M. Greenfield Research Fellowship. It is no stretch to say that without this assistance, this book would not exist. At the FDR archives, Mark A. Renovitch and Karen Anson were extremely helpful guides. More recently, Karen aided in the photo reproductions found in the book. A special note of thanks goes to archivist Bob Clark. Bob happily helped this research in countless ways. And, after many visits to Hyde Park over the years, I am glad to now count him as a friend. Joseph Hovish and Howard Trace, curators of the American Legion Library at the Legion National Headquarters in Indianapolis, helped tremendously as I navigated their archives and located photographs for the book. I am extremely grateful for their assistance and the American Legion's cooperation. Bowling Green State University's Department of History and College of Arts and Sciences provided invaluable time off for the writing of the manuscript. Scott Martin, the department chair, and then Dean Don Nieman graciously agreed to grant me course releases for a semester off in my first year as a faculty member—no small concession.

Special mention goes to the Veterans of Foreign Wars National Headquarters and the publisher and editor-in-chief of *VFW* magazine, Richard Kolb. Rich literally sat in a dark and cold headquarters building after a brutal Kansas City ice storm in order to let me have access to their materials. He has had a hand in this project since its inception. More recently, Rob Widener, the art director of *VFW* magazine, has helped with the reproduction of the wonderful cartoons that graced the old *Foreign Service* magazines. This book owes its existence to the good men and women of the VFW.

Many friends over the years have helped in ways large and small over drinks and coffee, kvetching at the proverbial water cooler, in small reading groups, and by simply being good, cheerful friends. Chris Nicely kept me sane throughout graduate school with his humor, his irreverence, and his total lack of ties to academic life. Mark Hove and Jason Parker heard more than they wanted to about this project and were great friends and colleagues at UF. At East Stroudsburg University, Mike Gray and Don Dellipriscoli were indispensably positive friends, supporters of my career, and wonderful colleagues during my first fulltime academic position. At BGSU, the fellow members of the junior faculty reading group—Becky Mancuso, Amílcar Challú, Tiffany Trimmer, Jessie Abel, David Haus, and Scott Martin—all provided thoughtful comments on chapter drafts. Leigh Ann Wheeler, Andy Schocket, and Gary Hess have been supportive colleagues. Ruth Herndon and Becky Mancuso are my departmental neighbors and have become great friends; both offered moral support and encouragement through the bleakest days of writing (and they get pretty bleak in the northwest Ohio winter).

Debbie Gershenowitz has been everything one could wish in an editor. At her instigation, we met at a Society for Military History conference in 2003 and discussed my work. As we talked, she gave a broad ray of hope that I might be on to something. As the years passed, her support of my work only grew. Throughout the writing of the manuscript, Debbie provided very keen and prompt editorial advice. She allowed space when space was what was needed and applied pressure when that was in order. Working with NYU Press and with Debbie has simply been a pleasure.

Finally, my family has nourished and supported me in so many ways during this project. My parents, Ramon and Adda Ortiz, never lost faith in my abilities or doubted that this book would be published—and, given my extended adolescence, believe me, they had every reason to lose faith! In elliptical ways that elude simple description, my father's career as a physician in the Veterans' Administration hospital system was the seedbed of my interest in veterans' issues. I am indebted to both of my parents for so many things but foremost for their unyielding love. And finally, and most important, it is to my wife, Renée, and my daughter, Bianca, that I dedicate this book. They make daily life a constant source of warmth, love, and joy. Renée good-naturedly made it though the writing of the manuscript, putting up with all of my surly, churlish "writing" moods and the long absences that went along with the project. She read more passages and chapters than I can count and always made insightful suggestions, all while caring for a toddler. How? I really don't know, but I am forever grateful to her for all she has done. Some of Bianca's first words were "Daddy's working." But, she, too, put up with an absent-minded and distracted father with unbridled joy and unconditional love. Every single day with her has been a blessing. Words cannot express my gratitude and love for you both. This book is for you and is possible only because of you.

Introduction

In 1930, a dozen years after the conclusion of World War I, the journalist Oliver McKee, Jr., predicted the impact that military veterans would soon have on the American polity. McKee's article in *The Commonweal*, "The Political March of the Veterans," declared that already the "veteran of the World War has won a secure foothold in American politics." By way of example, he pointed to the fifteen senators, sixty-three members of Congress, and multiple Cabinet members that had served in the Great War. McKee explained that the veterans' ascendancy in politics could be traced in great measure to the voluntary associations that nurtured them. Vibrant veteran organizations gave ex-soldiers a strong collective political voice and "the machinery" to enact national or state laws and served as a training ground for the development of valuable political skills. Thus, McKee determined, "The American veteran of the World War has arrived on the political scene and . . . brought a new force into our political life. Hereafter, we must reckon with him." He pointed to an emergent political terrain where military veterans and their organizations would once again, as in the years following the Civil War, play a significant role in national politics. McKee would be proven right, but not in ways that he anticipated. By 1932, veterans had launched a "political march," not through the respectable and conventional channels of government but in the form of some 40,000 mostly unemployed and homeless World War I veterans who descended on Washington, DC, in what became known as the Bonus March.[1]

The Bonus March dramatically catapulted veterans' issues to the forefront of national political affairs. In 1924, Congress had awarded World War I veterans adjusted compensation for their wartime service in the form of deferred interest-bearing certificates payable in 1945 or, in the event of the veteran's death, to the veteran's beneficiaries. In May and June 1932, during the Great Depression's worst year, tens of thousands of veterans flocked to the nation's capital to lobby Congress for immediate payment on their "Bonus." Dubbed the Bonus Expeditionary Force by the sympathetic District Superintendent of Police, the Bonus March grew from smatterings of veterans numbering in the hundreds to some 40,000 protestors. The veterans, many with families in tow, set up camps around the city and made daily walks to the Capitol for rallies and meetings with members of Congress. On July 28, 1932, after Congress refused to grant early Bonus payment and after weeks of mounting tension, the U.S. government forcibly evicted the Bonus Marchers and their families from their makeshift encampments. In the largest of these, "Camp Marks," on the Anacostia River flood plain, U.S. Army troops led by General Douglas MacArthur rousted the veterans with fixed bayonets, tanks, and cavalry forces and then torched the veterans' dwellings to the ground.[2]

The Bonus March is a prominent part of the Great Depression and New Deal-era narrative. Besides vividly capturing the pathos of the era's social dislocation, the violent conclusion to the Bonus March has become a historically freighted symbol. One the one hand, the episode hardened pre-existing perceptions of President Herbert Hoover's disregard for the suffering of average Americans and thus quickly became historical shorthand for the failures of his presidency. On the other hand, the Bonus March has been viewed as an electoral tipping point and as a point of comparison between Herbert Hoover and the Democratic presidential candidate, Franklin D. Roosevelt. To contemporaries and historians alike, the episode signaled the certainty of a new political era dawning after twelve years of Republican rule. Indeed, even Roosevelt privately declared the election won upon receiving news of the Bonus March rout. Moreover, New Deal chroniclers compare Roosevelt's magnanimous treatment of veterans in a far smaller 1933 Bonus March to the 1932 debacle to illustrate both the New Deal's concern for "the forgotten man" and FDR's considerable political savvy. And yet, despite this centrality of veterans to the New Deal era, after 1933 veterans normally retreat into the background in discussions of New Deal politics.[3]

In 1944, veterans re-emerged into the spotlight of national politics with the passage of the Servicemen's Readjustment Act, better known as the GI Bill. When FDR signed the legislation on June 22, 1944, sixteen million World War II servicemen and servicewomen found that their military obligations would qualify them for generous postwar social and economic benefits. The origins of the GI Bill lay in the concern over the postwar readjustment of veterans to civilian life and the political consequences if that process were to fail. To those who had experienced the prolonged aftermath of the Great War, the Bonus March remained a potent reminder of the dangers posed to American society if veterans' social and economic reintegration went unaddressed. The GI Bill avoided this threat by creating the largest social welfare program in the history of the country. Veterans enjoyed federally financed vocational training and education benefits, a liberal unemployment policy, easy access to home, farm, and business loans, and an expansive healthcare entitlement. Some nine million veterans took advantage of the provisions, making the GI Bill arguably the most significant piece of legislation both in the history of American social welfare policy and in the formation of postwar American society.[4]

Chronologically and, in many respects, interpretively, the Bonus March and the GI Bill bookend FDR's unprecedented time in office and attendant discussions of New Deal domestic politics. Scholars contrast FDR's veterans' policy with Hoover's expulsion of the Bonus Marchers and portray an amicable relationship ultimately consummated by the passage of the GI Bill. While many historical accounts take note of FDR's opposition to the "soldier's bonus" between 1932 and 1936, the early payment of the Bonus in 1936 over a presidential veto stands out only as an awkward political moment on the road to the GI Bill denouement. In short, if the Bonus March marks the sine qua non of New Deal–era veteran politics, the GI Bill stands as its successful, albeit delayed, conclusion. Unfortunately, this perspective has served to obscure the wide range of veterans' political struggles *between* 1932 and 1944. What is more, in failing to recount those battles fully, historians have failed to appreciate how veteran politics shaped the political contours of the New Deal itself.[5]

To address these shortcomings, this book employs a set of methodological and interpretive perspectives different from those used in previous studies. First, it moves beyond the narrow trajectory of the Bonus March to explore veterans' issues and the political activism over them—what I call in this book "veteran politics"—and follows the protracted, albeit less well-known, struggle for the Bonus between 1932 and 1936. It also expands our understanding of interwar veterans' issues to include pensions and, perhaps most important, the foundational issues of political economy that lay at the heart of veteran political activism. It is imperative to do this since the intensely political battles over veterans' special claims on the state already have been shown to greatly influence American partisan politics and state formation during other periods. Revolutionary War pensions, conflict over "the bloody shirt" and Civil War pensions, and World War I soldiers' benefits have located veterans at the heart of postrevolutionary political culture,[6] Gilded Age partisan politics,[7] and Progressive Era institutional development, respectively.[8] To use the Bonus March as a springboard is to better address these larger issues of the New Deal era, an era critical to the formation of the modern American state.[9]

Second, to study veterans and veteran political activism, scholars must come to grips with the organizations that advanced veterans' interests. To do this, one must go beyond inward-looking institutional histories of the major veteran organizations. National veteran organizations such as the American Legion and the Veterans of Foreign Wars mediated veterans' relationship with the state, both with elected officials and with the veterans' bureaucracy. They also provided the "machinery" that structured veterans' political involvement at the national, state, and local levels. Even the Bonus March, uniformly depicted as a spontaneous protest movement unsupported by veteran organizations, begs for a reevaluation that takes these structures of organization seriously. Indeed, as Oliver McKee, Jr., pointed out in 1930, at the center of interwar veteran politics stood veteran organizations.[10]

Finally, this study employs the methods and perspectives of an expanding subfield, policy history, to analyze veterans' issues of the era. The bifurcated nature of the existing literature on veterans of the interwar period reflects the lenses through which social historians and traditional political historians have addressed the issues: the Bonus March and Roosevelt's New Deal. Approaching the period from a policy history perspective offers an opportunity to reconcile the division between a grassroots approach and a top-down one.[11] Moreover, I focus on the ways federal policies created new political forces and actors, how policies themselves made politicized citizens.[12] This is not to suggest that the ideological nature of American involvement in the World War I did not matter to interwar political debates. It did, mightily, and several studies have shown the long-term ideological ramifications of the war "to make the world safe for democracy."[13] But tracing interwar federal veterans' policy and the "policy feedback" it generated offers a different path with different rewards. It shines a light on the nexus where civic organizations, citizens, and the state interact and on the connections that link social policy, state formation, and electoral politics.[14]

Using a broader chronology and range of veterans' issues, information from both of the major veteran organizations, and the insights from policy history enables alternative story lines to emerge that complicate the teleological Bonus-March-to-GI Bill narrative. Indeed, three narrative arcs interweave throughout this book. The first is the evolution of federal veterans' policy from 1917 to 1944. The second is the development of the institutional rivalry between the Veterans of Foreign Wars and the American Legion as each mobilized World War veterans to pressure the government for salutary legislation and to amend existing unfavorable policies. And last is the recasting of the New Deal political narrative to accommodate veterans' policy and veteran politics. A brief description of each of these is necessary before the organizational structure and arguments of the book can be laid out.

Federal policies for veterans underwent a fitful but ultimately sweeping transformation during the interwar years, one that paralleled the changes to twentieth-century American liberalism during the same period. In the 1910s, policymakers steeped in Progressive-minded ideals of bureaucratic efficiency and nonpartisanship sought to fashion a new system of benefits and pensions for Great War veterans. The corrupt, sectional, and partisan Civil War pension system created during the Gilded Age served as a negative point of reference when policymakers developed the Bureau of War Risk Insurance (1917), the Veterans' Bureau (1921), and, later, the Veterans' Administration (1930) to tend to soldiers and ex-soldiers of the Great War. The Republican presidents of the 1920s and FDR viewed an expansive veterans' welfare system suspiciously, seeing it as a continued pocket of governmental waste and corruption and as contrary to the tenets of fiscal conservatism that they all held dear. But, despite this, Congress continually voted to liberalize veterans' benefits and pensions, more often than not over presidential vetoes.[15]

By the early 1930s, two issues had come to dominate veterans' policy discussions: the Bonus and the liberalization of pensions. At the heart of the debate was the question of what the federal government owed to veterans for their service during war. Few disagreements arose over service-connected disabled veterans who were wards of the state—although exactly what constituted disability and whether or not a given disability could be proven to be service-connected continually dogged veterans, legislators, and administrators. But liberal pensions and the possibility of early Bonus payment rankled fiscal conservatives within and beyond the Roosevelt administration. In 1933, FDR announced, at the American Legion annual convention, that "no person, because he wore a uniform, must thereafter be placed in a special class of beneficiaries over and above all other citizens." He continued, "[T]he fact of wearing a uniform does not mean that [a veteran] can demand and receive from his Government a benefit which no other citizen receives." Congress, however, frequently disagreed. During election years especially, fear of the veterans' vote drove members of Congress from both parties to promote both Bonus payment and pension liberalizations. Moreover, veterans' policy became inextricably linked to the contentious national discussions on the need to increase Americans' "purchasing power" to combat the Great Depression. By the mid-1930s, while numerous plans to stimulate consumption through deficit spending and inflationary monetary policy circulated throughout Congress, a debt already owed—the Bonus—began to be seen as a ready-made vehicle to accomplish this goal.[16]

As resistance to government spending weakened, federal approaches to veterans' issues changed along with it. In 1936, Congress granted early payment on the Bonus. Moreover, the terms of veterans' pensions and health care were steadily liberalized to account for disability claims not proved to be service related. By the beginning of American involvement in World War II, the veterans' system had evolved from its Progressive-era origins into something more like the Civil War system in scale and generosity. However, this new system was national in scope, rather than sectional, and nonpartisan in nature—a prime example of the fitful rise of the modern American state. In 1944, when a new cohort of veterans prepared to return to American society, plans for servicemen's postwar readjustment dovetailed with the discussions over the avenues twentieth-century liberalism might take, avenues that included extensive European-style social welfare provisioning for all citizens.[17]

While aiding elected officials and agency bureaucrats in the formulation of federal policies, two major national organizations fought for further liberalization of the system and vied for the membership of American veterans: the American Legion and the Veterans of Foreign Wars (VFW). Other smaller organizations based on ideological orientation, ethnoreligious ties, and disability, groups such as the Communist Party-affiliated Workers' Ex-Serviceman's League, the Jewish War Veterans, and the Disabled American Veterans, also competed for veterans' affiliations. Yet, the American Legion and VFW far outdistanced the others in terms of membership and national political influence and became the major rivals among the associations. The Legion, founded in 1919 by members of the American Expeditionary Force, opened admission to all honorably discharged veterans of World War I. After its founding in Paris, the Legion became known as *the* Great War veteran organization. The VFW, however, traced its origins to veteran groups of the Spanish-American and Philippine-American Wars that formed in 1899: the National Association of the Army of the Philippines and the American Veterans of Foreign Service. After these groups merged, in 1914, the VFW offered membership to servicemen and veterans who had served "on foreign shores or in hostile waters in any war, campaign or expedition recognized by Congress with a campaign badge or service clasp." While active-duty doughboys were inducted into the VFW during the Great War, some time passed before the organization became a serious rival to the American Legion for those veterans' affiliation.[18]

In the interwar period, fundamental differences in ideology and in political power distinguished the VFW from the American Legion. In particular, the VFW's persistent and vehement demand for the immediate cash payment of the soldiers' bonus and the pointed critique of the political economy that informed its arguments offered veterans an alternative to the more conservative Legion. This is not to suggest that the two organizations' agendas were always in opposition. Undeniably, the VFW and American Legion agreed on a whole host of issues and worked in tandem to realize most of their shared goals. But when the then dominant American Legion mounted less strident challenges to federal policy than its rival, World War I veterans turned to the VFW, transforming it into an important vehicle for those disaffected by the Legion's stance. Prior to the emergence of this rivalry, the American Legion leadership had found it relatively easy to suppress veterans' excessive demands on the state. After 1929, veterans found in the VFW a newly energetic and increasingly powerful organization to champion their causes. Empowered by this new institutional rivalry for members and for the corresponding political muscle that came with increased membership, veterans could articulate a much more expansive understanding of what the role of the federal government should be, giving veteran politics a sharp ideological edge. The ultimate result of this intense rivalry was the creation of a twin-pillared, intergenerational, and powerfully entrenched veterans lobby that still continues to dominate veterans' issues.

As the investigation of veteran politics expands to include the wide range of veterans' policy matters and looks more closely at the workings of the veteran organizations, another theme emerges. In traditional political histories of the New Deal, veteran political activism is tied to the success or failure of Bonus Marches. As a result, depictions of Roosevelt's gentle disarming of the much smaller 1933 Bonus March render veterans as early beneficiaries and eventual supporters of the New Deal. Yet, a detailed examination of FDR's veterans' policy and the fierce political mobilizations against it reveals that veterans played a critical role in the politics of the New Deal era, even if no single demonstration on the scale of the Bonus March materialized. What is more, the handling and the eventual resolution of politically controversial veterans' issues such as the Bonus and pensions offer insight into the era's changing relationship between citizens and the federal government, a process normally associated with New Deal labor, social welfare, and relief programs. Therefore, the inclusion of veteran politics does not just supplement the New Deal narrative; it alters it.[19]

As this discussion suggests, the triangular relationship involving veterans' policy, the Legion and VFW organizations, and the larger political milieu is the focus of this book. I contend that interwar federal policies provoked repeated political mobilizations by veterans and veteran organizations seeking to reverse or amend those policy decisions. Elected officials in Congress, bureaucrats, and presidents all were forced to conceptualize and implement veterans policy—and in many cases, to reconceptualize it and re-implement it—in response to the strength of veteran organizations' political activism and in deference to the "soldiers' vote." In the process, veteran issues and veteran politics were at the epicenter of larger political battles.

Most important, this book reconsiders the political origins and the political triumph of the "Second" New Deal.[20] From 1933 to 1936, veterans' protests against the Economy Act's draconian cuts in veterans' benefits and the bitter struggle for early payment of the Bonus pitted veterans against the Roosevelt administration. This critical response to early New Deal policy situated veterans in the vanguard of the "New Deal Dissidents," the social protest movement led by Senator Huey P. Long and Father Charles E. Coughlin. Indeed, in the late spring of 1935, the Bonus provided the glue that held a politically threatening coalition of Long, Coughlin, and veterans together while the battle for its passage brought the dissident movement to a crescendo. The payment of the Bonus in 1936 deprived the dissidents of their one common rallying cry, helping to undermine the strength of their third-party electoral challenge. Moreover, the massive cash infusion into the economy in the summer before the election made the fall of 1936 the most prosperous since the Crash and contributed substantially to Roosevelt's reelection. Thus, the political origins of the "Second" New Deal and Roosevelt's electoral triumph of 1936—standards in the New Deal narrative—are reinterpreted to posit veteran politics as a central causal factor.[21]

Equally important, this book explores the creation of the modern veterans' lobby during the interwar period. The passing of the GI Bill was the denouement not just of the Bonus March but of years of continual political activism by veteran organizations. In describing those struggles and the competitive dynamics between the American Legion and the VFW that shaped them, I trace the rise of organized veterans as a powerful interest group in modern U.S. politics. The Legion and VFW's roles in the creation and implementation of the GI Bill only consolidated their positions as the leaders of a robust, nonpartisan, and intergenerational political lobby that would serve veterans and influence political affairs throughout the twentieth century.

By examining the development of veterans' policy and the establishment of the World War I veterans' organizations between 1917 and 1929, the opening chapter lays essential groundwork for the rest of the study. The creation of the Progressive-minded World War veterans system is recounted, followed by a description of the two major veteran organizations. Then I turn to the transformations in federal veterans' policy prompted by the lobbying power of veterans, especially the two legislative landmarks passed in 1924: the World War Veterans Act and the Adjusted Service Compensation Act. Before 1929, Republican hegemony in Congress and in the White House, coupled with American Legion dominance in veterans' affairs, made conditions unfavorable for the politics of veterans' issues to spill over into larger political battles. But, in 1929, a new set of circumstances emerged. Dissatisfaction with federal Bonus and pension policies empowered a new organizational voice in World War veterans' issues just as the ebullience of the 1920s came to an abrupt, shattering end. This chapter ends, then, in 1929 with two precipitous events: the VFW national organization's vote to push for more expansive veteran benefits, including immediate payment of the Bonus, and the stock market crash that would lead to the Great Depression and fundamentally transform the nation's politics.

Chapter 2 explores the Bonus March as the starting point of New Deal–era veteran politics. In doing so, the chapter argues that the supposedly unprompted Bonus Army that moved on Washington in the summer of 1932 actually responded to organized political activism orchestrated by the Veterans of Foreign Wars between 1929 and 1932. The federal policy that outlined the Bonus's deferred features inadvertently led to the rapid political mobilization by veterans. When the largest of the veteran organizations, the American Legion, failed to challenge federal policy, veterans first flowed into the VFW and then onto the streets of the capital. In short, the federal policies aimed at benefiting veterans instead transformed them into activist citizens. Moreover, the rise of the Veterans of Foreign Wars as an organizational rival to the American Legion during the late 1920s and 1930s bolstered the institutional resources and choices for veterans, helping them make further demands on the state. Only by rethinking the role of the veteran organizations in the March can the role of organized veteran political activism in the ensuing years be fundamentally recast.

Chapter 3 examines veterans' initial reaction to FDR and the New Deal. The chapter discusses the ways in which the two organizations tackled the sharp reductions in veteran pensions called for in the 1933 Economy Act. The Economy Act, the second piece of legislation passed in the New Deal's "Hundred Days," reduced veteran benefits by more than $400 million. In response to the Economy Act, many veterans immediately broke ranks with the Roosevelt administration and questioned the authenticity of the New Deal's claims to helping the forgotten man. Members of both organizations expressed outrage at this piece of legislation and its implementation by the administration. Each organization, however, adopted different tactics to push for its repeal. Legion leaders preferred behind-the-scenes lobbying. The VFW leadership, on the other hand, blasted the administration publicly and began to align itself with more radical voices in and beyond Congress. In their forceful response to the Economy Act, veterans, in particular those in the VFW, joined with other early critics of the New Deal who chastised FDR's unwillingness to reconfigure the nation's political economy. These differences in methods—not necessarily in goals—intensified the ideological differences between the organizations. And, yet, their combined tactics helped produce tangible results for individual veterans when Congress repealed the Economy Act in 1934 over a Roosevelt veto.

In Chapters 4 and 5, I return to the battle over the Bonus. Chapter 4 describes the re-emergence of the Bonus as a political issue in 1934 despite opposition from a popular president and the most powerful veteran organization. The struggle to pass the Bonus over Roosevelt's objections drew two of the era's dissident voices, Father Charles E. Coughlin and Senator Huey P. Long, to the veterans' cause. Chapter 5 explains how the Bonus issue further aroused veterans against the administration, precipitating widespread veteran political activism. The Bonus battle of 1935, I contend, was also the point of convergence for a powerful and controversial alliance of Long, Coughlin, and veterans that raised the specter of a new party consisting of Long and Coughlin supporters, buttressed by the veteran vote. The chapter ends with FDR's dramatic and unprecedented Bonus bill veto, delivered on May 22, 1935, to a joint session of Congress and a rapt national radio audience. The re-evaluation of veteran politics in this chapter offers a new interpretation of the political origins of the "second" New Deal.

Chapter 6 picks up the story in the wake of FDR's veto, carrying it forward through eventual Bonus payment to the presidential election of 1936. Roosevelt used his veto of the Bonus as a springboard for the special legislative program of the "Second" New Deal, the landmark session that included the passing of the Social Security Act and the National Labor Relations Act. The Bonus issue, however, would not lay quiet. On January 27, 1936, the Bonus passed over another FDR veto. But the passing of the Bonus in 1936 may well have been the must successful piece of "second" New Deal legislation, even if FDR did veto it. When veterans began receiving payments in June, nearly $2 billion flowed into the national economy, making 1936 the best economic year since the Crash. This fiscal stimulus boosted the economy just in time for the 1936 election. Moreover, the removal of the Bonus issue as the point of convergence, coupled with the death of Huey Long, meant that the dissident movement's electoral challenge to Roosevelt amounted to very little. The resolution of the Bonus, therefore, contributed significantly to Roosevelt's electoral landslide that November and the political triumph of the New Deal.

The concluding chapter explores the veteran organizations' rivalry and the creation of the GI Bill in light of New Deal–era veteran political activism. If veterans had once criticized the New Deal for not doing enough to recalibrate the political economy, the GI Bill would stand as the apotheosis of the type of federal support that they had imagined in early 1930s. To be sure, the Bonus March was an important contributing factor in the origins of the legislation, but I contend that the New Deal mobilization by veterans, the political rivalry between the veteran organizations, and renewed concerns about the "soldiers' vote" were equally responsible. During World War II, the VFW originally supported a new Bonus policy for returning veterans, hoping to rekindle the dynamism of its halcyon days from 1929 through 1936. In 1943–1944, however, it was the American Legion that pushed for expansive GI Bill benefits. The competition between these organizations—negligible before the Bonus issue arose in the late 1920s—drove the Legion to outdo its fierce rival for the allegiance of World War II veterans. Competition for new members and for the new bureaucratic jobs that an expanding federal veteran welfare system might create moved the Legion to promote a federal policy antithetical to its founders' avowed conservatism. And, while federal veterans' policy as written in the GI Bill emerged as a symbol of the new path postwar liberalism might take, it also cemented the dominant position of the American Legion and the VFW as the cornerstones of the twentieth-century veterans' lobby.

In the period from 1918 to 1944, veterans battled with the federal government over pensions, entitlements, and adequate compensation for wartime military service. The ultimate success of these battles over the federal governments' obligations to veterans dovetailed with a larger transformation in twentieth-century American political life: the changing relationship between citizens and the federal government. While this process is typically associated with New Deal labor, social welfare, and relief programs, veterans' issues resonated throughout the American political and social order well beyond the end of World War II, and, indeed, beyond the New Deal political consensus forged in the 1930s. Despite the waning of New Deal liberalism and the conservative resurgence in the late decades of the twentieth century, veterans' entitlements continue to be generous, and most Americans—and certainly most politicians—take for granted veterans' special claims on the federal government.

1

Veterans' Policy and Veteran Organizations, 1917–1929

For the disabled veterans of the war and the dependents of those who fell the country cannot do too much. . . . But the fit and able-bodied veterans are offered the opportunities open to every other citizen.

—President Calvin Coolidge's annual budget message, December 10, 1923

In the 1920s, American citizens engaged in an extended political debate over the treatment of military veterans. The debate served as a constant, sometimes unpleasant, reminder that the consequences of the Great War would unfold well after the peace. This came as something of a surprise. After all, the federal government had created and implemented innovative wartime veterans' policies in the hope that the kind of drawn-out, partisan disputes that had erupted over Civil War pensions could be avoided by an efficient new bureaucracy administering judiciously crafted policies. But the legacy of the Civil War era animated a new generation of veteran organizations, too. The Grand Army of the Republic's success in building the Civil War pension system offered a sterling example for the organizations that would lobby the government on behalf of World War veterans. While the new bureaucracy and new civic associations such as the American Legion weighed in on World War veterans' issues, Congress and the president continued to control the reins of policymaking. Even then, although Republicans controlled both the legislative and the executive branches of the government, the politics of veterans' issues proved divisive enough to pit Congress against the era's popular presidents. But two factors—the American Legion's dominance in veteran circles and the conservative Republican hegemony in national electoral politics—successfully created a system of levees that kept veteran politics from cresting over into larger political battles. In 1929, however, those levees failed and a rising tide of veteran activism overflowed into the national political arena.[1]

Creating the World War Veterans' System

During the Great War, Progressives applied the same intensity and earnestness to soldiers' welfare issues as they did to the experiments in labor relations, economic coordination, and social reforms such as Prohibition. On April 6, 1917, when Woodrow Wilson signed the declaration of war against Germany, the United States set out to "make the world safe for democracy" with one of the smallest armies among the warring nations. Six weeks later, Congress passed the Selective Service Act, putting the mechanism in place through which the United States ultimately would raise an armed force of 4.7 million men. Even before the first American doughboys experienced the grim taste of combat in France, a framework had already been created for how the country would handle the long-term needs of its soldiers and their dependents. On October 6, exactly six months after the United States officially became a belligerent, Congress passed the War Risk Insurance Act (WRIA), effectively establishing a new veterans' system.[2]

The WRIA held out the promise that the Great War veterans' system of benefits would be based on Progressive principles of impartiality and efficiency. More than anything, legislators sought to avoid, in the words of Representative Sam Rayburn (D, TX), "another saturnalia of pension frauds." The WRIA utilized an agency formed in 1914, the Bureau of War Risk Insurance (BWRI), housed in the Treasury Department, to serve new veterans, rather than the much-maligned Pension Bureau. By giving this agency control over veterans' issues, the WRIA successfully bypassed the administrative apparatus of the Civil War era and built a firewall around the old pension system. Initially created to insure ships and seamen traveling into war zones when private insurers balked, the new agency would take over the government's efforts for soldiers and, eventually, veterans by administering to soldiers in four areas: family allotments for those in service, life insurance, disability payments for those with service-connected conditions, and long-term hospitalization for disabled veterans. Former President Theodore Roosevelt endorsed the measure, explaining that its features put "the United States where it ought to be, as standing in the forefront among the nations in doing justice to our defenders." Congress passed the bill unanimously, desiring to do right for the men in arms but also to prevent the problems of fraud, corruption, and partisan cronyism that had plagued the nation for more than fifty years after the Civil War's end.[3]

The WRIA created one of the largest centralized federal bureaucracies in the nation's history when it tapped the Bureau of War Risk Insurance as the agency to administer soldiers' welfare. The War Department deducted money from active-duty soldiers' pay in order to provide for their wives and children, but the BWRI was responsible for the disbursement of family allotments directly to the dependents. Moreover, the BWRI handled life insurance coverage, also with payments withheld from soldiers' paychecks. The insurance provision included up to $10,000 of term life insurance for servicemen with a pay deduction of only $8 per year for every $1,000 of coverage. For veterans, the WRIA constructed a schedule of payments for those who had suffered service-connected disabilities. Congress set the initial rate of $30 per month for the totally disabled, plus an additional $15 for the veteran's wife and $10 per dependent child. In 1919, Congress raised the rate to $80 per month, a more reasonable reflection of the inflated cost of living. In addition, veterans who had suffered the loss of both hands or feet or total blindness qualified for a payment of an extra $100 per month. The BWRI calculated partial disability payments on the basis of the severity of the injury, adhering to a formal schedule of reductions in earning potential attributable to specific injuries and ailments.[4]

The WRIA also mandated that the federal government provide vocational rehabilitation training and long-term hospitalization coverage for the service-connected disabled. It did not, however, delineate the methods or the agencies responsible for these provisions. To address this, in 1918, Congress passed the Vocational Rehabilitation Act, which gave control over the rehabilitation program to the Labor Department's Federal Board for Vocational Education. The program only served the needs of disabled veterans who demonstrated an inability to find work because of their disabilities. In fact, over 300,000 disabled veterans who applied were denied the training they sought because they did not meet the threshold of this requirement. Even so, more than 128,000 veterans completed vocational training between 1919 and 1928. On the issue of hospitalization, in 1919, Congress passed legislation giving the Public Health Service control over veterans' long-term hospital care. At that time, the Public Health Service provided medical care to merchant seamen in twenty government-run hospitals. After the rapid demobilization of 1919, veterans requiring hospitalization inundated the Public Health Service facilities, leading to overcrowded and dangerous conditions. As an example of the dire hospital situation, as late as 1922, the Public Health Service somehow crammed 26,869 veterans into only 17,792 available beds. Veteran organizations issued vehement calls for the construction of new hospitals and expanded vocational training to accommodate the volume of veteran claimants, but neither provision provoked much in the way of political controversy because they applied to the genuinely disabled. And both provisions continued to be seen as bulwarks against the feared clamor for general veterans' pensions.[5]

This veterans' system replaced the Pension Bureau with important new agencies for implementation and took most, if not all, of the ambiguity and room for potential manipulation out of veterans' welfare provisioning. While soldiers and ex-soldiers complained about the speed of implementation and about how little of their wartime paychecks remained after the mandatory deductions—not an insignificant complaint because it led to the postwar push for retroactive "adjusted compensation," or a Bonus—the federal government succeeded in setting up a seemingly judicious and incorruptible new veterans' system. In very short time, however, a new cohort of veteran organizations proposed to alter it to better serve veterans' needs.

World War Veteran Organizations

After the Armistice, Great War veterans negotiated the terrain of veterans' policy through their organizations. The American Legion quickly developed into the foremost of these. Founded in Paris in 1919 by members of the American Expeditionary Force, the Legion sought to become the representative organization of all Great War veterans. While soldiers serving overseas had started the organization, the Legion offered admission to honorably discharged veterans of the conflict regardless of their stationing. This gave the Legion a pool of some 4.7 million potential members. A little over a year after its creation, 843,013 veterans swelled the Legion's ranks. Thanks to this significant membership, on September 15, 1919, Congress granted a charter to the organization in acknowledgment of its contributions to the national public interest. Moreover, the War Department gave the Legion official recognition and offered assistance with members' war records and bureaucratic problems too tangled for individual veterans to contend with on their own. These gestures from the federal government confirmed and further enhanced the Legion's rapid ascension to the forefront as the dominant World War I veterans association.[6]

The Legion's growth to prominence, however, hinged on more than membership growth and official recognition. A group of men drawn from the nation's political and economic elite dominated the Legion's national leadership and steered the fledging organization through its first steps. Relying on wealthy leaders' creditworthiness and on the assistance of financial backers such as Morgan Guarantee Trust, the Legion founders quickly created a solvent national organization. Never far from the reins of national political power, founding members such as Theodore Roosevelt, Jr., Eric Fisher Wood, Ogden Mills, William J. Donovan, and Bennett Champ Clark correspondingly exerted a tremendous amount of control over the Legion's policies. While rank-and-file veterans often complained about this Legion oligarchy—referred to usually as "the kingmakers"—there was no question that the Legion's powerful leadership and financial stability helped it gain its immediate national standing among veterans and among elected officials across the nation.[7]

The Legion rapidly became the dominant veteran organization, but World War veterans did have other options. Veterans' groups sprang up from across the ethnic, religious, racial, and ideological mosaic of the United States. Some of the largest of the ethnoreligious variety included the Catholic War Veterans, the Jewish War Veterans, and the Polish Legion of American Veterans. African American veterans quickly formed two organizations, the Grand Army of Americans and the more militant League for Democracy, marrying martial camaraderie with the struggle against racial discrimination. A radical group known as the World War Veterans arose and then quickly fell victim to the first Red Scare. (After 1930, the Communist Party–affiliated Workers' Ex-Serviceman's League took its place, offering veterans another radical, albeit small, organization to channel their revolutionary zeal.) An organization was founded in 1920 on the basis of service-connected disability, but the Disabled American Veterans of the World War (DAV) enrolled only 25,000 of the 350,000 disabled veterans. Furthermore, the organization focused almost exclusively on issues affecting the disabled, which meant that the DAV was not regarded as an important voice for the vast majority of veterans. Another smaller organization, the Veterans of Foreign Wars (VFW), would ultimately prove quite significant for Great War veterans.[8]

The VFW traced its origins to relatively obscure veterans' groups that formed after the Spanish-American and Philippine-American Wars: the National Association of the Army of the Philippines and the American Veterans of Foreign Service. In 1914, these groups in Colorado, Ohio, and Pennsylvania officially consolidated into the Veterans of Foreign Wars of the United States. Unlike the American Legion, which sought an exclusively doughboy membership, the VFW opened its doors to all honorably discharged veterans who had served "on foreign shores or in hostile waters in any war, campaign or expedition recognized by Congress with a campaign badge or service clasp." In 1917, the VFW added veterans of the Great War to those of the Spanish-American and Philippine-American Wars, the Boxer Rebellion, and various expeditions into Latin America. Many members had served in multiple conflicts. For example, in late 1917, VFW national commander Albert J. Rabing boasted that some 15 percent of the organization's members were in military service for the second time.[9]

Throughout the 1920s, the VFW did not seem a likely candidate to challenge the American Legion for the allegiance of World War veterans. Even though the VFW inducted active-duty doughboys in France, the organization struggled mightily to get World War veterans into the fold. In 1920, the VFW's membership stood at 20,000 veterans, not appreciably larger than it had been in 1917 and minuscule in comparison to the 800,000 Legionnaires. Even as late as 1927, the VFW had just 70,000 members. A difference in potential membership partially explains why the VFW never approached the size of the American Legion. After all, the organization's pool of potential members was only around 2 million—fewer than half of the 4.7 million from which the Legion could recruit. As important, the organization faced the perception that it was for an older generation. In 1920, seeking to alter this perception and to bump membership recruitment higher, the VFW tried touting the news that a World War veteran had been elected to the position of national commander. While this was true—two-time national commander Robert G. Woodside was a high-ranking VFW official even before his second tour of service during the Great War—the VFW continued to struggle with the younger generation as the WWI-age cohort remained reluctant to join and, when they did, slow to assume leadership positions throughout the organization.[10]

The VFW lacked not only the Legion's size and attendant lobbying strength but also its prominent, politically connected leadership. Throughout the 1920s, VFW leaders were older veterans of the Spanish-American

War era and rarely came from the nation's economic or political elites. Commander Woodside, for example, was one of the most advantaged of the VFW leaders. The Pennsylvanian parlayed his law practice and military experience into a position as Allegheny County sheriff, and then as County controller. These were no small positions in Allegheny County, but they paled in comparison to the Wall Street and Washington connections of the Legion leadership. Yet the absence of "kingmakers" in the VFW did have one benefit. VFW leaders proved slightly more responsive to the membership than their Legion counterparts because they were less entrenched in positions of power within the organization. The VFW leadership's lack of economic and political stature, however, translated into a shocking and perpetual shortage of organizational funds. Individual leaders of far lesser means than their Legion counterparts lent the organization not inconsiderable sums of money just to keep it afloat. Thus, in the 1920s, the power-brokering Legion towered over the VFW not just in membership but also in power and prestige, however they were measured.[11]

While marked differences existed at the leadership level and in the national status of the Legion and VFW, more subtle differences could be found in their rank-and-file memberships. Both organizations took pride in a cross-class national membership. The thorny issue of race, however, tested the supposed inclusiveness of the organizations. Each allowed state departments to decide on racial matters in tacit complicity with the southern Jim Crow system and the racial system that was emerging in the north during the 1920s. Therefore, while both the VFW and the Legion included African American veterans as members, typically they were shunted into segregated posts in both northern and southern states. As far as class composition is concerned, however, there was a key difference between the Legion and VFW.[12]

Limited existing evidence from Legion polling and VFW post rosters suggests that rank-and-file Legion and VFW members differed in their class origins. Legionnaires tended to be from the middle or the upper-middle class. A 1935 membership survey conducted by the Daniel Starch advertising agency in New York found that 22.4 percent of Legionnaires came from the ranks of the professional and managerial class. The survey discovered that 43 percent of the members either owned small businesses (22.2) or were sales or clerical workers (20.8). Only 3.8 percent of the Legionnaires surveyed were farmers, while just 16.1 percent and 6.2 percent were skilled and unskilled workers, respectively. In 1938, another marketing survey confirmed this class composition by revealing that some 64 percent earned more than $2,000 a year at a time when the average family income was $1,244.[13]

The VFW's membership, on the other hand, hailed from the middle or lower rungs of the social ladder. Very large numbers of skilled workers joined with small businessmen such as barbers and grocers and clerical workers of the lower-middle class to make up the majority of the VFW membership. A much larger percentage of unskilled laborers filled the ranks, too. In 1935, for example, skilled workers made up 44 percent of the 111 locatable members in Kankakee, Illinois, Post 2857. The post had nearly the same percentage of unskilled workers (10 percent) as of professionals and managers (11 percent). Clerical workers and small-business owners constituted 21 and 14 percent, respectively, of the membership. Home ownership statistics corroborate this social portrait. Only 28.8 percent of the members owned homes valued at or above the median home price for Kankakee County. Fourteen percent owned homes worth less than the median value, while the majority of the members (56.7 percent) were renters. Members of Post 2350 in Elko, Nevada, were of a similar class composition: 47 percent were skilled workers, and every other category, including farmers and unskilled workers, accounted for 11.7 percent. Only 17.6 percent of the Elko veterans owned homes over the median county value of $2,555. Nearly 65 percent of the Elko VFW members rented. In this regard, the nonelite VFW leadership more accurately reflected the social makeup of the group's rank-and-file members. These class differences between the organizations would play a large role in the future of interwar veteran politics.[14]

Despite their differences, between 1919 and 1929, the Legion and the VFW shared a number of organizational characteristics and positions on veterans' issues. After all, given the overlapping membership requirements, some veterans could—and did—belong to both of them. The organizations fought diligently for expanded medical benefits and the construction of veteran hospitals and clinics. Each sought to strengthen the existing system of pensions and benefits for ex-servicemen and their widows and families. Both the Legion and the VFW attempted to make the Bureau of War Risk Insurance and its replacement, the Veterans' Bureau, more efficient and more responsive to veterans' needs. The organizations also served an important shared role in veterans' policy, a mediating role that claims agents had played during the Civil War pension era. The American Legion and the VFW established National Service Bureaus in

Washington, DC, to help veterans navigate the new system. Thus, beyond proposing and promoting legislation, the veterans' organizations became part of the implementation structures of the federal veterans' bureaucracy itself, effectively mediating veterans' claims on the state.[15]

On issues other than the veterans' welfare system, the Legion and the VFW also shared similar agendas and perspectives. They called for a strong national defense and military preparedness, supporting increased defense spending and the maintenance of civilian military training camps. Despite the Legion's elite provenance, rank-and-file veterans in the Legion and the VFW expressed a critical view of the patriotism undergirding a political and economic system that would send soldiers off to die in the trenches and pay them a mere pittance while industrialists and capitalists profited handsomely safely at home. To address this discrepancy, each organization repeatedly called for measures that would "take the profits out of war." While this critique of the American political economy struck some as radical, both organizations fervently opposed any semblance of Bolshevism and stridently promoted the emotionally charged goal of "Americanism." Finally, the Legion and the VFW claimed to be "out" of politics, by which they meant the overtly partisan politics epitomized by the Grand Army of the Republic and its members' status as the shock troops of the Gilded Age Republican Party. This overlapping of agendas and attributes allowed critics to comment on a singular "veterans lobby," but the American Legion undeniably held the upper hand and wielded the most power in the efforts to amend the veterans' system initially created by the War Risk Insurance Act. And those efforts began almost immediately after the war's end.[16]

Amending the Veterans' System, 1919–1924

The first five years after the war witnessed an overhaul of the system initially laid out by the War Risk Insurance Act. With the necessary assistance of veterans' groups, legislators refashioned the policies and consolidated the bureaucratic agencies that implemented them. In the process, a rigid "iron triangle" emerged that consisted of new congressional committees, a new federal veterans' agency, and the veteran organizations. Consolidation did not mean the centralization of the bureaucratic apparatus. In fact, the decentralization of the veterans' bureaucracy through the creation of regional and branch offices drew some of the loudest praise from veterans and their advocates because it led to a greater level of responsiveness. That said, the policymaking structures were centralized into a tight "iron triangle," bounded by the Veterans' Bureau, the newly created House Committee on World War Veterans and the Senate Sub-committee on Veterans' Affairs, and the national legislative committees of the veteran organizations. This consolidation produced legislative results, first in the area of retroactive compensation for veterans but also in the form of liberalized disability pensions. In this period, the impact of the American Legion on World War veterans' legislation can hardly be exaggerated. Its size, influence over elected officials, and access to the corridors of power made the Legion a formidable lobbying force. And the new policies that emerged in the years between 1919 and 1924 reinforced the Legion's standing, giving it a virtual monopoly on the expression of World War I veterans' demands.[17]

The American Legion was among the Bureau of War Risk Insurance's first critics. At the first national convention, in 1919, some Legionnaires sought to condemn the BWRI outright for its failures, notably the severe backlog of 100,000 disability claims. Instead, the Legion convention issued a resolution demanding that the Bureau "employ more ex-servicemen, give prompter attention to inquiries directed to the Bureau, and Get Busy!" By 1920, dissatisfaction with the Bureau and the tripartite distribution of veteran care led to a broad overhaul of the veterans' bureaucratic structure. Robert Cholmondeley-Jones, the War Risk Insurance Bureau director (and a Legionnaire), cooperated with Legion officials in planning the end result of this overhaul: the Veterans' Bureau.[18]

In 1921, the Sweet Act created the Veterans' Bureau, charging it with the combined responsibilities of the three distinct agencies that were dealing with postwar veterans' issues: the BWRI (Treasury), the Board of Vocational Rehabilitation (Labor), and the Public Health Service (Interior). Allocated a $500 million budget and led by Charles R. Forbes, the Veterans' Bureau reconfigured the veterans' bureaucracy. In addition, the Sweet Bill chipped a crack in the edifice of service-connected disabilities by allowing veterans who had been diagnosed with tuberculosis and neuropsychological disorders in the two years after the war to claim disability. After a promising launch, however, the Veterans' Bureau suffered a debilitating setback. In 1923, Director Forbes precipitated one of the defining scandals of Warren G. Harding's administration because of his outright fraud and corruption in the handling of Bureau funds and contracts. Suspicions of corruption in veterans' pensions had dogged all efforts for veterans even before the scandal. But the black eye for the Bureau, while quite dark, eventually faded. After Forbes left the Bureau—ultimately receiving a two-year prison sentence—Brigadier General Frank T. Hines assumed the directorship and proved an able and honest administrator for the next twenty-two years. For all of the negative publicity surrounding the scandal, the Veterans' Bureau succeeded in streamlining the veterans' bureaucracy, making it more responsive to veterans' needs and more accountable to Congress. Not coincidentally, the Veterans' Bureau also provided a haven for veteran employment. As early as 1925, veterans made up half of all Bureau employees, thanks to preferential civil service hiring policies. As the Legion had played a significant role in the Bureau's creation, its members benefited greatly from the reorganization.[19]

The other two sides of the veterans iron triangle also emerged in the years from 1920 through 1924. Both the American Legion and the VFW formed national legislative committees staffed by permanent lobbyists in Washington, DC. John Thomas Taylor, head of the Legion's National Legislative Committee and chief lobbyist from 1920 to 1950, became one of the most important behind-the-scenes figures in the Capitol. Taylor once replied to a question concerning the "veterans' lobby" by exclaiming, "The veterans' lobby? You're looking at it." Taylor perfected what was called the "barrage technique" of influencing members of Congress. When congressional support needed shoring up, Taylor would issue the call for a "barrage" of letters on a specific issue. Legion members would oblige, inundating their representatives with demands to show broad support for veterans—or face the consequences. But after 1924, the need to barrage a wide array of members of Congress became less important as the House of Representatives created a new committee based on Legion recommendations solely to handle veterans' policies, the World War Veterans Committee. Royal C. Johnson (R, SD), a member of both the Legion and the VFW, chaired the committee. Thirteen of the twenty other members were Legionnaires, too. Further reinforcing the triangle, the Senate joined the House the next year by creating a new permanent subcommittee in the Finance Committee that would concentrate on veterans' policy. The Subcommittee on Veterans Affairs also included a Legionnaire among its five members.[20]

During the early 1920s, the creation of the new agency and of the veterans' iron triangle were significant developments, but adjusted compensation, or the soldiers' Bonus, proved to be the most controversial and contentious veterans' issue. Immediately following World War I, ex-soldiers began to call for a retroactive correction of their wartime pay. Soldiers

Royal C. Johnson (R, SD), chairman of the House Committee on World War Veterans, and John Thomas Taylor, director of the Legion's National Legislative Committee and chief lobbyist, undated. Courtesy of the American Legion.

complained that wages of $30 a month, minus mandatory war-risk insurance and family allotment payments, left them with paltry compensation, especially in contrast to the inflated wartime wages—as much as $10 a day—paid to those in the booming war-related industries. To be sure, the fortunes made by industrialists during the war exacerbated the feelings of inequity as critics pointed out that between 1917 and 1919 more than 1,000 new members joined the "millionaires club" while doughboys earned less than a dollar a day in the trenches. As early as 1919, sympathetic members of Congress already had introduced fifty-five different plans granting veterans some form or another of retroactive adjusted compensation. Two hurdles stood in the way, however. President Woodrow Wilson opposed any Bonus plan beyond the $60 discharge pay given to demobilized men. Moreover, Congress seemed reluctant to coalesce around any one plan without some formal endorsement by the American Legion.[21]

Between 1920 and 1924, both the Legion and the VFW fought for the passage of Bonus legislation. From the start, the VFW echoed soldiers' calls for a Bonus, but the Wilson administration opposed any such payment as a beginning of a pension movement and found initial support from the newly organized American Legion. While many veterans within the Legion voiced the desire for additional compensation, Legion leaders suppressed the issue, fearing that the bitter divisions among the members over the Bonus would rend the fledgling organization in two. Finally, in 1920, Bonus advocates forced the Legion to back some form of adjusted compensation legislation. The National Executive Committee could no longer tamp down rank-and-file discontentment over the issue and made public the organization's support for a Bonus. On October 16, 1920, in a show of political strength and veteran solidarity 75,000 veterans paraded down New York's Fifth Avenue demanding a Bonus. One hundred thousand spectators witnessed hundreds of Legion and VFW posts joining the national commanders of both organizations to form the "Petition in Boots." It appeared likely that, with the Legion's full support, some kind of adjusted payment legislation would emerge in the upcoming congressional session.[22]

Between 1921 and 1923, however, presidential opposition derailed congressional action on a Bonus. With a number of proposals circulating through the House, Warren G. Harding, the newly elected president, importuned the Republican-led Senate to recommit a bill that had already cleared the Finance Committee. When this unlikely move succeeded, administration allies kept Bonus bills buried in committee throughout 1921.

Like the presidents who would follow him, Harding opposed the payment on principle and for fiscal reasons, contending that to pay a Bonus demeaned the spirit of patriotism and wartime sacrifice shared by the entire mobilized citizenry. More important, he condemned the Bonus as a fiscal impracticality, incompatible with Republican calls for tax reduction and government contraction after years of Progressive-era growth. Yet, in the midterm election year of 1922, a Bonus bill supported by the veteran organizations broke through the administration opposition as members of Congress sought to mollify their veteran constituents. Secretary of the Treasury Andrew W. Mellon provided the administration's ammunition against the bill, arguing—incorrectly, as it turned out—that the country already faced a large looming budget deficit even without some $4 billion in costs associated with a Bonus. Pierre S. Du Pont and the U.S. Chamber of Commerce joined the loud business community chorus against payment. In the end, while the bill passed both houses of Congress, it lacked enough strength in the Senate to override Harding's veto. In his veto message, Harding linked patriotism with fiscal conservatism, proclaiming, "These ex-soldiers who served so gallantly in the war . . . must know that nations can only survive where taxation is strained from the limits of oppression."[23]

But calls for the Bonus would not cease. Indeed, the lobbying pressure from both the Legion and the VFW intensified. The fact that a number of states passed bonuses for their ex-soldiers bolstered rather than dampened Bonus advocates' demands. By the end of the congressional term in 1923, many predicted the passage of the bill in the next election-year term. Representative Royal C. Johnson (R, SD), citing Legion sources, announced that there were enough votes in the Senate to override Harding's next veto by four votes. Indeed, Reed Smoot (R, UT), the chairman of the Senate Finance Committee, confirmed this, saying, "As sure as God lives and the sun rises in the morning there will be a soldier bonus law passed by the next Congress."[24]

When Calvin Coolidge ascended to the presidency after Harding's death, he, too, declared his opposition to a Bonus. This was despite the fact that, during Coolidge's term as governor, Massachusetts had passed a Bonus bill—the first state Bonus—for its ex-servicemen with his approval. Before the 1924 congressional term started, Secretary of the Treasury Mellon again led the efforts to prevent a Bonus. Mellon wrote to William R. Green (R, IA), chairman of the House Ways and Means Committee, explaining that Congress could enact a Bonus or a tax cut, but not both.

Mellon put the pressure on his fellow Republicans who were caving on the Bonus question. He wrote, "A soldiers' bonus would postpone tax reduction not for one but for many years to come." *Time* described the choice as a Bonus for four million veterans or a tax cut for fourteen million citizens, seemingly an easy political choice in the upcoming election year. But, the writer contended, "Any politician's answer would be obvious were it not for the fact that as voters and lobbyists the bonus advocates have a much better organization than the taxpayer."[25]

In the election year of 1924, a Republican-led Congress passed the Adjusted Compensation Act over the objections of their party's nominal leader. But the objections outlined by Coolidge and Mellon led to a congressional compromise through which veterans would receive a Bonus for their soldiering experience but not as an immediate cash payment. Rather, the Bonus would be awarded as a deferred interest-bearing certificate payable in 1945 or, upon the veteran's death, to his beneficiaries. In 1945, veterans would receive additional compensation of a dollar for every day in service, overseas veterans $1.25 per day, plus the accumulated 4 percent interest. Including interest, the total face value of the certificate could reach as high as $1,600; the average was around $1,000. Moreover, as part of the bill, after two years, veterans would be allowed to take out a 22.5 percent loan from the Veterans' Bureau in the amount of their certificates' face value. The legislative compromise proved significant because the fiscal outlays could be spread over time and would not derail the additional tax cuts demanded by the Coolidge administration. Regardless, Coolidge remained true to his word and vetoed the bill, declaring, "Patriotism which is bought and paid for is not patriotism. . . . There is no moral justification for it." The Republican majority in Congress felt enormous pressure to stand by their party's leader, but they were also eager to please a large and vocal voting bloc. In the end, the Senate barely overrode the Coolidge veto, making the Bonus law and handing veterans a long-sought victory. While Coolidge's opposition caused a rift in the Republican Party, it was neither a deep nor irreparable one. The Bonus passage allowed both the president and the Republicans in Congress to enter the 1924 campaign with heads held high.[26]

Yet, the success of the Bonus's passage proved problematic for veterans and ultimately laid the seeds for future political activism. The American Legion leaders supported the deferment and insurance policy provisions that emerged in the compromise. The VFW leadership argued against the deferment, but, lacking the size and lobbying stature of the Legion, relented, preferring the measure to no Bonus at all. Some 4.1 million veterans ultimately applied to the Veterans' Bureau for their certificates, a percentage so large that it destroyed the arguments of those like Coolidge who said that "veterans as a whole don't want it." The American Legion crowed over yet another achievement, turning 1924 into a "harvest year," in the words of the national commander. To the VFW, however, the victory proved woefully inadequate. The organization's opposition to what many veterans derisively called the "tombstone" Bonus would increase as the decade wore on.[27]

In 1924, Congress also passed the sweeping, albeit less controversial, World War Veterans Act. This bill streamlined and codified the tangle of piecemeal veterans' legislation added after the War Risk Insurance Act. More important, it expanded the parameters for disability pensions. It achieved this by extending the pension deadline exactly as the earlier Sweet Bill had, granting service connection pensions to all veterans who reported tuberculosis or neuropsychological disorders before January 1, 1925. It also ended the application of a misconduct clause to cases of venereal disease. While an act of undoubted compassion toward veterans whose disabilities had emerged or been diagnosed well after the war, this liberalization of disability terms created an enormous increase in claims. Ultimately, some 80 percent of disability benefits accrued to this new group of claimants. In immediate terms, however, the financial impact of the World War I Veterans Act was less staggering than expected. In fact, the cost of veteran benefits rose modestly between 1925 and 1929, from $612 million to $659 million. Yet, in the Coolidge era of shrinking budgets, these expenditures accounted for approximately 20 percent of the federal budget in each of those years. Indeed, outlays for veterans made up the largest single category of federal expenditure.[28]

Veterans' Policy Feedback, 1925–1929

After 1925, the newly created veterans' policies drew a powerful yet unexpected reaction from veterans. Beginning in 1927, veterans' policies created a new round of political activism among veterans seeking to redress their continued grievances. The first of the precipitating events was the setting in of the 1927 Bonus loan provision. As allowed by the Adjusted Compensation Act, veterans began to draw loans on their adjusted service certificates as soon as they were eligible to do so. Between 1927 and 1929, 1.65 million veterans (more than 40 percent of all certificate holders) borrowed $133.4 million against their certificates at the Veterans' Bureau and nearly $30 million more at banks. Second, the revised retroactive disability ratings that took effect in 1925 proved an important precedent for expanding disability claims temporally and categorically. In each of these areas, the VFW, a seemingly moribund veterans' group, began to speak out forcefully for additional revisions to enhance its standing with the former doughboys while the American Legion leadership rested on the laurels of the organization's previous victories.[29]

The Legion played the dominant role in the administrative and legislative victories for veterans' benefits and in the creation of the new veterans' bureaucracy, but the VFW increasingly parted company on major veterans' issues. Between 1926 and 1928, the policies of deferred payment and partial loans against that payment provided the grist for the VFW's challenge to federal veterans' policy. The VFW leadership began to renege on the adjusted service certificates compromise, offering instead proposals that would chip away at the Bonus insurance policy by pushing for immediate payment to those rated permanently and totally disabled. In resolutions issued from multiple national encampments, the VFW argued that the "permanent total" invariably suffered a shortened life span and, therefore, should "enjoy the benefits derived from the value of his adjusted compensation during the remaining months of his life." Yet, the organization's calls for any adjustments to the Bonus provisions went unheeded by both the Legion and veteran advocates in Congress. The VFW's association with Spanish-American War veterans continued to hinder the organization's ability to speak for the World War veterans with much authority, even though ex-doughboys counted themselves as members. More important, the VFW simply lacked the Legion's size and corresponding political strength. The Legion maintained a membership in 1928 of nearly 800,000 veterans, while the VFW struggled to keep 70,000 dues-paying members between 1926 and 1928. In early 1929, the chairman of the House Committee on World War Veterans Legislation, Royal C. Johnson (a member of both the Legion and the VFW), explained it quite simply to the newly inaugurated Herbert Hoover: the VFW's "membership is not sufficiently large to make it a vital factor in public sentiment." That year, however, the VFW embarked on a new course of action that would eventually transform the fortunes of the organization as well as the nation's politics.[30]

In 1929, while the Legion leadership remained mostly contented with its legislative bounty, the VFW pressed for greater demands on the government as a way to attract more former doughboys into the fold. To accomplish this, VFW leaders increasingly used the legislative victories of 1924 as a wedge to win even more concessions from the government. The Legion had recommended a very modest amendment to the World War Veterans' Act that would grant small pensions to widows and orphans of the World War I deceased. Seeking to make inroads with Great War veterans, however, the VFW supported measures that would broaden the pension rolls considerably. Eugene P. Carver, the national commander of the VFW, issued a statement on the twelfth anniversary of the United States' entry into the war, calling upon Congress to grant service pensions "to every disabled veteran who has thus far been denied compensation in some form." He proclaimed, "the least this nation can do . . . is to lend a helping hand to the veteran handicapped by physical and mental disabilities as a result of his loyalty to the flag." To achieve this, the VFW legislative committee sought to extend the deadline once again for tubercular and neuropsychiatric claimants. More important, the VFW leadership proposed a qualitative structural revision to the veterans' welfare system that would amend the list of "service-connected" infirmities to include dubious ailments like obesity and gout. This, of course, smacked of a move toward a general pension, but it was also a response only made possible by the 1924 legislation.[31]

Then, bolstered by the level of veterans' loan activity from 1927 to 1929, VFW national leaders began to argue more forcefully that the federal government must uphold its obligations to veterans permanently disadvantaged by their war service. In September 1929, the leadership derided the "Grave Yard Bonus" in an editorial published in *Foreign Service*, the organization's monthly publication. It declared, "The large percentage of loans made on the compensation certificates, since the first of 1927, proves how seriously was—and still is—the need of the average world war veteran." That same month, at the national encampment held in St. Paul, Minnesota, the VFW delegates went on record as endorsing the proposal by the populist Iowa senator Smith W. Brookhart (R, IA) to pay the Bonus immediately. The encampment resolution ordered the VFW leadership to "take appropriate action to further the passage and administration of the measure." Prior to the stock market crash and the social dislocation of the Great Depression, then, the VFW made the government's payment of the Bonus a signature issue based on the rationale that wartime service severely and irreparably disrupted the economic lives of veterans. The federal policy of a deferred Bonus coupled with the loan provision cracked the door ajar for future veteran political activism; the VFW's drive for new members blew it wide open. [32]

Just weeks after the members of the VFW met at their annual encampment, the stock market crashed in a spectacular and devastating fashion. As the U.S. economy ground to a halt and economic anxiety inexorably engulfed the nation, the VFW's new advocacy brought the organization the previously withheld support from World War veterans and located the organization in the middle of the swirling controversy precipitated by Great Depression over the proper relationship between citizens and the federal government. The VFW's sharper ideological edge matched the transformed national political mood, no longer dominated by the pro-business conservative orthodoxy of the Republican era. And the American Legion leadership and popular presidents could no longer suppress veterans' rising discontent with the government's treatment of its former defenders. By openly challenging the Legion's dominance on veterans' policy, VFW leaders watched energized and politicized World War veterans flock to the banner. A new suitor had cut in between the American Legion and the federal government, ending the virtual pas de deux that had characterized the ten years from 1919 to 1929.

2

Rethinking the Bonus March

Their remedy, obviously, is to pool their political strength . . . and
bring irresistible pressure to bear upon the politicians. Various altruistic leaders, eager for the ensuing jobs, already whoop them up
to that end. I suspect that they will be heard from hereafter, and
in a most unpleasant manner. We are just beginning to pay for the
war.
>   —H. L. Mencken on the veterans' Bonus in "The Case for the
>   Heroes," *The American Mercury* 24 (December 1931): 410

Political consciousness is as much a result of political mobilization
as a cause of mobilization.
>   —Richard Oestreicher

In the late 1920s, the Veterans of Foreign Wars appeared des-
tined for historical obscurity. Despite desperate attempts to recruit from
the ranks of the more than two million eligible World War veterans, the
VFW lagged behind both the American Legion and even the Spanish War
Veterans in membership. And yet, by 1932, in the middle of an economic
crisis that dealt severe blows to the membership totals of almost every
type of voluntary association, the VFW's membership tripled to nearly
200,000 veterans. Between 1929 and 1932, the VFW experienced this sur-
prising growth because the organization demanded full and immediate
cash payment of the deferred Soldiers' Bonus while the American Legion
opposed it. By challenging federal veterans' policy, the VFW rose out of
relative obscurity to become a prominent vehicle for World War veterans'
political activism. As important, by doing so the VFW unwittingly set in
motion the protest movement known as the Bonus March. Indeed, the

supposedly unprompted Bonus Army that moved on Washington in the summer of 1932 was a culminating response to the VFW's initiatives over the prior three years. When the American Legion, the largest of the World War veteran organizations, failed to challenge federal policy, veterans first flowed into the VFW and then onto the streets of the capital. And veteran politics, contained throughout the 1920s, burst like a shell into the watershed presidential campaign of 1932.

As discussed in the previous chapter, the Great Depression did not trigger veterans' calls for immediate cash payment of the Bonus. It did, however, impart a new intensity to their demands. While veterans' arguments for immediate payment hinged on the notion that wartime service unfairly and permanently disadvantaged them economically, they—like many Americans—began to bear the additional burdens brought on by the Depression. As evidence of the immediacy of the economic crisis that veterans were facing, over a nine-day period in January 1930, 170,000 needy World War I veterans applied for first-time loans on their Bonus certificates. Indeed, the scant existing evidence suggests that the Depression disproportionately affected veterans. In May 1931, the Legion issued a report claiming that 750,000 veterans were out of work, some 16 percent of the World War veteran population. More extensive Veterans' Administration studies conducted in 1930 and 1931 found that veterans experienced a nearly 50 percent higher unemployment rate than nonveterans of the same age cohort. Another Depression-era VA report concluded that veterans experienced longer stretches of unemployment and more dire financial need than did nonveterans. In 1931, American Legion Commander Ralph O'Neil summed up the situation—perhaps a bit too tidily—by proclaiming, "It is reasonable to assume that a majority of the unemployed are world war veterans."[1]

Both the Legion and the VFW attempted to address the issue of World War veterans' unemployment, but they did so in entirely different ways. In 1930, the Legion kicked off a series of employment drives to find jobs for veterans. As they had in similar efforts during the 1922 recession, Legion officials relied on the organization's middle-class and elite membership to assist out-of-work veterans. Commander O'Neil explained that the organization would be responsible in the 10,000 communities where it had posts for "providing the contact necessary between the veteran out of a job and the man who has a job." In announcing another plan in 1931, O'Neil explained that each Legion post would now have an appointed employment officer to help dispirited and jobless veterans. While the Legion's initial efforts made little headway in the struggle against unemployment, they proved a boon to the organization's membership rolls. Great War veterans scrounged up the $3 to $5 membership fee in order to utilize the organization's connections and influence to find work. By 1931, more than a million veterans belonged to the Legion, up from the roughly 900,000 who belonged at the start of the Depression.[2]

The VFW national leadership, in contrast, immediately turned to the government for aid. As early as November 1929, the VFW leadership witnessed the impact of the stock market crash on veterans' economic livelihoods. Hezekiah N. Duff, the VFW national commander, wired President Hoover asking that he employ the bully pulpit and urge business leaders to provide additional assistance to veterans through preferential hiring programs. On veteran unemployment, the VFW Commander reported to the president, "The local units of the VFW throughout the country are being besieged daily with appeals for help from veterans unable to secure employment." Duff painted a grim picture, "Thousands are shuffling along the streets of our cities, thinly-clad and hunger-driven, in futile search for employment and a chance to exist in the country for which they fought and were willing to die on the field of battle." As the Depression deepened in 1930, Commander Duff again wrote Hoover asking for federal assistance. Duff explained that the citizenry recognized the federal government's obligation to veterans, noting that "All these citizens know is that these veterans were hale and hearty before they went into service during the World War, and that they are physical and mental wrecks as well as industrial losses today." The VFW employed this rationale to continue the organization's call for the Bonus into the 1930 congressional session.[3]

In 1930, Congress, ever eager to please this important constituency, sought to alleviate some of the worst financial hardships facing veterans. The 1930 congressional session, however, focused on veterans' issues other than the Bonus. In the summer, Congress passed substantial legislation, including the granting of nonservice-connected disability pensions and the consolidation of all existing veterans' agencies into the Veterans' Administration. (A full discussion is found in chapter 3.) Many commentators suggested that the renewed interest in veteran affairs, although a typical election-year concern, could be seen as an attempt to curtail demands for the Bonus. Indeed, the expansion of disability pensions meant that many desperate veterans would now receive some federal financial

support. Meanwhile, the Bonus remained tabled in Congress for the remainder of the year. Nevertheless, World War veterans tried mightily to
get their representative organizations to resume the Bonus drive.[4]

At the 1930 national encampment in Baltimore, the VFW delegates
maintained the organization's mandate to fight for immediate payment.
Yet, the VFW's relationship with Herbert Hoover proved amicable, despite the organization's demands. The organization approved of Hoover's
positions on the pension bills passed during the summer and welcomed
the executive orders that restructured the unwieldy veterans' bureaucracy.
Many in the leadership believed that Hoover had their best interests at
heart, despite his opposition to the Bonus. The national commander even
told the encampment delegates that Hoover offered "the best administration for the overseas veteran which the country has ever had." Indeed,
Hoover made the trip to Baltimore to review the VFW's encampment
parade but declined the invitation to speak to the delegates, finding no
pressing political reasons to discourage the VFW from supporting the
Bonus. The larger, more powerful Legion proved a different matter.[5]

When the American Legion met in Boston just weeks after the VFW
encampment, the Legion leadership enlisted Hoover to squelch the plans
of its most unruly member, the congressional sponsor of immediate Bonus
payment, Wright Patman (D, TX). Prior to the convention, Patman announced his intention to raise the question of the Bonus before the assembled Legion delegates. This so worried administration officials and sympathetic members of the Legion that Hoover, joined on the dais (silently)
by Calvin Coolidge, gave the first presidential speech to the organization.
In a speech prepared with the aid of John Thomas Taylor, the Legion lobbyist, Hoover appealed to the Legionnaires' patriotism and, pointing to
the summer of veterans' legislation, explained that the federal government
had been very generous already to its former soldiers. Hoover's address
enabled Legion leaders to turn back the Bonus tide at the convention with
relative ease. The Legion national leadership's victory over Patman—a
Legionnaire but ineligible for VFW membership—changed the congressman's tactics and improved the fortunes of the VFW.[6]

In December 1930, Patman made overtures to the VFW national leadership, hoping to convince the VFW to join forces on the Bonus. By
this point, the VFW had been supporting the issue for well over a year.
Patman's solicitation of the VFW resulted from his frustration with the
intransigence of the Legion leadership. In December, as he wooed the
VFW leadership, Patman berated the conservative element in the Legion,

claiming that "Mr. Mellon's cohorts were successful in applying the gag rule" on the Bonus at the Legion convention.[7] Throughout December, Patman also spoke with Washington, DC, area VFW posts, often debating with Representative Hamilton Fish, Jr. (R, NY) over the respective merits of the Bonus bills they would submit at the beginning of the new congressional session. Patman's efforts bore fruit as District VFW posts began reporting their endorsement of the Patman plan in the weekly veterans' section of the *Washington Post.* The Federal Post described its members' support for Patman's bill, even though they reported that not one of its members was in need of relief.[8]

In January 1931, at the start of the congressional session, some forty-seven Bonus-related proposals circulated through Congress. If a proposal such as Patman's was accepted, payment of the full face value of the Bonus certificates would require a $2.2 billion federal expenditure. The Bonus, however, was not a strictly partisan matter. Of the forty-seven bill proposals, twenty-eight came from Democrats, eighteen from Republicans, and one from a Farm-Labor congressman. As this pressure mounted, Congress and the capital witnessed an explosive month of VFW activities.

President Herbert Hoover addresses American Legion national convention in Boston, October 6, 1930. General John Pershing looks into camera; former President Calvin Coolidge is seated fourth from right. Courtesy of the American Legion.

Congressman Wright Patman of Texas debates Donald A. Hobart, national commander of the American Veterans Association, on the question of Bonus payment, January 12, 1935. Courtesy of Bettmann/CORBIS.

The VFW's aggressive public lobbying tactics, official testimony before both houses of Congress, and leadership of Bonus marches to the Capitol thrust the organization into the spotlight.[9]

On January 21, the VFW ramped up the public pressure for the Bonus. A thousand veterans, led by the VFW, marched at the Capitol in a procession, delivering petitions supporting immediate payment. The gathering of the petitions itself had become an issue in late December when Royal Johnson attacked Patman and the VFW for signature gatherers' practice of asking for dime contributions. Johnson claimed that the petition drive smelled like a racket and denied its validity. Nevertheless, 124 members of Congress who publicly supported the Bonus accepted the petitions on the Capitol steps, drawing cheers from the assembled veterans. Three days after the Bonus rally, two hundred veterans congregated in Philadelphia's Independence Square, proclaiming their intentions to march to Washington in support of immediate Bonus payment. After speeches by their leaders, John Alfieri and Terrance B. Cochran of the Cochran VFW post in Philadelphia, and music from the VFW Darby post band, the marchers began a walk to Washington, carrying flags and a handmade sign reading "Philadelphia to Washington." Only twenty-six of the marchers made it to Washington, but the hungry and exhausted men managed to buttonhole the Pennsylvania congressional delegation and to call on Patman, the Bonus advocate. Some of the marchers hoped to appear before the Ways and Means Committee meetings on the Bonus planned for that week. When asked if the march had been a failure, the veterans prophetically explained to the contrary that "the hike might serve as a motive to other veterans' groups to actively back the [adjusted] pay bills with similar demonstrations."[10]

Yet, ultimately, as with all previous World War veterans' issues, the American Legion determined the course of legislative action on the Bonus. On January 25, bowing to internal pressure from fifteen State Legion Departments, the American Legion National Executive Committee (NEC) met to review the Legion's position. The Legion NEC made an unexpected reversal and endorsed the principle of immediate payment, noting in the resolution that the Bonus "would benefit immeasurably not only the veterans but the citizenry of the entire country." Livid Republican "kingmakers" such as Hanford MacNider and Stephen Chadwick privately condemned the members of the NEC as "the weakest since our organization began" and lambasted their failure to "hold the Legion against the selfishness of individuals" who wanted to "impose the ex-servicemen and his program as a burden upon the country." Nonetheless, the Legion NEC's decision imparted a new weight to the Bonus hearings in the Ways and Means Committee scheduled for the following week.[11]

The new Legion position turned the tide in Congress in favor of some liberalization of the Bonus, be it full cash payment or some partial measure. The VFW continued to voice its support for full and immediate payment. In testimony before both the Ways and Means Committee and the Senate Finance Committee, VFW Commander Paul Wolman argued that the Bonus would have three positive results. It would help relieve veterans' suffering, prove a "marvelous stimulant to existing economic conditions," and relieve the federal government of an existing debt. Wolman explained, "The Government would simply transfer an obligation, already assumed, from the shoulders of the veterans—who can not carry the burden—into the strongboxes of bondholders."[12] When a proposal to increase the amount veterans could borrow against their certificates from 22.5 to 50 percent received backing from the Legion's chief lobbyist, John Thomas Taylor, however, Congress jumped at the opportunity to satisfy veteran demands without fundamentally altering the established Bonus policy. This compromise legislation, like the original Adjusted Compensation Act, encountered intense opposition from the administration and from business groups. Secretary of the Treasury Mellon assumed the point for yet another Republican administration, characterizing any Bonus loan or payments as fiscally ruinous. The Republican National Committee released a statement claiming that if the Bonus loan passed, "we can expect a business depression and a period of acute human suffering the like of which this country has never known."[13]

On February 12, 1931, Congress took action, passing the 50 percent loan bill despite assurances from the administration that it would be vetoed. Hoover's promised veto message challenged the arguments for the Bonus loan and warned of the financial hardships it would inflict on the government. He derided the notion that the loans would stimulate business, calling the money veterans might spend from their loans "wasteful expenditure" and "no assistance in the return of real prosperity." Hoover rejected the moral arguments for the Bonus, noting that "The patriotism of our people is not a material thing." Moreover, he warned that paying the Bonus threatened the moral fiber of the country by eroding the virtues of "self-reliance and self support." Despite these arguments, Congress quickly overrode the veto. *Time* referred to the decisive vote to override as Hoover's "most serious congressional reversal."[14]

Veterans gladly took advantage of the newly available loans. On the first day, 18,000 veterans applied for loans in the New York City Veterans' Bureau offices alone. At the end of the first week, officials sorted through 985,793 loan applications. By January, 1932, 2.5 million veterans had borrowed the full 50 percent. Senator Arthur Vandenberg of Michigan later explained to Hoover that the loan liberalization was the only way to curtail the drive for full payment. Vandenberg wrote, "I shall always believe that if [Congress] had not embraced the loan plan . . . there would have been no escape from the full payment of these compensation certificates at that time."[15]

Yet, the federal government's continued reluctance to completely satisfy the admitted obligation only led to further veteran political activism. As they had in the 1924 Bonus compromise, VFW leaders relented, accepting the compromise measure for practical reasons, even though the organization continued to call for full payment. The VFW leadership still bemoaned "the injustice of the tombstone bonus," but they "accepted the compromise measure . . . because we realized this was the best we could hope for under existing conditions." Ironically, the 50 percent loan bill, and the political turmoil surrounding it, provided the VFW leadership with new ammunition in their fight for full payment. The sheer quantity of loans extended served as incontrovertible proof that veterans were in need. Moreover, the overwrought concerns of the Hoover administration and business groups about the catastrophic financial impact of even the 50 percent provision gave the VFW leaders a sharp retort. One month later, the editors of *Foreign Service* heaped scorn on those arguments in an editorial titled "No Chaos Yet." The editors dryly noted that, "despite gloomy predictions of a terrible calamity, impending bankruptcy, industrial chaos, and a tumultuous financial crisis nothing has actually been exploded but the myths."[16]

The VFW's militant position on the Bonus brought the organization unaccustomed success with World War veterans. In terms of membership growth and the expansion of the organization into new communities, the Bonus struggle paid substantive dividends for the VFW. From 1929 to 1931, the VFW grew from just less than 70,000 to 138,620 dues-paying members, nearly doubling its membership. As impressive, the VFW expanded its organizational structure into new communities with the formation of seven hundred new posts, a 43 percent increase. Post growth began to increase dramatically in the late fall of 1930, coinciding with the Legion's stated opposition to the Bonus. In October and November 1930, the VFW chartered fifty new posts each month, setting records for the organization. The growth in 1931 proved most remarkable, with 350 new posts being established and 70 more regaining their charter after becoming defunct for nonpayment of dues. By the end of 1931, the VFW's institutional strength was greater than at any other time in the organization's existence. To the upper echelons of the organization leadership, their position on the Bonus had made the difference. The VFW Legislative Committee chairman noted in his annual report that "it is felt that our legislative stand on the bonus . . . provided the working tools for our recruiting drive." With a swipe at the Legion, he added, "It certainly confirms the statement that the Veterans of Foreign Wars truly represent the veterans."[17]

The 1931 national encampment, organized by a VFW member from Independence, Missouri, Harry S Truman, reflected the organization's new standing. VFW officials with Republican ties wrote to the Hoover administration, fearing that the nominally nonpartisan VFW encampment would turn into a "Democratic Rally" in the friendly confines of the Kansas City Pendergast regime. A VA official with connections to both the administration and the VFW deemed an appearance by a high-ranking administration figure "darn near essential" to stemming a Democratic veterans "promenade" that would push the Bonus with malicious partisan glee. Frank T. Hines, the director of the VA, did attend and address the delegates, but his arguments against the Bonus proved futile.[18]

Hines's remarks to the delegates underscored the changing fortunes of the VFW. He congratulated the VFW delegates on their recruiting success but cautioned them in thinly veiled terms about demanding the Bonus. Hines remarked, "You have increased your membership greatly and with that increase comes a greater responsibility, because we must remember that before we were veterans we were citizens of this great country of ours and we are still citizens." He advised the VFW delegates and leaders to tell the next Congress, "because we realize the situation existing in our country and because we are patriotic citizens of this country . . . that we are going to be exceedingly cautious in our demands, because we are not going to be put in the position of asking for something and then be blamed later on because we caused a greater depression or a greater problem in our Nation." Commander Wolman immediately and sharply rebuked Hines in front of the delegates: "[W]e do not think we have ever made any demands as an organization which were unfair, and we certainly pledge that we shall not make any demands that our members believe to be unfair, sir." The encampment promptly and unanimously passed a resolution reaffirming the VFW's commitment to immediate cash payment of the Bonus.[19]

Weeks later, the American Legion convention met in Detroit. The National Executive Committee's decision in the January to reverse the official position against the Bonus complicated matters for those trying to suppress the Patman forces in the Legion. Concerned Legion "kingmakers" feared that the delegates were poised to swing over to a full cash payment position. To undermine calls for the Bonus, the Legion enlisted a reluctant Hoover to speak to the convention yet again. Despite warnings from Royal Johnson that a riot over the Bonus might break out in the convention hall, Hoover accepted the invitation and addressed the Legionnaires for the second consecutive year. Hoover appealed to the Legion's "character and idealism" and history of service, asking for "determined opposition by you to additional demands upon the nation until we have won this war against world depression." In response, the Legion delegates passed a resolution using language almost identical to Hoover's and beat back a Bonus vote, 902-507. The Legion resolution called upon "the able-bodied men of America, rich and poor, veteran, civilian, and statesmen, to refrain from placing unnecessary financial burdens upon National, State, or municipal governments." Legion leaders attributed the defeat of the Bonus to Hoover's address. One wrote Larry Richey, the president's secretary, "I firmly believe the Chief's coming to Detroit changed the vote from two to one for to two to one against payment of the bonus."[20]

In late 1931, as they realized that the Legion would not join in the fight for the Bonus during the next congressional session, the VFW leadership started staking an even more vigorous claim to the issue. Moreover, the VFW's Bonus position took on a sharper ideological cast as the issue began to be conflated with both inflationary economic thinking and the calls for increased "purchasing power" to defeat the Depression. In the process, the VFW made a prophet out of Baltimore's resident cynic, H. L. Mencken, who predicted that the fight for the Bonus would turn ugly. In a December editorial, Mencken admitted that "the damage the heroes suffered by being thrust into the war is much under-estimated, and that the amount of compensation they have got since they came home is equally over-estimated." He called Hoover's Legion speech, and the Legion national leadership's response a "spit in the eye" to veterans. Moreover, Mencken predicted that veterans would "pool their political strength" under "various altruistic leaders" who "already whoop them up to that end." Between December 1931 and May 1932, the VFW would "whoop them up" even more, establishing the immediate context from which the Bonus March would emerge.[21]

In late 1931, in response to the Legion leadership's success in squelching a favorable Bonus resolution, the VFW national organization undertook a massive publicity campaign to demonstrate World War veterans' support for immediate payment. Cognizant still of the Legion's larger membership and stature, the VFW attempted to demonstrate that the Legion leadership misrepresented the rank-and-file veteran on the Bonus issue. The VFW national organization published veteran "bonus ballots" in 162 metropolitan newspapers, newspapers with a combined circulation of twenty-three million copies. The VFW received 254,324 ballots from veterans in favor of the bonus and only 596 against. *Foreign Service* candidly framed the disconnect between the Legion leadership and veterans' views: "[T]he heart of the American Legion is sound to the core—with the rank and file of its membership wholly in sympathy with the problems of the great mass of veterans who are suffering from economic distress, due to widespread unemployment, and bureaucratic control of agencies that affect their welfare." For proof of the wrongheadedness of the Legion's official stance, the editorial staff pointed to the "thousands of individual Legion posts and members . . . working hand in hand with the VFW in the present crisis of the fight for immediate cash payment of the adjusted service certificates." Thus, even while reaping the benefits of their position and moving aggressively out in front of the issue, VFW leaders needed to confront the perception that the Legion spoke for the average World War veteran in order to obtain legislative results in the upcoming congressional session.[22]

While the VFW leadership solicited rank-and-file veterans' feelings on the Bonus, they did little to squelch veterans' rumblings about a march to Washington to promote the issue. Even in late 1931, small groups of veterans moved on the city, including the "Veterans Bonus Brigade" from Philadelphia led by the irrepressible John Alfieri. The VFW leadership issued a specific word of warning to marching veterans in the pages of *Foreign Service*. The leadership did not oppose the lobbying technique; rather, VFW leaders hoped to discourage insolvent veterans from flocking to the District. The warning stated that "all VFW members are urged to refrain from going to Washington to lend their personal influence to the campaign in behalf of cash payment *unless they are financially able to take care of themselves during the interim.*" The VFW leadership discouraged less solvent members from making the trip because the District of Columbia posts were already straining to provide relief for local unemployed veterans and for additional down-and-out veterans who journeyed to Washington in order to wrestle with the Veterans' Administration bureaucracy. The Washington, DC, posts told the national leadership that they could provide no more assistance to homeless and hungry veterans. That inability, not the VFW's disapproval of the lobbying technique, determined the organization's national policy on veterans coming to Washington. Instead, the VFW steadfastly supported the veterans' right to petition their government and continued to lead veterans in petitioning efforts.[23]

In 1931–1932, the VFW's mobilization for the Bonus intensified at both the national and the local level. Wright Patman and the dynamic future national commander James Van Zandt began a series of speaking engagements across the country. The Bonus barnstorming tour touched off veteran rallies in cities from Providence, Rhode Island, to St. Paul, Minnesota. *Foreign Service* reported that veteran audiences of as many as 2,500 persons attended these rallies. The VFW national organization also coordinated a grassroots push by holding four sectional conferences in Washington, DC; Chicago; Boston; and Kansas City. These conferences trained departmental and state leaders in publicity and lobbying tactics. The VFW leadership published petition blanks in *Foreign Service*, furthering the ongoing petition drive. VFW posts around the country reported to the national organization that they had amassed thousands of signatures for the Bonus. Members from Camp Bowie Post No. 78 in Fort Worth, Texas, secured 55,000 signatures in just eighteen days. The national organization published reports highlighting local posts' publicity and recruiting activities for others to emulate, activities that included renting out small storefronts in depressed commercial districts where VFW members combined heavy recruitment of veterans with the aggressive signature drive. Moreover, VFW and Women's Auxiliary national officers called upon members of the local posts and the auxiliaries to write their legislators demanding action on the Bonus. In short, the entire organization mobilized in the election year push for the Bonus.[24]

The VFW national organization also expanded its lobbying efforts into new media platforms. In January, the VFW planned a radio program for the NBC network that would combine lobbying for the Bonus, organizational recruiting, and patriotic entertainment. The "Hello America" broadcast featured an address by Wright Patman and a novel recruiting method in which the commander would conduct the induction ceremony's oath of obligation over the radio. Heard in more than fifty radio markets, Patman's speech refuted Bonus opponents' claims and cemented his public affiliation with the VFW. The VFW found the evening an enormous success as just over 21,000 new members joined the organization during the swearing-in ceremony. Twenty-one thousand new members equaled an over-night 15 percent increase in the existing membership. The VFW leadership found the radio an extraordinary publicity tool, one to be utilized at both the network level and in local broadcasts for years to come.[25]

From March to May 1932, the VFW lobbied Congress aggressively for the Bonus. The VFW legislative committee offices served as the headquarters for congressional supporters of the Bonus, a radical departure from the Legion's thirteen-year stranglehold on lobbying power. The VFW legislative chairman, L. S. Ray, mailed letters to every representative and senator asking for their support. Those who declared their intentions to vote for the bill went on a public list. Ray kept tabs on the list, periodically releasing it to the newspapers to maintain the pressure. On April 2, prior to the scheduled Committee on Ways and Means Bonus hearings, Ray reported that 166 "pledged" legislators supported the Bonus, even though the VFW explained that "in no instance had the organization threatened any member who refused to support the legislation." The VFW hoped that the Committee would rule favorably on the Patman bill, but, just in case, the VFW also tracked the signatures on a discharge petition that would bring the bill to a House vote regardless of the recommendations in the Committee report.[26]

On the eve of the House Ways and Means Committee meeting, those veterans who looked to the American Legion to join with the VFW and come out for the Bonus found their hopes dashed. Between the 1931 convention and the committee meeting, the Legion remained pointedly silent. Although pressed by state and local leaders and rank-and-file veterans to announce for the immediate payment of the Bonus, the Legion's national commander, Henry L. Stevens, kept his pledge to follow the dictates of the delegates who had elected him at the 1931 convention, even if it meant he would be "boiled in oil" at the next annual meeting. Still, veterans held out hope that Legion backing would once again carry the day. Instead, on April 5, the White House announced that Stevens had contacted President Hoover to assure him that the Legion "stands solidly behind him" against the Bonus payment. From his home town in North Carolina, Stevens declared that he was convinced he spoke for the Legion membership; he had toured thirty-seven states and found that only twenty-three out of the thousands of Legion posts supported immediate payment. He explained that "legionnaires recognize that as much as they would like to have the bonus money, the government is just not in any position to pay it now." This was no small matter in the Bonus struggle. As the *New York Times* pointed out, "Without Legion support it is admitted that the bill will never be passed over the veto certain to be applied if it ever reaches the White House." For this reason, Stevens's comments set off a firestorm.[27]

Bonus advocates in Congress, the VFW, and even the Legion all blasted Stevens's repudiation of the Bonus fight. Elmer Thomas (D, OK), a Senate sponsor of a Bonus payment bill, exclaimed that Stevens's assertion "absolutely could not be and is not true." Wright Patman rebuked Stevens, explaining "this goes to show that he does not know about his own organization." Darold D. Decoe, the VFW national commander, archly commented that Stevens could find on just one page of the March 1 *Congressional Record* resolutions supporting the Bonus from 330 Legion posts. He added that, by making such patently untrue statements, Stevens was "making himself ridiculous in the eyes of Congress and the veteran world." Legion state departments and posts fired off public statements supporting the Bonus and repudiating Stevens's comments. A Legion post in Hot Springs, New Mexico, told the Associated Press that if Stevens did not retract his statement, it would withdraw from the national body. The post commander added that Stevens had "played traitor to the ex-servicemen, does not merit the confidence of the membership, and has sold out." Veterans across the country joined the chorus of criticism. E. M. Luther wrote Stevens from Los Angeles denouncing his "trying to make a monkey out of the rank and file." He added bitingly, "As for the Legion being behind Mr. Hoover solid in his stand against . . . the Graveyard Bonus, so called, you are in very plain English, 'ALL WET.'" In Greensboro, North Carolina, a "near riot" occurred at a veterans' Bonus rally where the Legion's national commander was assailed for his comments. When a veteran from Stevens's hometown took exception to the calumny heaped on the commander, "two pistols and some whiskey bottles were brandished over the . . . man's head." Police were called in to calm down the thousands in attendance. Clearly, Stevens's comments had touched a very raw nerve.[28]

To counter Stevens's statements and to show the strength of veteran support, the VFW escalated the public pressure. In a precursor to the Bonus March, three days before the House Ways and Means Committee proceedings on the Patman Bonus bill, the VFW organized a large march and rally to the Capitol in support of the Bonus. On April 8, 1932, Paul C. Wolman led the Bonus procession with members of VFW posts from Pennsylvania, Maryland, Virginia, West Virginia, and the District of Columbia taking part. Defiant members of eight Legion posts joined the rally. Between 1,500 and 2,000 veterans marched in a "picturesque" parade up to the Capitol steps, led by the VFW band from Clarksburg, West Virginia, and two hundred flag bearers. Members of the House and Senate, including Representative Wright Patman and Senator Elmer Thomas, the leaders of the Bonus legislation, met with the leaders of the procession and drew loud cheers from the assembled veterans. The VFW leaders presented the members of Congress with twenty packing cases of petitions bearing more than two million signatures—281,000 from ex-servicemen—supporting immediate cash payment. Newsreel cameras and

VFW-led Bonus demonstration at Capitol, April 8, 1932. Underwood and Underwood, courtesy of the Library of Congress.

photographers thronged around the ceremony on the Capitol steps. Veterans yelled, "Give us cash!" The *New York Times* noted, "Occasionally there was a shout of 'to the White House' but the mass meeting was an orderly one." Five hundred policemen stood by just in case.[29]

When the Committee on Ways and Means finally met on April 11, the VFW national leaders alone represented World War veterans' demands for the Bonus. VFW Commander DeCoe explained to the Committee that "the Bonus will be the biggest and best payday this country has had in months." Paul C. Wolman, a former VFW commander and now the chairman of the VFW's Cash Payment Campaign Committee, testified that veterans needed the Bonus since they suffered disproportionaly compared to the rest of the working population. Legislative chairman Ray submitted to the Committee a state-by-state tabulation of the VFW's newspaper ballot results and excerpts from letters written by desperate veterans to the VFW Legislative office. The VFW and Patman also called on celebrities to bolster their arguments for the Bonus. Sgt. Alvin York, the popular and highly decorated World War I hero who had joined a VFW post in April as the organization reached into the Tennessee countryside, sent a telegram supporting the Bonus. The recently retired Marine general Smedley D. Butler also wired the House Committee at the behest of his VFW comrades. Father Charles E. Coughlin, the radio priest, offered his opinions on the social and economic merits of the Bonus. Despite these efforts, however, the Legion remained aloof and opposed to the bill because of the 1931 convention's decision against prepayment. Moreover, Hoover had assured members of Congress in no uncertain terms that he was "absolutely opposed to any such legislation." As a result, on May 6, 1932, the Ways and Means Committee shelved the Patman Bonus bill. Both Patman and the VFW vowed to send the bill from committee to the House floor by a discharge petition and continued to press for the measure, even though the congressional calendar afforded little time to complete the necessary parliamentary maneuvers before the end of the session. [30]

While the VFW failed in its Bonus push, the organization collected concrete benefits from the mobilization begun in December. John A. Weeks, a member of the Minnesota House of Representatives, wrote the White House about the VFW's gains in stature and membership relative to the Legion. He bemoaned to Walter Newton, "A good many of the boys have lost their heads [about the Bonus] because the Legion membership has dropped 25%, while it is claimed that the VFW have doubled their membership." Weeks miscalculated slightly; the Legion lost 162,000 members between 1931 and 1932, a 15.4 percent decline. Weeks did come closer, however, in describing the VFW's success with the Bonus issue. In April, May, and June of 1932, for example, the VFW mustered 71,100 new members and 74 new posts, shattering all organization records. In May alone, nearly three posts a day chartered into the VFW. [31]

The VFW's growth resulted from the organization's aggressive promotion of World War veterans' demands while its larger, more powerful rival stayed in the background. A May *Foreign Service* editorial touted the VFW's new strength, asserting that "veterans throughout the country are awakening to the fact that they owe their support to a veteran organization that truly represents the rank and file of ex-servicemen." Even the unsympathetic editors at *The Christian Century* framed the Bonus fight in terms of the rivalry for World War veterans' affiliation. "So great are the stakes," they explained, "that the rivalry between the various organizations is constantly increasing in bitterness." The editors admitted that the Legion opposed the Bonus, "but their position is made difficult by the knowledge that a rival body is supporting this proposal, that many local legion posts are in favor of it, and there is a possibility that if the legislation passes the rival body will take the credit for the act, and will be able to transfer to itself the allegiance of hosts of ex-service men who have previously been members of the legion." Tunis Benjamin, a veteran of the Great War from Watervleit, Michigan, confirmed that this transfer in membership was under way. In a letter dated the day the VFW marched on the Capitol, he wrote the White House demanding immediate payment and added pointedly, "I am a veteran and belong to the American Legion. I do not belong to the VFW but am changing to an honorable vets organization soon." More important than the significant organizational gains, the VFW national organization provided an outlet for veterans' Bonus agitation all spring and fostered the conditions necessary for the subsequent Bonus March.[32]

In this spirited context of organized veteran political activism, three hundred veterans in Portland, Oregon, set out for the nation's capital, beginning what came to be known as the Bonus March. Spurred on by an unemployed overseas veteran named Walter W. Waters, the group departed on May 10, 1932, and rode the rails across the country, encountering widely publicized difficulties with railroad companies and various local authorities. By the time the Oregon contingent made it to Washington on May 29, waves of veterans around the country had joined the trek. The VFW's refusal to relent on the Bonus and its feverish promotion of the discharge petition as a last-ditch effort both kept the issue in the media and, more important, gave the marchers a concrete goal. Indeed, after the veterans set up camps around the city, they walked to the Capitol daily to convince members of Congress to sign the Bonus discharge petition. Dubbed the Bonus Expeditionary Force (BEF) by the sympathetic District Superintendent of Police, Pelham D. Glassford, the veteran crowd grew at an astonishing rate. By June, as many as 40,000 veterans, many with families in tow, had crowded into the capital. A group of Communist veterans affiliated with the Worker's Ex-Servicemen League also moved into the city, but their attempts to recruit the other marchers met with little success. BEF leaders denounced their revolutionary zeal; more proactive veterans physically expelled them from the camps with unequivocal shoves.[33]

As the BEF settled in Washington, congressional Bonus supporters finally gathered enough discharge petition signatures to vault the Patman bill over the Ways and Means Committee and put it to a floor vote. On June 15, the House quickly passed the Patman Bonus measure despite the

Veterans protesting at the Capitol during the Bonus March, July 5, 1932. Courtesy of Bettmann/CORBIS.

fact that (or, as cynics argued, because) the bill stood little chance in the Senate and faced a promised veto from Hoover. On June 17, with thousands of veterans awaiting news on the Capitol steps, the Senate decisively defeated the Patman Bonus bill. Deflated by the loss, more than 5,000 veterans accepted the government's offer of transportation back home—the cost would be deducted from their remaining Bonus balances. The remaining veterans stayed in the various camps and other abandoned buildings around the city, promising to stay until they got their Bonuses, even if that meant waiting until 1945. The Communist Party contingent stayed, too, becoming a larger and louder percentage of the veterans in the city but still making few inroads with the larger BEF. For more than a month, the situation simmered as supplies became critically short and sanitation a major concern. Government officials grew increasingly anxious. One source described the situation as "a pile of dynamite on Washington's doorstep."[34]

The Legion's national officers disassociated the organization from the ragtag Bonus Army as assiduously as they did from the Patman Bonus bill. In fact, for some time the Legion national officers simply remained silent on the Bonus March. Royal Johnson wrote Hoover to explain that the Legion leadership had kept mute despite his pleas that it begin to work on getting the veterans out of the city peacefully. He explained, "I tried to get the Commander of the American Legion to take the initiative, but he seems to be afraid of it." A statement of sorts finally came from Commander Stevens during a trip to Paris where, to his surprise, people believed the Legion was behind the March. He asked members of the American Club in Paris to help correct the French misunderstanding, adding that "Legionnaires are too good American Citizens to ask Congress for anything in these times." He insisted, "They prefer to set an example of forbearance and sacrifice." Lesser Legion officials, however, slammed the veteran marchers. A New York Legion leader explained, "I want to state that we have not sanctioned any such demonstration as is now going on and we have no sympathy for the bonus hunters who are besieging Washington." Post Commander Joseph C. Paul, of South Orange, New Jersey, wired the White House offering "to organize and finance 100,000 World War veterans to come to Washington . . . and clear the Capital City of our misinformed brothers-in-arms, administering a sound spanking to the leaders for good measure."[35]

Despite this mixture of indifference and contempt, "renegade" Legion posts and individual veteran members had supplied the Bonus Army at every step on the way to Washington and continued to do so throughout the occupation. As just one of countless examples, on June 18, fifty members from the Frank C. Hall Legion Post in Newark carried seven carloads of food for the Bonus camps. Moreover, despite the national organization's stand on the Bonus and the March, Legionnaires became part of the BEF. On June 5, the *New York Times* reported that two hundred veterans from Brooklyn Legion posts had set off to the capital to join their comrades. [36]

For their part, VFW members followed this logical extension of the organization's Bonus campaign and, as a result, left an indelible mark on the Bonus March. Eleven days before the celebrated Bonus Army from Oregon arrived in Washington, in fact while they were still in the train yards of East St. Louis, twenty-five veterans from VFW Post No. 1289 in Chattanooga, Tennessee, had already arrived in the capital demanding the Bonus. The Chattanooga VFW members parked their truck, with "We Want Our Bonus" painted on the side, near the White House. One historian of the Bonus March postulates that the Portland veterans perhaps borrowed the idea that they would not leave the city until they got their

Veterans from Chattanooga VFW post parade past White House in truck
with signs demanding Bonus, May 18, 1932. New York World-Telegram
and the Sun Newspaper Photograph Collection. Courtesy of the Library
of Congress.

money from a statement by the VFW members published in an AP report. A *New York Times* column described a contingent of 125 veterans,
half of whom belonged to the VFW's Fred C. Hall Post in Jersey City,
who had left Hoboken to join the BEF and bring relief supplies,. A group
of 450 integrated veterans from the VFW's post in Harlem, the Dorrence
Brooks Post No. 528, reported its plans to join the festivities in Washington. By June, local VFW leaders close to the situation claimed, much to
the dismay of the national leadership, that "60 percent of the veterans in
the Capital are members of the VFW waving the colors of their respective
posts."[37]

Additional evidence suggests that overseas veterans—the membership
pool of the VFW—made up a disproportionately large percentage of the
veterans coming to the capital. Using data from District police officers
who registered veterans as they came to town, the *New York Times* reported that 83 percent of the veterans moving into Washington claimed to

be overseas veterans. After the Bonus bill's defeat, when the federal government provided transportation to more than 5,000 veterans, Veterans'
Administration officials indicated that 66.5 percent of those accepting the
offer had served overseas during the war. Overall, only half of World War
I veterans served overseas. Whether overseas veterans suffered disproportionately from the Depression or rallied more energetically to the VFW's
agitation is unknowable, but the proportion of overseas veterans in Washington for the March far exceeded their proportion of the World War veteran population.[38]

Whatever the percentage of VFW members in the BEF may have been,
local posts in Washington and around the country generously provided
the Bonus Army with material and moral support. The VFW District of
Columbia Council, representing fourteen local posts, donated $500 to help
feed the marchers. The VFW Front Line Post of Washington offered the
use of a theater that the post had at its disposal. The Front Line Post told
a BEF assembly that the theater would be "turned over to the BEF for the
purposes of collecting funds for the BEF treasury." The BEF would need
only to supply "the talent." On June 7, when some 7,000 Bonus Marchers
paraded up Pennsylvania Avenue, a local VFW band led the procession.
Posts from around the nation provided material assistance. For example,
VFW members in Asbury Park and Bradley Beach, New Jersey, solicited
food and materials for the BEF from local merchants. The Jersey posts accumulated enough to fill two trucks and headed toward Washington with
twelve veterans eager to join the March. Whether as members of the BEF
or as sympathetic supporters, VFW members aligned themselves in solidarity with the Bonus Army.[39]

Adding to the linkages between the Bonus March and the VFW, key
figures from the episode maintained extensive VFW ties. Chief of Police
Glassford's personal rapport with the veterans and his patient handling
of the crisis made him immensely popular with the BEF, so popular that
Glassford served as the treasurer of the BEF's funds. Not only did Glass-
ford belong to a local VFW post; he had also been a chief recruiter for
the VFW in 1931 just prior to his taking the police chief position. Joseph
Heffernan, the former mayor of Youngstown, Ohio, and a prominent
VFW state leader, moved to Washington to begin the publication of *The
BEF News*, a weekly newspaper published for the Bonus Army veterans.
Heffernan's publication, with its scathing editorials, became the officially
sanctioned publication of the BEF, ending its publication run in August
at 75,000 copies. Rice Means, publisher of the *National Tribune*, the only

national veteran publication unaffiliated with the veteran organizations, supported the Bonus March from the start in print and with coin. Means, a former senator from Colorado, worked extensively with a number of veteran organizations. He was known, however, as the VFW's first national commander and continued to serve on the VFW's legislative committee. Smedley Butler, the popular Marine Corps general who came to Camp Marks to cheer on the men and who actually bivouacked overnight in one of the dwellings, belonged to the VFW and would go on, from 1933 to 1936, to be the VFW's main recruiting speaker. This is not to say that all of these prominent VFW figures gave the Bonus March VFW sanctioning. But the fact that all of these high-profile men publicly supported the Bonus Army linked the VFW to the episode in visible and important ways.[40]

The VFW leadership had not anticipated that its lobbying efforts for the Bonus would spark such a massive demonstration. Yet, given the level of VFW involvement, it is easy to see how the organization that had supported the Bonus since 1929 would be associated with the episode. Statements from the VFW leadership reflected concerns that the March was being viewed as a VFW-sanctioned event. As early as May 24 (five days before the Portland contingent arrived in Washington), the VFW national organization felt compelled to deny any official connection with the demonstrations and discouraged members from coming to the city. In early June, as the BEF grew to more than 20,000 members, the national leadership sent communiqués to every post prohibiting members, on threat of expulsion, from taking part in the March and adding to the crisis. The VFW adjutant general in Kansas City, R. B. Handy, Jr., denounced the Communist agitation in the March as an effort "to capitalize upon the unrest and discontent of unemployed veterans." Handy argued that this could only prove counterproductive to the organization's Bonus strategy, "embarrassing existing efforts on the part of our legislative committee and those individual members of Congress who are advocating immediate cash payment." Even so, Handy noted that the goals of most of the marchers coincided with the VFW's call for immediate payment. Handy explained that, "without doubt, the groups of former service men marching on Washington are inspired by patriotic motives and have no other purpose than assisting in the campaign for cash payment of the Bonus." Handy and the VFW leadership feared that those men would set the Bonus drive back, not advance it.[41]

While the national leaders of the VFW failed to back the Bonus March for pragmatic reasons, VFW officials in proximity to the veteran camps blasted the leadership for not commandeering a march it had unintentionally instigated. At the height of the BEF occupation, the Maryland Department of the VFW met to elect state officers and national encampment delegates. The Maryland delegates became embroiled in a passionate debate over the Bonus March and the failures of the national leadership. The state encampment passed a resolution denouncing the national leadership and requesting an explanation for the national headquarters' actions. Claiming that the VFW had initiated the March as evidenced by the "60 percent" VFW participation, the Maryland VFW decried that "when the big throng moved on Washington nothing was done by way of leadership." Why, they asked, were "no officials sent to lead the 20,000 or more veterans in their fight to urge passage of the Bonus Bill in Congress?" These state leaders suggested that, instead of leading the March, the VFW had abdicated responsibility for the BEF, giving the Communists the opportunity to appropriate what the VFW had started. Had the VFW appointed leaders to the Bonus Army, the Maryland delegates proclaimed, "the great body of veterans in this country would not be branded radicals." The following day, after VFW chief of staff, Joseph Ranken, addressed the delegates, cooler heads prevailed and the delegates withdrew the resolution. The resolution, however, exposed both the belief that the VFW had caused the March and the equally troubling proposition that the VFW had played into the hands of the Communists by not leading the BEF.[42]

Others echoed the Maryland VFW delegates in making this accusation. An intelligence memorandum circulated to the FBI and the White House explained that the VFW bore responsibility, even though the March was becoming a Communist rally. The memorandum described the situation in terms almost identical to those in the Maryland accusations. It began, "The present march on Washington is the direct result of Communist agitation, pure and simple." The memo continued, however: "The Communists have taken advantage of Veterans of Foreign Wars internal politics and the urging of the Bonus by the leaders and are trying to turn this agitation to their, the Communists' advantage." Accusations blaming the VFW and the VFW national leadership for causing the Bonus March reverberated through other private and public channels that summer.[43]

Prominent figures in veteran circles attributed the descent of the marchers on the city to the VFW's Bonus agitation. In a private letter, Royal C. Johnson cautioned President Hoover that the Bonus Army might reach 100,000 people. He explained that perhaps any veteran "who thought

[he] had a bonus due would join with them, particularly when they have been excited to such a move by the Veterans of Foreign Wars, members of Congress, newspapers, and even the clergy." Johnson thought that the VFW had recognized its mistake, however, claiming, "I feel certain that by this time the commander of the Veterans of Foreign Wars would also urge them to leave." On June 11, Johnson made similar statements on the House floor, solemnly declaring, "one great organization . . . the Veterans of Foreign Wars, is partially responsible for this migration." He acknowledged that the VFW leadership now sought "to move [the marchers] out, but they helped get them in." Johnson explicitly linked the VFW's promotion of the discharge petition with the descent of the marchers and proclaimed that "the men who started that [petition] have their share of responsibility." As chairman of the House Veterans' Committee and a former judge advocate of the VFW national organization, Johnson was in a better position than most to cast blame for the Bonus March.[44]

To some in the media, the "veterans' lobby" bore ultimate responsibility for causing the Bonus March. The editors of *The Christian Century* cast blame on the Legion and "other organizations" for "the descent of veterans on the capital." The editors explained that "it is a short step" from veteran lobbying "to the idea that veterans would fare even more profitably should they make their demands in person." But it was a sidestep that the marchers took. The Bonus March took place because veterans *bypassed* the entrenched World War veterans' lobby domineered by the American Legion. Urged on by an interloping organization looking to secure a more prominent position with them, Great War veterans turned first to the VFW and then took to the streets of the nation's capital in their efforts to change federal policy.[45]

On July 28, 1932, the U.S. government moved to expel the Bonus Marchers from the city. When the police tried to disperse BEF squatters' camps located in partially demolished federal buildings, clashes broke out, leaving two veterans dead and several police wounded. District commissioners finally appealed to the federal government for assistance with the precarious situation. The Hoover administration called upon the U.S. Army to restore order at the sites, but Chief of Staff General Douglas MacArthur exceeded his orders and deployed troops, tanks, and cavalry to drive the veterans out of all of their encampments. At the largest of these, on the Anacostia River, the Army chased out stragglers with fixed bayonet and then torched the dwellings to the ground. The Hoover administration immediately defended the Army's tactics during the veteran removal, branding the BEF a dangerous gathering of Communists and criminals that threatened the security of the nation's capital. Dazed and angry veterans now marched out of the District, their quest over. But the specter of the Bonus March's ignoble end lingered, permeating the political consciousness of Americans and, for many, making inevitable a new chapter in U.S. politics.[46]

The Bonus saga caused veteran politics to spill over into the national political arena. In the pivotal 1932 presidential election year, the Bonus had become weighted with intensely ideological baggage, the veteran supplicants becoming symbols of a collapsing political and economic order incapable of addressing the problems created by the Great Depression. From its inception, the Bonus had reflected a fundamental critique of the American political economy. After 1929, however, veterans and their many sympathizers viewed the struggle for the Bonus as one where ordinary Americans faced off against the wealthy and powerful who continued to exert an unchecked and damaging influence on the polity. The formation of the National Economy League, an organization of prominent financiers and business leaders who denounced the Bonus and called for dramatic reductions in veteran benefits, in the late spring of 1932, proved what lengths the economically advantaged would go to oppose veterans' and, by extension, ordinary citizens' welfare.[47]

As Americans began to reassess the role of federal government, for many the Bonus March came to represent the country's unmet obligations to its citizens. And the Hoover administration's rout of the BEF exposed the callousness of austere conservatism during a time of great national need. Lawrence G. Pugh, an attorney and a former American Expeditionary Force officer, explained in a letter to Hoover that the Bonus March had been "foolish and useless." But, he continued, "the cause of their presence was the failure of the leaders of this country in furnishing relief." Pugh added caustically, "Clubbing these men, women, and children from Washington will not remove the cause of their pilgrimage." Frank Murray, a veteran, wrote a letter to Hoover declaring that "the unemployed in this country owe a debt of gratitude" to the BEF because, prior to the March, "poor relief was a local problem and should have no assistance from the federal government." John Henry Bartlett, a Republican Roosevelt supporter who had offered his own land to the BEF as an encampment, summed up the relationship by claiming that, while the marchers had failed in their quest for a Bonus, "they won a principle of relief for all of the poor in the land and helped establish the new federal policy wherein the paramount concern is the uplift of the . . . people."[48]

Despite its ideological trappings, the Bonus issue failed to become fodder for national partisan politics. Split as they were between conservative and populist or progressive wings, neither party took command of the issue. In June, many Progressive Republicans had supported the issue, much to the consternation of Hoover. Indeed, thirty-four Republican signatories had allowed the discharge petition to advance. Fifty-seven Republicans opted to go against their chief's directives when the Bonus passed the House. That said, Wright Patman, Elmer Thomas, and other populist Democrats who supported the measure continued to see it as a traditional Democratic issue. Elmer Thomas explained very clearly that the Bonus transcended mere monetary relief for veterans. Thomas viewed it as a Jacksonian class issue: a battle between the "bondholding creditor class" and the "debtor class." After the defeat of the Bonus, the rising populist star of the Democratic Party, Senator Huey P. Long (D, LA) believed that all Democratic candidates for national office should use the Bonus vote to bludgeon their Republican opponents. Despite this pressure within his party, however, Governor Franklin D. Roosevelt of New York resisted entreaties that he seize on the Bonus as a campaign issue.[49]

As a Democratic candidate for President, FDR did all he could to keep the Bonus March and the Bonus issue out of his campaign. On the stump, FDR spoke movingly about the "forgotten man" who needed the government's helping hand. Moreover, New York's state government had provided a great deal of relief to the unemployed during Roosevelt's term as governor. Yet, FDR hewed to his own fiscally conservative sensibilities and commented that he saw no reason that the Bonus should be paid in advance, given the economic conditions and the soaring federal deficit. Moreover, Roosevelt viewed the Bonus as a benefit to only a small group of citizens no more deserving of aid than millions of other suffering Americans. At the 1932 Democratic convention, however, pressure to pledge for the Bonus reemerged. During the grueling nominating session, FDR received a phone call from Senator Huey P. Long, a supporter, begging him to declare for immediate payment. Long told FDR, "Whether you believe in it or not, you'd better come out for it with a strong statement, otherwise you haven't got a chance for the nomination." When Roosevelt told Long that he would not do it, the Kingfish sighed, "Well, you are a gone goose." As the convention went to the tense third round of balloting, many of FDR's advisers worried that Long had been right.

Nevertheless, Roosevelt clinched the nomination—just barely—without supporting the Bonus, and the resulting Democratic platform remained awkwardly silent on the issue.[50]

If FDR's stance on the Bonus more or less removed it from the campaign, the rout of the Bonus marchers nonetheless weighed heavily on the election. Foremost, the removal of the BEF by the Army just one month after the convention allowed FDR to profit politically from the Bonus issue even without supporting prepayment. Indeed, FDR and his innermost circle viewed the rout as an unequivocally auspicious development. Rex Tugwell recorded in his memoir that FDR realized he had sewn up the election as he lay in his Hyde Park bed reading the newspaper accounts of the rout. In another account, FDR declared to Felix Frankfurter upon hearing the news, "Well, Felix, this will elect me." For Roosevelt, as for most historians since, Hoover's removal of the Bonus Army was the symbolic ending of one political era and the tenuous beginning of another.[51]

Veterans' reaction to the Bonus Army's removal gave sustenance to the notion that the country had reached a political watershed and that veteran politics would prove decisive in the election. As expected, countless Democratic veterans issued condemnations and threats to Hoover's continuance in the White House. But letters from Republican veterans who had voted for Hoover in 1928 provided an indication of the potential impact of the Bonus March dispersal on the November election. Lawrence G. Pugh, a former American Expeditionary Force (AEF) officer, protested Hoover's actions and concluded, "The members of the AEF can but express themselves at the polls and I will vote against you every time I have the opportunity." George E. Parker wrote to Hoover's secretary lamenting that his vote for Hoover had been a mistake because "it is all too evident that he is incapable of measuring up to the grave responsibilities and duties of his position." Parker continued, "It is . . . a matter of deep regret to one who has been a life-long Republican, to realize that yesterday Mr. Hoover kicked out of the Republican column some five million votes." He concluded, "We will answer yesterday's events at the polls in November, and that in unmistakable tones." A letter from a disabled veteran in Los Angeles dripped with venom, explaining to Hoover what the rout had meant to him. He wrote, "As a Republican I'm going to help revile you and bury you in November." He admitted that Hoover probably would not read the letter, but just the same he told him "you are going to *Feel* our *Power* in November."[52]

As expected, veterans affiliated with the VFW also reacted fiercely to the Bonus Marchers' removal. The VFW leadership reproached the officials involved in no uncertain terms. Calling the episode "a national disgrace," the leadership defended the rights of the BEF to assemble in Washington. The editorial explained that "those men who assembled with the belief that their presence would win recognition of their demands, were sincere in their conviction that their cause was just and their methods proper." Moreover, even if the BEF had exercised poor judgment and had to be disbanded, the editorial argued, "there were dozens of effective methods . . . that could have been used in this evacuation in preference to tear bombs, sabers, tanks, and machine guns." The VFW leadership issued a warning to Hoover and congressional Bonus opponents, predicting that "evacuation orders will be heard again in Washington when the ballots are counted next November." Hostile letters and telegrams stacked up in the White House from VFW posts condemning Hoover in equally vituperative language. The Argonne Post of Flatbush (Brooklyn), New York, protested the "inhumane and brutal treatment of the veterans" and commented that "certainly bread is cheaper than tear bombs, Mr. President." The Glendon Post, of Philadelphia, described the rout as the "most cruel and shameful act of ingratitude towards its defenders as ever perpetrated by the constituted authorities of a civilized nation." The Herbert Dunlavy Post of Houston, Texas, explained the episode in the ideological terms associated with the Bonus. The writers concluded that "this foul act reflects only class discrimination, for had these unfortunate veterans the power of millions of dollars, they would have been welcomed with outstretched arms."[53]

Much as they had split over the Bonus, Legionnaires had varying reactions to the Bonus March rout at the national, state, and local levels. National leaders remained publicly silent, resisting pressures to censure the president and his administration. Theodore Roosevelt, Jr., a kingmaker and a Republican, argued that the Hoover administration had acted sensibly to put down Communists bent on "riot and revolution." But the serving national officers tried very hard to place some distance between the organization and the Hoover administration. When Assistant Attorney General G. Aaron Youngquist requested that the Legion publish the official administration version of the March and rout in its monthly magazine, Legion officials politely declined. Some conservative Legion posts and state departments offered the administration support. The Crosscup-Pishon Post of Boston wired Hoover, endorsing the "action you have taken regarding the so-called bonus army" who had "neither the support, sympathy nor respect of the true veterans of this country." The Vermont Legion's state convention passed a resolution condemning the marchers and "viewed with satisfaction" the eviction of this "threatening force."[54]

A larger number of Legion posts and state encampments blasted the president for the removal of the BEF and, in defiance, came out in favor of the Bonus. South End Post 105 of Boston wrote the president a terse letter protesting the rout. "These men merely asked for what was promised them when they were called heroes," the members explained. Instead, they continued, "they are treated as hoboes." The post promised to "do all in its power to see that this will be kept before the public, 'Lest we forget' in November." Vincent B. Costello Post 15 in Washington, DC, passed a resolution denouncing Hoover and the officials "responsible for the brutal, Un-American, and unlawful manner in which these hungry and destitute veterans . . . were driven from the District." The Pennsylvania Legion's state convention condemned the president's removal of the BEF as a "spectacle alien to our history." The resolution charged that Hoover "handled the whole situation in a regrettable manner, which contributed to this sad incident." When a minority group—presumably Republican faithful—sought to strike out all specific references to the president, they were voted down 864 to 124. Ohio Legionnaires also decried the "unnecessary force" and voted to endorse Bonus payment at the national convention. Indeed, by the end of August, thirty-one Legion state departments had adopted resolutions in support of the Bonus, including the largest department of New York. Eight state departments urged formal censure of the president, including the normally Republican strongholds of Illinois and Pennsylvania. Whereas the Bonus March had failed to push the Legion to support immediate payment, the Hoover administration's rout of the Bonus Marchers and its clumsy handling of the aftermath succeeded in moving Legionnaires unequivocally into the pro-Bonus camp after years of deep division on the issue.[55]

Barely one month after the removal, the VFW gathered at the annual encampment in Sacramento, basking in the organization's membership success and ready to take the fight to Hoover and to Bonus opponents. The organization had a right to boast. Indeed, in 1932, the VFW grew at an amazing clip. More than 50,000 new members joined, raising the membership total to nearly 200,000 overseas veterans by the time of the convention. The outgoing national commander claimed a 67 percent one-year increase in membership. This put the organization at three times

TABLE 2.1
VFW Membership and Post Growth, 1929–1932

	1929	1930	1931	1932
Total membership	76,669	95,167	138,620	187,469
Membership gained in year	6,693	18,498	43,453	48,849
Total posts	1,767	1,945	2,313	2,757
Posts gained in year	154	178	368	444

its size in 1927. Moreover, post growth broke records just set in 1931. The VFW gained 442 new posts in 1932, by all accounts the direst year of the Depression and a horrible year for voluntary association membership. One hundred and eighty-six suspended posts rechartered. For the year, 52.3 posts chartered per month, an average that bested the all-time highs for any one month in the organization's history. In other words, in 1932, the VFW's membership and distribution throughout the country simply skyrocketed.[56]

The VFW encampment turned into a spirited political rally. The slate of speakers attacked the veterans' enemies, issuing stinging indictments of the Hoover administration and the organization's congressional adversaries. Wright Patman traveled to California to address the delegates, drawing boisterous and prolonged applause for his attacks on Bonus opponents. The VFW delegates swore continued vigilance on the Bonus, demanding from the leadership that the Bonus campaign not only continue but "be intensified and extended in every way possible as far as finances and facilities permit." The organization then passed a resolution "seriously censuring those Government officials . . . responsible for the un-humanitarian and un-American manner that was used in clearing the camps occupied by the so-called marchers." In another extraordinary resolution, the delegates looked to the November election to punish the Hoover administration, decrying the "action of the President of the United States with the BEF" as "criminally brutal, and uncalled for, and morally indefensible." They described the ballot as "the veterans' strongest weapon of defense" against such presidential misdeeds. Then, so that the American people would be aware of the organization's attitude, the VFW delegates commanded that all posts "be urged to mount sandbags and post a military guard from now on until November so that the Washington evacuation begun in July may be fully completed in November."[57]

The Legion's national convention in Portland was only slightly less raucous. Hoover and his allies realized that nothing could stop the Legion delegates from supporting the Bonus, but they hoped to avoid the political embarrassment that an act of censure might bring. The *New York Times* described the threat of censure as the "greatest political danger facing the administration." *Time* explained that "the prospect sent cold chills up & down the spine of the Republican high command." Legion leaders succeeded, with some difficulty, in suppressing resolutions censuring Hoover and governmental officials, but encampment speakers proved more than willing to take the occasion to criticize the administration. The celebrated Hearst syndicated columnist Floyd Gibbons spoke movingly about the marchers and their shameful removal. Boston's Democratic mayor James Curley exclaimed that the veterans had been "shot down like dogs." Indeed, George Leach, a Republican operative, wrote to the White House from Portland describing the situation as "vicious" and the convention as

Herbert Lake, "Another Zero Hour—November 8," *VFW (Foreign Service)* Magazine, September 1932. Courtesy of the Veterans of Foreign Wars.

"a mob." With no apparent irony, Leach told the White House, "I am not discouraged—all the voters in this country are not veterans." The "non-partisan" Legionnaires read the electoral writing on the wall and voted in a Democratic stalwart from West Virginia, Louis Johnson, as national commander. On the Bonus, the Patman pro-Bonus forces finally carried the day, overwhelmingly (1,167–109) and enthusiastically.[58]

By November of 1932, it remained uncertain whether the electoral process would resolve the Bonus question. Just weeks before Election Day, the Bonus issue finally made its way into the presidential campaign. The Hoover camp and the Republican press blasted FDR for what they viewed as willful obfuscation on the Bonus. In an address at Madison Square Garden, Calvin Coolidge contended that the potential for a $2.2 billion "raid on the Treasury" needed to be rejected outright by Roosevelt to give "a great encouragement to business, reduce unemployment and guarantee the integrity of the national credit." Coolidge continued, "While [FDR] remained silent economic recovery was measurably impeded." *Time* reported that the Republican gambit was gaining traction, declaring "'Yes or No?' on the Soldier Bonus remained last week the question most voters wanted Governor Roosevelt to answer." In response, FDR made an address to 35,000 faithful in Pittsburgh's Forbes Field in which he called Coolidge's charges "baseless and absurd." FDR restated his position against payment and remarked that balancing the federal budget should be the first priority of his presidency. Both prospects—no Bonus and a balanced budget—sounded ominous to veterans, echoing the National Economy League's plans for achieving a balanced budget through drastic cuts in veteran benefits. Despite this, veterans still hoped a Democratic administration and Congress might serve their purposes. But a vote against Hoover, however satisfying, certainly did not assure veterans of a compliant White House occupant.[59]

Between 1929 and 1932, the federal veterans' policy that explicitly recognized a financial obligation to veterans but continually delayed discharging it gave life to an otherwise moribund veteran organization, the VFW. As the VFW grew as a result of its demands for the Bonus as well as the Legion's recalcitrance, it raised the organization's public profile even further, creating a positive feedback loop for political activism. By the end of 1932, the VFW had asserted itself as an important national political actor by staking an unshakeable claim to the Bonus issue. In the process, the VFW stood ready to challenge the American Legion as the dominant voice speaking for World War veterans and their demands on the federal government. Meanwhile, the Bonus evolved into an ideologically explosive national political issue, melding with the pressing Depression-era questions about the American political economy and the proper role of the federal government in the maintenance of its citizens. As the following chapters explore, attempts to organize additional Bonus Marches in the New Deal period proved futile, but neither demands for immediate payment of the Bonus nor the controversies over veterans' issues went away. On the contrary, veterans' relationship with the New Deal soured from the start, and veteran politics exerted as powerful an influence on the Roosevelt presidency as it had in launching it.

3

The "New Deal" for Veterans

The tragic consequences of the 'new deal' in veterans' legislation
become more and more apparent.
—VFW editorial, *Foreign Service*, May, 1933

On March 9, 1933, as the Roosevelt administration initiated the
New Deal in a flurry of legislative activity known as "the Hundred Days,"
veteran politics exploded into the national political arena once again. Historians of the New Deal emphasize the significant structural reforms in
banking, securities, and agriculture and the relief measures that emerged
in those "Hundred Days." [1] But the lesser-known "Bill to Maintain the
Credit of the United States Government" became the second piece of legislation pushed through the 73rd Congress. The Economy Act, as it was
more popularly known, precipitated a $460 million reduction in veteran
pensions and benefits.[2] In turn, the federal retrenchment triggered a rapid
political mobilization by military veterans against New Deal policy. When
the American Legion adopted more conciliatory tactics to remedy the
consequences of the Economy Act, the Veterans of Foreign Wars (VFW)
spearheaded yet another confrontational veteran mobilization. Although
obscured by the long shadows of the Bonus March, this veteran political
uprising laid the foundations for organized New Deal dissent. In fact, the
VFW served as an important early meeting ground for what I call the
"New Deal Dissidents," the political faction that would eventually develop
around Senator Huey P. Long and Father Charles E. Coughlin. With the
Economy Act as the catalyst, VFW-led veterans raised some of the original voices in protest against the "first" New Deal.[3]

From 1929 to the passage of the Economy Act, World War veterans' policy underwent a fitful sequence of expansion and contraction. In 1929,

veterans renewed their attempts to amend the World War pension system. The VFW led the charge, proposing further liberalization of disability terms. When a minority faction within the Legion looked to follow suit, Representative Royal C. Johnson (R, SD), chairman of the World War Veterans Committee, wrote to Hoover, predicting that a "general service pension for World War veterans [will] a year from today . . . be of pressing importance to the country, the Congress, the service men and the taxpayers." If successful, Johnson warned, "expenditures for World War veterans will be doubled within the next five years, and will progressively increase for many years." Johnson held out hope that, despite the rumblings from the VFW, the more important Legion would maintain its longstanding opposition to pensions. To help the Legion nip enthusiasm for general service pensions from welling up from the rank and file, Johnson urged Hoover to work with the Legion leadership. He explained, "Much of the difficulty can be obviated if responsible governmental authority can arrive at an agreement with responsible veterans' organizations." As Johnson predicted, pensions became an election-year issue the following summer. Although long delayed by the original World War veterans' policies and opposed by the Legion and conservatives within both political parties, general pensions would become a reality.[4]

In the summer of 1930, insurgent Republicans joined Democrats hoping to grab majority control over Congress in pushing for liberalized pensions. Legislators desperately wanted to take this achievement home for summer campaigning, their minds "riveted on the soldier vote in their states." James E. Watson (R, IN), the Republican leader of the Senate, cracked that "you could not drive the House out of Washington until it provides pension legislation." The expansive—and expensive—bill sponsored by Representative John Rankin (D, MS) furthered the revisions associated with the previous decade's Sweet and World War Veterans Acts by expanding the time frame and the conditions that would qualify a veteran to receive service-connected disability benefits. The Rankin bill extended the presumptive date for service connection from January 1, 1925, to January 1, 1930. Then it added to the list of "service-connected" infirmities ailments such as gout, scurvy, rickets, leprosy, and obesity. Frank T. Hines, director of the Veterans' Bureau, attacked the measure, estimating the costs associated with the Rankin bill at $181 million a year, with the possibility of reaching $400 million in the future. Hoover once again deployed Secretary of the Treasury Mellon to warn of the unavoidable necessity of raising corporate and individual taxes to pay for such legislation.

Nevertheless, in late June, both the House and Senate narrowly passed versions of the Rankin bill.[5]

Despite Hoover's opposition to the Rankin bill, nonservice pensions came into existence with his approval. On June 26, Hoover vetoed the Rankin bill, explaining that "this measure is a radical departure . . . into the field of pension to men who have incurred disabilities . . . having no relation to their military service." But on July 3, after House Republicans successfully sustained the veto and just one hour before the summer adjournment, both houses hurriedly passed a compromise replacement bill drafted by Royal Johnson and blessed in advance by the White House. Hoover hastily traveled to the Hill in his evening wear to sign the World War Disability Act into law. The compromise bill reduced the payment for nonservice-connected disabilities substantially from that provided for in the defeated bill and removed all of the language related to deadlines and diseases that qualified as disabilities. Well after the fact, Walter H. Newton, Hoover's personal secretary, claimed that Hoover promoted and signed the compromise legislation "with the idea of preventing the overriding of the Presidential veto and the breaking down of the World War Veterans Act and its fundamental principles." But Hoover caved on the pension issue, signing the bill that significantly reduced the proposed cost but now allowed for nonservice-connected pensions.[6]

The resulting 1930 legislation opened wide a door that had been only slightly ajar since 1924. *Time* declared the pension bill "a major reversal of the policy of compensating World War soldiers for service disabilities only." Thanks to this new policy, a veteran with a nonservice-connected disability rated at 25 percent disability would receive a pension of $12 a month; a veteran with a nonservice-related disability rated as 100 percent disabled received $40. Both figures were well below the rates for service-connected disabilities. All of the Rankin bill's liberalized time limits and legal presumptions expanding the window for service connection were removed. Only two restrictions remained: veterans who contracted venereal disease through "willful misconduct" and those who paid federal income tax (i.e., had $1,500 or more in income) were denied pensions. The Veterans' Bureau estimated it would cost from $31 million in the first year to $82 million in the fifth. Senator William Borah (R, ID) predicted that it was only "a short time until the question of service alone will be the basis upon which pensions will be granted." *Time* anticipated worse: "small though the amount of the pension appeared, they were large enough to establish the principle of civil disability payments which in the course of years will undoubtedly dwarf the pension outlays after all other U.S. wars." Symbolic of the new pension system, Congress nearly simultaneously granted the president the authority to reorganize the veterans' bureaucracy by combining the Pension Bureau, the Veterans' Bureau, and the National Home for Disabled Veterans into the Veterans' Administration. The 1930 legislation and the federal restructuring literally and symbolically tore down the bureaucratic barriers protecting the initial World War veterans' system from its corrupt Civil War predecessor.[7]

During the pension debate, the VFW and the Legion offered contradictory and somewhat confusing counsel to Congress. In order to capitalize on the Legion's opposition to pensions, the VFW leadership championed more liberal veterans' provisioning, including the nonservice-related pensions. In fact, after the bill's passage, Walter Newton presented the pen used by Hoover to sign the legislation to the chairman of the VFW's National Legislative Committee, Edwin S. Bettelheim. Newton commented, "This pen should be of unusual significance to the VFW knowing your long-standing interest in establishing a pension system for veterans of the World War." On the other hand, Legion leaders initially opposed general pensions. Nonetheless, Commander O. L. Bodenhamer and the top tier of leaders uncharacteristically changed their minds in the middle of the Senate battle over the Rankin bill to avoid appearing insensitive to the demands of rank-and-file veterans. When Royal Johnson bluntly questioned the wisdom and integrity of this conversion experience, Bodenhamer curtly replied, "Because the Legion has been fair and conservative in their programs and because of the shortness of time, we are now willing to support if necessary legislation more extreme than we had originally requested." Senator James Watson, an administration ally, wryly commented that the Legion "promised when we passed the bonus act that they would not ask for pensions; and yet, because of present conditions, they came to endorse this bill." *Barron's* explained it more acerbically: "The American Legion regarded the new bill with amazement, then it hastened to endorse it. That, briefly, is the story of how pensions came to the American taxpayer." As with its stance on the Bonus, the VFW gained in national stature by commandeering the successful pension battle. Meanwhile, the pension issue divided Legionnaires into hostile camps; not everyone in the organization embraced the leadership's change of heart.[8]

The national leadership's tactical reversal on pensions chagrined many Legionnaires. Some of the old guard who had consistently renounced the idea of general pensions withdrew their membership in dismay and disgust. Ray Murphy, chairman of the National Legislative Committee, later commented piquantly on the Legion's role in the general pension system: "Many felt that the Disability Allowance [the World War Disability Act] whose paternity the American Legion has many a time and often rejected was the doorstep baby that had brought disgrace upon our house." John Thomas Taylor, the Legion's chief lobbyist, warned veterans and Legion leaders of the backlash the bill would provoke against the Legion even though the pension revisions originated elsewhere. Taylor foresaw the "terrible effect the tremendous cost of this legislation will have on the news stories, placing the entire responsibility for it on the Legion . . . [as] the public generally look upon the Legion as the spokesman for the servicemen."[9]

Taylor's concerns about a public relations disaster were prescient. Americans who had been resentful of veterans' political clout and of the costs and corruption that stemmed from it, now voiced their displeasure with the "veterans' racket." Critics published a stream of books and articles chastising veterans and their organizations, calling them by epithets such as "Treasury raiders" and "plunderers instead of patriots." In one example, the *Christian Century* published a jeremiad masquerading as an editorial entitled "The Soldier Racket." The editors bemoaned the enormous federal outlays and the power of the veterans' lobby, asserting that "Year by year . . . the veterans are becoming a more separated, and a more privileged, class. And year by year the taste of power is spurring them on to demand even larger extractions." Indeed, these critics who raised the alarm about the costs of the new provisioning proved correct rather quickly. Between 1930 and 1932, new veteran pensioners accounted for an alarming increase in federal expenditures. Some 407,581 nonservice disabilities were now being compensated by the federal government. The VA estimated the yearly cost of the new pensions to be between $153 million and $181 million. By 1932, the rising expenditures on veterans—now totaling more than $800 million a year—and the concurrent bitter Bonus struggle provoked a countermobilization.[10]

In 1932, the worst year of the Great Depression, the revulsion against the new pension system finally bred a political initiative of its own. Early in the year, the U.S. Chamber of Commerce began to attack the veterans' system. Then, in the heat of the Bonus March, the National Economy League (NEL) formed in New York City, with chapters following in most major U.S. cities. Led by Archibald Roosevelt, Calvin Coolidge, Grenville Clark, and Admiral Richard Byrd, the NEL dedicated its efforts toward the continued pursuit of fiscal conservatism. The NEL's Declaration of Purpose, therefore, stated opposition to both the Bonus and the wasteful extravagance of veteran benefits as part of the organization's core values. But Clark gave away the organization's true motive in a letter to Hoover in which he explained that "real economy is virtually synonymous with a radical cut in the billion a year for veterans." [11]

Aware that retired senior officers and business elites might not be the optimal messengers for shaping public opinion on veterans' issues, the NEL joined forces with a newly founded veteran organization, the American Veterans' Association (AVA). The AVA was created by disgruntled, typically elite Legionnaires who broke with the Legion after the 1932 convention supported the Bonus. The organization's charter promoted a return to strict and parsimonious service-connected pensions and spoke out against Bonus prepayment. Other veteran organizations accused the NEL and the U.S. Chamber of Commerce of sponsoring the creation of the AVA to suit their purposes, but no conclusive proof exists for this. Nevertheless, the NEL and 4,000 AVA members together publicly attacked the veterans' welfare system, finding easy access to print and radio media outlets, not to mention the corridors of Congress. Given the Depression's political climate of hostility toward Big Business, it would be reasonable to assume that these initiatives fell on deaf ears. But the two presidential candidates, Hoover and Roosevelt, also opposed the Bonus and dedicated substantial time in their campaigns trying to outdo each other when it came to fiscal discipline. Neither spoke specifically about cutting veterans' benefits, but any mention of the federal excesses that needed trimming invariable drew comparisons to the NEL's plans. After all, veterans' welfare costs accounted for one out of every five federal dollars spent. [12]

After the conclusion of the 1932 election, the lame-duck Hoover administration initiated in earnest a drive for reductions in federal expenditures. Hoover proposed budget cuts of $500 million to $700 million to remedy the burgeoning federal budget deficit, caused mostly by the steep decline in revenues over the preceding years. Congress also took up the issue, appointing a joint committee to address the relationship between the budget deficit and the expensive veterans' welfare system. The Joint Congressional Committee on Veteran Affairs met throughout the winter of 1932–1933 to investigate the feasibility of cutting veterans' benefits by nearly 50 percent, or more than $400 million. Spokesmen for the National Economy League, the American Veterans Association, the U.S. Chamber of Commerce, and the National Association of Manufacturers all provided testimony explaining how the deficit was the primary hindrance to economic recovery. All complained that outlays for veterans' pensions exceeded fiscal sustainability and needed dramatic trimming with a return to stringent service-related pensions. In testimony in late December, former Solicitor General William Bullitt, representing the National Economy League, dueled verbally with Senator Arthur Robinson (R, IN) over the proposed reductions. When challenged by Robinson on pensions, Bullitt smirked, "I would recommend that the Senator read some of the veto messages of Grover Cleveland." As expected, the Hoover administration, Congress, and the "economy" groups encountered stiff resistance from veteran organizations bent on tabling any legislation detrimental to veterans' compensation.[13]

The American Legion quickly mobilized to oppose plans for reductions in veteran benefits. The American Legion leadership denounced the supporters of such cutbacks as the forces of Big Business. Legion leaders ridiculed the NEL as "the speckled colt," the "spiritual adopted son," and the "more or less (legitimate or illegitimate) secret stepdaughter" of the U.S. Chamber of Commerce. The *Virginia Legionnaire* editorialized that the economy forces were "inspired by the same selfish class which knows only the patriotism of dollars." John Thomas Taylor, the Legion's lobbyist, called the economy countermobilization a "deliberate attempt to destroy the influence of this Legion." He described the economy plans as a "very canny and cunning scheme . . . to shift the burden of taxation from the back of the big fellow to the back of the little fellow." Commander Johnson sent a Christmas message over the NBC radio network deriding the NEL for "misinforming the public through erroneous statements and misleading figures." He pledged the Legion's continuing diligence, noting, "Our problem now is to maintain the gains that have been made . . . and to see that the hysteria of false economy does not destroy the structure that has been carefully built." In early January, Taylor and other Legion representatives, including tuberculosis specialists and psychiatrists, testified before the Joint Committee, arguing against the economy plans to reduce and/or eliminate liberalized pensions.[14]

Although the VFW remained only secondary representatives of the World War veterans, the organization's role in the 1930 legislative effort gave the organization an additional stake in retaining the existing pension system. Therefore, VFW leaders likewise characterized the economy forces as merely the stalking horses of Big Business and mobilized the membership to oppose the plans to overturn the 1930 legislation. In the

January issue of *Foreign Service*, the VFW published a lengthy defense of the 1930 Disability Act so loathed by the economy advocates. The editorial blasted the NEL, claiming that it "knows but one God and one Creed—the well known Dollar." The leadership wedded the VFW to the new pension system, proclaiming, "This is the legislation that must be preserved at all costs against the onslaught of the National Economy League and other selfish groups who refuse to recognize the theory that those who made the largest profits during the war must expect to assume the resultant burden of cost in the sad aftermath." The New York State Department of the VFW followed the national headquarters' lead, publishing a pamphlet titled "An Expose of the National Economy League" to discredit the economy group. The pamphlet explained, "Big business—represented by the National Economy League and Chamber of Commerce of the United States—is back of this scheme to knife the average taxpayer and the veterans at the same time." "Don't be fooled," it continued, "success of the National Economy League program means the destruction of the entire veteran rehabilitation structure!" In February, L. S. Ray, the vice chairman of the VFW National Legislative Committee, refuted the "anti-veteran testimony" before the Joint Committee.[15]

The veteran organizations' determined resistance appeared to be effective; no legislation resulted from the committee's work. But veteran leaders knew that the lack of cooperation and resolve exhibited by a lame-duck administration and Congress determined that outcome rather than their own efforts. Consequently, both Legion and VFW leaders cautioned that, while the economy plan stood defeated, the issue was not dead. They nervously awaited a new Democratic Congress acting in lockstep with the Roosevelt White House. An article in the *American Legion Monthly* on the Legion's battle against the economy forces explained that "Economy is economy. The new Congress is certain to strive in every way possible to find means to cut down government expenditures." VFW leaders warned the membership that "the cause of the veteran is by no means out of danger . . . [from] those who would pounce upon the issue of economy as a means of wiping out existing veteran legislation."[16]

Despite FDR's campaign promises to cut the federal budget and their leaders' insistence that the storm had not passed, rank-and-file veterans outside the capital still hoped that the incoming administration and Congress would handle the issue of veteran benefits benevolently. Indeed, some VFW and Legion posts expressed a profound sense of optimism over the Roosevelt presidency. In the first weeks of March 1933, congratulatory telegrams and letters poured into the White House. From Neponset, Massachusetts, VFW Post 2235 wrote Roosevelt with barely contained zeal, "It's zero hour. We are ready to go over the top with you and drive old man depression out of his trenches by X-mas." Raymond Price, the commander of VFW Post 518, in Camden, New Jersey, thanked Roosevelt, noting, "It is gratifying to know we have at last a president that *all* the people can look to for leadership. The prayers of the American people have been answered." Legion Post 480, in Cincinnati, sent a copy of a resolution conveying "to our comrade the newly elected President of the United States God speed in the fulfillment of his undertakings." Albert Marquis, commander of a New York City Legion post, expressed his view that FDR would deliver to the people "an administration that will go down in history as the outstanding one of the century." Comrade W. E. Dowling of VFW Post 1941, Irvington, New Jersey, however, offered Roosevelt a less giddy welcome, enunciating a common veteran understanding of the 1932 election. Dowling wrote, "The War Veterans who secured your election beg to have you beware of the Republican treachery."[17]

Veterans soon realized that treachery had come to pass, but not of the Republican variety. Indeed, March 20, 1933, marks the beginning of organized New Deal dissent. Less than two weeks after his inauguration, FDR signed the Economy Act, forcing veterans to reevaluate their confidence in the Roosevelt administration. With little publicity, Roosevelt and Lewis Douglas, the conservative former Arizona congressman and FDR's Budget Director appointee, worked during the interregnum on legislation to balance the budget through sharp reductions in veteran benefits. Lewis and Roosevelt both viewed the federal deficit of $22.5 billion, an unprecedented peacetime amount, with alarm. In fact, only the calamitous banking crisis derailed FDR's plans to offer an economy bill as the administration's first piece of legislation. When the economy bill was introduced in Congress on March 10, 1933, a strongly worded presidential message demanding immediate action accompanied it. Administration allies obliged, steamrolling the bill through Congress with rules stipulating minimal debate and sharply limiting amendments. The resulting legislation gave the chief executive discretionary powers over veteran benefits. By delegating those powers to Budget Director Douglas, a decorated World War veteran and a leading congressional advocate of fiscal austerity, FDR attempted simultaneously to remove veteran benefits from congressional oversight and to distance himself from this politically sensitive issue. FDR, however, failed at both. Instead, when the Economy Act became law, on March 20, the Roosevelt administration provoked a confrontation with disgruntled veterans and a bipartisan coalition of congressional dissenters vowing to repeal the bill. [18]

With the Economy Act, Congress mandated budget reductions and then handed the chief executive the axe. Totaling 20 percent of the federal budget, veteran-related expenditures were naturally on the block. Between March 20 and March 31, therefore, veterans and their organizational leaders held their breath until Roosevelt and Douglas revealed their plans for reductions with the issuing of Executive Orders 6089 through 6100. Roosevelt issued the orders with an accompanying message asking that veterans "share the spirit of sacrifice" and reassuring them that he did "not want any veteran to feel that he and his comrades are being singled out to make sacrifices." Despite the administration's assurances that the cuts would be handled justly and humanely, the reductions proved even more draconian than veterans originally feared. [19]

The executive orders authorized $460 million dollars in cuts almost precisely as proposed by the NEL. The new regulations removed 501,777 veterans and their dependents from the pension roll, including approximately 100,000 veterans suffering from tuberculosis who were unable to prove that they had contracted the disease during their time in the service. The vast majority, some 390,000, had received pensions only after the 1930 liberalization. Even more galling to veterans, men who retained disability benefits—those with documented service-connected injuries— shouldered anywhere from 25 to 88 percent reductions in their benefits. In one especially poignant case, VA authorities informed Vincent Carver of Lansing, Michigan, a veteran of the Great War, that his pension would be cut from $150 to $40 a month, a 73 percent reduction. Married and with four dependent children, Carver was rated as permanently and totally disabled due to wounds he had suffered in combat that left him completely blind in both eyes and with gunshot wounds to his thigh, neck, shoulder, hand, and knee. Other heartrending stories of World War veterans committing suicide because of their reductions—or their removal from the pension roll altogether—ran in veteran and national publications throughout the late spring and summer. In many cases, veterans opted for suicide so that their needy families would at least receive the remainder of the Bonus owed them. [20]

At the onset, FDR received important political cover when the American Legion's national leadership appeared to side with the administration on the Economy Act. During debate over the bill, Legion leaders offered to assist FDR in coming up with proposed reductions in veteran benefits of up to 25 percent. National Commander Louis Johnson, like many of the conservatives within the Legion appalled by the 1930 pension legislation, found some level of cutting warranted. He explained that the Legion was "not without blame in the overburdening of the World War Veterans Acts with benefits which made it so top-heavy that it was certain to destroy itself sooner or later." So FDR's March 5 appearance on a national Legion radio broadcast in which he asked for the support of men "who know the meaning of sacrifice" gave the impression that the Legion leadership knew and tacitly approved of the Economy Act.[21] Moreover, Democratic stalwart Johnson's cozy relationship with the administration only fueled veterans' suspicions of complicity. Indeed, Johnson did everything possible to squelch the uproar from veterans. He informed FDR that the Legion leadership would start a "publicity" campaign in *American Legion Monthly* to convince veterans to "Support the President." On March 16, despite the fact that he had admitted the Economy Act might have the "gravest consequences to the disabled veteran," Johnson issued a "battle order" insisting that Legionnaires back FDR on the issue. Johnson explained that "the Legion has every faith in the discretion, firmness, and justice with which the President will deal with this problem." He also asked that special meetings be held in every Legion post to pass resolutions in support of the President. Johnson affirmed the Legion's loyalty, stating "Many may disagree with the new law, but now in this crisis we must take [FDR's] orders."[22]

Johnson's comments and actions did not sit well with all of his comrades. Legion posts, State Departments, and even the National Executive Committee (NEC) questioned the wisdom of their commander in chief's public stand. In an early May meeting at Legion headquarters in Indianapolis, the NEC rejected Johnson's appeal that the organization continue to offer FDR support, refusing to endorse "Roosevelt's attitude toward veterans and their dependents." The DC Department adopted a resolution protesting the "fake economy" act. The Newark, Ohio, Legion post proclaimed, "We disapprove of the attitude of National Commander Johnson in so completely surrendering the Legion to the victories of the National Economy League and for promising Legion support for policies and doctrines . . . contrary to its views and aims." The Dennis-Butler Legion Post of Stillwater, Oklahoma, condemned the National Economy League and called for Johnson's resignation.[23]

When the Douglas plan proved more drastic than even Legion officials had imagined, the Legion initiated efforts to repeal the most glaring injustices of the Economy Act. Legion leaders believed that outraged confrontation would exacerbate the antiveteran attitudes developed since 1930. In agreement, the *Legion News* of the Wayne County Council in Detroit explained that Legionnaires must "take it like men" because "to whine at the situation, to curse and blaspheme those responsible, to refuse any cooperation . . . and to take the position of obstinacy . . . would never . . . do the disabled one bit of good, but might render them irreparable damage." For this reason, the Legion hierarchy set out to reverse the damages wrought by the Economy Act quietly, patiently, and mostly out of the public spotlight. On April 12, Legion lobbyist John Thomas Taylor visited the White House and told FDR the reductions were "all wrong." Louis Johnson met with Lewis Douglas to discuss the executive orders. After the meeting, press secretary Steve Early told reporters that "as a result of the appearance of the veterans' representatives, it now seems that the cut in compensation of service-connection world War veterans with special disabilities has been deeper than was originally intended." The Legion then worked tirelessly to rectify the most severe reductions in benefits for service-related disabilities. Legislative Committee chairman Ray Murphy urged Legionnaires to look forward by looking *back* to the pre-1930 days during which the Legion "built up a system of veterans' legislation and surrounded it with the stone walls of service connection." In spite of the behind-the-scenes efforts and genuine concern over the harm done, many veterans still believed that the Legion national offices had acquiesced in the president's plan.[24]

In contrast to the Legion's contradictory response, a united VFW mobilized immediately and fiercely against the Economy Act. Undoubtedly the VFW's lead role in the 1930 pension legislation, legislation entirely rescinded by the new policies, rankled VFW leaders. VFW national officers and posts throughout the nation vehemently protested passage of the bill and the new regulations. Aghast at the drastic cuts in disability pensions and new stringent guidelines for proving service-related disabilities, the VFW assaulted the plan in no uncertain terms. VFW officials and members disparaged the New Deal in blistering attacks. The VFW monthly publication, *Foreign Service*, editorialized, "[T]he so-called economy bill virtually destroys the basic structure of veterans' legislation created during the past fifteen years." In the editorial titled "Blood Money," the VFW national leadership explained veterans' case against the Economy Act. The VFW leadership argued that veterans would gladly agree to some cuts in benefits for the sake of economy if Congress had spread them evenly across the federal budget. But the Economy Act considered only economies in veteran benefits, thus reflecting the agenda of "Big Business." The editorial continued, "The obvious fact that the Economy Bill reflects the very language that featured [*sic*] the propaganda of the National Economy League indicates that this new legislation achieves the objectives of those who found it profitable to sponsor and finance that organization—those who control the wealth of the nation."[25]

The VFW's critique of the Economy Act folded into a larger indictment of the political and economic system. Cuts in benefits alone would have touched off heated criticism, but the VFW's argument against the reductions enumerated in the Economy Act employed veterans' understandings of the World War, the causes of the Depression, and the prevailing political economy. Veterans widely considered corporate avarice and greed, the concentration of wealth, and the corruption of the political system by "Wall Street" and "Big Business" to be the causes of both the Great War *and* the Depression. Thus, the VFW leadership concluded its editorial: "It is apparent that the veteran has been forced to bear the burden of a depression that was actually caused by his enemies—the predatory interests that have their hands in the public till. The money that will be withheld from the disabled veteran . . . can only be regarded as blood money."[26]

Drawings by the VFW's artist and political cartoonist, Herbert E. Lake, accompanied the vitriol on the editorial pages of *Foreign Service*. Lake graphically depicted the VFW's sentiment regarding the Economy Act. In the panel titled "Some Call This Economy," Lake portrayed the proponents of the Economy Act as executioners. The firing squad was made up of figures wearing top hats and tails and labeled "National Economy League" and "U.S. Chamber of Commerce," while three veterans—one each from the Civil War, the Spanish-American War, and the World War—calmly but sternly faced their executioners. In "The First Casualty of America's 'War on Depression,'" Lake depicted a World War veteran prostrate and bleeding from a vicious bayonet wound in the back. The rifle to which the bayonet is affixed read "economy." As the caption suggests, Roosevelt's "War on Depression" carried dire and unexpected consequences for veterans. In a short time, the expressions of distrust and dissatisfaction with the Roosevelt administration became even more pronounced.[27]

By April 1933, the VFW's national leadership had begun to assail not just the rapacity of the Economy Act but the New Deal more generally. VFW leaders recognized that Roosevelt had not been duped into the

Herbert Lake, "Some Call This Economy," *VFW (Foreign Service)* Magazine, April 1933. Courtesy of the Veterans of Foreign Wars.

passage of the Economy Act. On the contrary, the Roosevelt administration had openly sided with the business community on veteran issues and had continued some of the conservative fiscal policies of the vilified Hoover administration. The VFW, therefore, concluded that the New Deal's policies threatened to undermine irrevocably the privileged positions veterans and their supporters had come to expect. From this point, the VFW leadership began referring to the Roosevelt administration's relief and recovery efforts with ironic quotation marks around the phrase "new deal." One characteristic editorial began, "[T]he tragic consequences of the 'new deal' in veteran legislation become more and more apparent," while an article outlining the specifics of veteran benefit reductions was entitled, "An Analysis of the 'New Deal' for Disabled Veterans."[28] The VFW also communicated this message through the very effective use of critical humor. The back page of *Foreign Service*, the VFW monthly, contained a list of jokes and comic drawings known as "Jest-A-Minute." This section began to include jokes critical of the Roosevelt administration. In the following jokes, veterans lampooned the New Deal:

Dealer's Choice
A gagster in Judge says the new deal started with the jack left out.
The veteran apparently sat at the dealer's right because he got the cut!

Jeers or Cheers?
Cheer Leader: Three cheers for the New Deal!
Veteran Rooters: Raw! Raw! Raw![29]

In a similarly mordant way, VFW editorials deployed the well-known "forgotten man" theme of the Roosevelt election campaign as a rhetorical weapon. A May 1933 editorial huffed that, while "legislation is being enacted for the relief of agriculture; the railroads, banks, and other financial institutions," the veteran absorbed "a reduction in income amounting to $460,000,000." The VFW warned, "If the present session of Congress ignores the plight of these former defenders of the nation then truly history will record the veteran as the real 'forgotten man' of the depression and democracy will have failed its saviors." Once again Lake rendered the VFW's position into visceral drawings. The drawing "The Forgotten Man" depicted the numerous grabs at the federal Treasury that the New Deal had come to signify. The hands clutching at the Treasury gold glistened with jeweled rings while Congress, characterized by a portly, well-dressed figure, shunted the veteran in puttees off his feet. The veteran "forgotten man" was not so much forgotten as knocked down by the New Deal legislation.[30]

The VFW leadership urged members and local posts to express their outrage over the Economy Act by writing to their elected officials. Many VFW posts and members voiced their complaints directly to the White House. The L.M. Tate Post 39 of St. Petersburg, Florida, wired FDR that the members were "ready to do our part in the interests of economy" but suggested that cuts should not be made "at the expense of the private in the rear rank." The Huntington Park (California) Post 952 forwarded to the White House a resolution passed by the Los Angeles County VFW Council reversing its decision to participate in a Roosevelt Day program. The Los Angeles County VFW Council explained that it refused to participate "in view of the fact of the arbitrary assumption of dictatorial and unconstitutional powers, especially in veterans affairs." Minnesota VFW officers informed FDR by telegram that "delegates of all posts, Veterans of Foreign Wars, Minnesota . . . voted unanimously—oppose granting of dictatorial powers to President and are absolutely opposed cutting veterans benefits—emphatically demanding our Government that its defenders be not betrayed." Harry Hoffman, commander of City of Detroit Post 334, ominously warned FDR's personal secretary that "the sober thinking veteran is getting tired of sitting idly by, he is thinking and some of these

Herbert Lake, "The Forgotten Man," *VFW (Foreign Service)* Magazine, July 1933. Courtesy of the Veterans of Foreign Wars.

days you're going to have a real Bonus Army in Washington, men who served overseas."[31]

Democratic allies within the VFW had even more direct admonitions for the new administration. James Farley, the Democratic Party chairman, received a letter from Joseph Heffernan written from the Ohio state convention of the VFW, where there was "a strong undercurrent for open censure of President Roosevelt because of the Economy Act." Heffernan—a VFW member, a Democrat, and a former mayor of Youngstown—claimed that he was able to keep the issue off the convention floor and that he had prevented "a *direct* expression." Nonetheless, he urged Farley, "Please do not underestimate the dynamite in the veteran situation." Heffernan put the controversy in the strict electoral terms that Farley understood: "They feel that they were a great influence in the defeat of Hoover, and, frankly, I should not like to see them turn en masse against Roosevelt." He reiterated, "They can cause trouble, so do not underestimate such a concerted opposition."[32]

As with the Bonus saga, the differences between the VFW's militant protest and the Legion's perceived acquiescence on the Economy Act affected the institutional vitality of the two veteran organizations. The VFW clearly gained a competitive advantage over the Legion by leading the public charge against the Economy Act. In 1933, the American Legion suffered a nearly 20 percent loss of membership; some 160,000 veterans dropped their Legion membership. In the same year, the VFW continued the rapid expansion begun in 1929. In 1933, the VFW signed up more than 40,000 new recruits, including 21,000 first-time members inducted during the second "Hello America" broadcast over the NBC radio network. The VFW experienced a net growth of 165 new posts, with 74 more posts regaining their charters by paying their overdue fees. In the middle of the uproar, the VFW national headquarters issued a statement proclaiming that the organization was "rapidly forging to the forefront in veteran circles." After mentioning the membership difficulties of a rival unnamed veteran organization, the VFW statement claimed that "The continued growth of the VFW, despite economic handicaps, indicates that the rank and file of veterans are in thorough accord with the militant and unselfish policies of our organization." Highlighting the perceived betrayal by Legion Commander Johnson, the statement coolly added, "Our leaders have remained loyal to the mandates of our membership." In case the reference was missed, the statement continued, "[Our leaders] refused to accede to the wishes of political leaders and they have spurned every compromise that would in any way betray the cause of the disabled veteran."[33]

The VFW continued to flourish because the organization tapped into a deep vein of seething veteran resentment over the Economy Act. A steady stream of letters and telegrams sent to the White House expressed veterans' disappointment. E. Burns of Rochester, New York, voiced the disillusionment of veteran FDR supporters confronted by the administration's veteran policy. In a telegram to FDR, Burns proclaimed that "Every veteran voted for you and stands back of you but the whole of us will consider it rank injustice to tamper in any way with the pension of any veteran." Likewise, after wishing FDR success, L. Cole of Chicago decried FDR's decision to side with the National Economy League. Cole pointedly announced that "The men of the service in nineteen seventeen and eighteen protest your contemplated action and we regret that you have listened to politicians and the Economy League rather than to stand upon fundamentals of Americanism." M. E. Depew wired a terse message: "We veterans protest cutting poor to exempt rich from taxation."[34]

Other veterans employed the rhetorical strategies and imagery adopted by the VFW. In a letter pleading with FDR to rescind the Economy Act, a disabled veteran expressed the frustration of a disappointed supporter in the "New Deal" who "never expected [it] to become a raw deal." Floyd O. Jellison of South Bend, Indiana, sent a telegram to FDR, stating, "Your forgotten man campaign followed by the assumption of dictatorial powers wherein the veteran becomes the forgotten man will cause the President's memory to be cherished with the high esteem as is that of Benedict Arnold." Recalling the imagery of "Some Call this Economy," Carrell S. Huston of Illinois asked FDR, "Why not send [the financier and economy advocate Bernard] Baruch out with his men to gather us all in and let us dig a ditch, line us up, backs to Baruch and let his men drop us all in the ditch?" When Fred B. Thomas, a Great War veteran, committed suicide in despair over the Economy Act by running a garden hose from his car's exhaust pipe into the passenger compartment, he left behind a note proclaiming, "I am out of work and of no use to the people who praised me during the war. We are forgotten now and just a bunch of bums."[35]

Reports from allies in the field confirmed for the White House that the deluge of outraged veteran letters corresponded to the new reality of veteran activism protesting the New Deal. Democratic operatives and friends of key FDR administration staff gathered evidence of the growing storm and passed it to the White House. A letter forwarded to FDR's secretary, Marvin H. McIntyre, from Dallas described the uproar in Texas. The letter emanated from the "'papa' of the ex-servicemen" in Dallas, W. E. Talbot. Talbot, a Republican but a "great admirer of Mr. Roosevelt," warned that the Economy Act was "causing a restlessness and feeling of antagonism that I have never before seen in ex-servicemen." Talbot claimed to have controlled veteran passions in the past but said he was "powerless to even discuss the matter calmly with them, as they are not open to reason. They feel they have been done a great injustice." An unsolicited report from Kansas City, home of VFW national headquarters, echoed those impressions. In a letter to FDR's press secretary, Steve Early, one of Early's newspaper contacts at the *Kansas City Star* passed along his impressions of veteran sentiment, accompanied by an internal memorandum outlining the specifics of veteran grievances. Roy Roberts expressed "amazement at the amount of furor that has been stirred up in the veterans by the cuts made on the service connected disabilities." He continued, "I am afraid there is a great revulsion in feeling on the part of veteran organizations toward the administration." Roberts concluded his message to Early: "It gives the Communists and Reds material to work on."[36]

As Talbot's and Robert's letters suggest, the Economy Act resonated with veterans in ways that made progressive New Deal supporters uneasy. After all, veterans' reactions rested on ideological foundations shaped by the historical memory of the Great War. Spurred on by a wave of revisionist history throughout the 1920s and 1930s, veterans increasingly viewed the Great War as a conflict whose origins lay in the financial ties between the United States' financial institutions and those of Great Britain. According to this interpretation, American involvement in the Great War secured the House of Morgan's loans and created thousands of new millionaires in the economic boom while veterans risked life and limb for little over a dollar a day. For this reason, figures that personified the influence of wealth and power on the American political and economic system, such as J. P. Morgan, Bernard Baruch, and Andrew Mellon, received a disproportionate share of veterans' vituperation. More important, these enemies and the organizations that they spoke through—the National Economy League, the U.S. Chamber of Commerce, and the National Association of Manufacturers—unwaveringly supported the reductions in veteran benefits effected by the Economy Act. Veterans often reflexively attacked "Big Business" and "Wall Street" as their enemies, but the ambiguity of those terms should not obscure the consistent pattern of opposition to veteran demands that emerged from conservative business and financial leaders. Whether FDR realized it or not, in veterans' eyes—and in the eyes of many progressives—he had tied his administration to this cast of villains.[37]

Within three months, the political mobilization of veterans against the Economy Act and the Legion's behind-the-scenes lobbying produced legislative results. On June 6, FDR attempted to forestall legislative revision of the Economy Act by issuing Executive Orders 6156–6159 liberalizing some of the Act's harshest reductions. Nonetheless, Congress passed the Independent Offices Appropriation Act on June 16, 1933, rolling back some $100 million in cuts, limiting reductions for those disabled in war to 25 percent, and creating ninety review boards to which veterans could appeal their new disability classifications. FDR grudgingly signed the legislation, but only his threat of a nationally broadcast veto message capped the restored benefits at $100 million. Several proposed amendments pushed for significantly greater benefits restorations. *Literary Digest* noted that the "Roosevelt 'Honeymoon'" had ended, adding that "only in deference to veterans . . . did Congress interrupt its willingness to accept White House leadership." Budget Director Douglas privately commented, "This veteran uprising is an outrage. . . . To think that a small group can intimidate Congress and what's more FDR [*sic*] is discouraging."[38]

Both the VFW and the Legion could find reason to continue their respective tactics against the Economy Act. In September's *American Legion Monthly*, Louis Johnson published a long, flattering list of newspaper endorsements for his strategy, including a *Baltimore Sun* editorial proclaiming Johnson's wisdom. The *Sun* wrote, "To veterans who demand an angry attack on the administration, the commander of the Legion says he 'is not going to bite off his nose to spite the President's face.'" The VFW leadership, on the other hand, touted "its militant aggressiveness and its steady advance under fire of opposition." The leadership pointed at the VFW's continued recruiting success as proof that rank-and-file veterans gave their "enthusiastic approval" to the organization's tactics even though it was "resented by the conservative elements in certain veteran and political circles who prefer compromises and 'withdrawals' in contrast to bold and vigorous attacks."[39]

Veterans' allies in Congress differed on whether the behind-the-scenes lobbying or the full-scale assault had caused the June restorations. Senator Frederick Steiwer (R, OR), a VFW member and Senate leader in the push for more generous restorations, wrote to an Oregon veteran that "we raised so much hell that I am reasonably hopeful that the President will further liberalize his regulations." Legionnaire Representative Wright Patman, who earlier had castigated Commander Johnson for not fighting the Economy Act "tooth and nail," wrote a conciliatory article in *American Legion Monthly* in which he admitted that, "with a policy of stubborn opposition to the President, the servicemen would have batted against a stone wall of popular sentiment—sentiment solidly confident of the President's good intentions." According to Patman, the Legion's tactics "led to the later modification of the law, and any other road would have led to defeat, discredit, and loss of public confidence." In any event, despite the attainment of these more amenable terms, veterans continued to absorb nearly $360 million in benefit reductions. The Independent Offices Appropriation Act only temporarily placated veteran unrest.[40]

For the VFW, the continuing fight over the Economy Act came to a climax at the 1933 VFW national encampment in Milwaukee. The VFW held a raucous convention with a roster of speakers openly hostile to the Economy Act. As the list of invited speakers suggested and the boisterous reception of the speeches confirmed, the delegates agreed with the sentiments of Representative Everett Dirksen (R, IL) when he noted that the Economy Act had become such a watershed in the relationship between veterans and the federal government that veterans would record events in the future "as something that happened before the twentieth of March, on the twentieth of March, or after the twentieth of March."[41]

The roster of guest speakers to the 1933 VFW encampment reflected the VFW's new position as an important rival to Legion. Prior to 1933, local dignitaries and leaders of smaller veteran organizations dominated the podium at VFW national encampments. In 1933, however, the VFW received a wide range of national figures who opposed the Economy Act and were to become prominent during the 73rd and 74th Congresses. In 1933, encampment attendees heard addresses from Senators Elmer Thomas (D, OK), Arthur R. Robinson (R, IN), and Huey P. Long (D, LA) and from Representatives Gerald J. Boileau (Progressive, WI) and Everett M. Dirksen (R, IL). These men led the floor fights in support of the summer's successful Independent Offices Appropriation Act and proposed further amending if not outright repeal of the Economy Act. Robinson, Boileau, and Dirksen belonged to the organization; Boileau sat on the encampment's Committee on Legislation. While the speakers at the VFW encampment ran the gamut of partisan politics—Republicans, Democrats, Farm-Laborites, and Progressives—conservatives from any party were in short supply. Unsurprisingly, President Roosevelt declined an invitation to address the hostile encampment.[42]

The call for political mobilization against the administration's policies echoed throughout the Milwaukee proceedings. The 10,000 veterans in attendance roared their approval at the lengthy denunciations of the Economy Act emanating from the speakers' platform. In numerous addresses, the call was militant, expressed in the well-worn rhetoric of the Great War and in thinly veiled gender and class terms. Senator Arthur Robinson (R, IN) proclaimed, "There is no time for mollycoddling, no time for silk stockings, but the moment has arrived . . . when the veterans of all wars must put on their shining armor and go forth to battle once again . . . and when this war is won, no one will dare again attempt to stab the veterans in the back." Robinson denounced "the so-called economy bill" as the "most cruel, brutal, and utterly indefensible act ever passed by a cowardly Congress." Rice W. Means, past national commander of the VFW and publisher of the national veteran publication, *National Tribune*, continued the assault in a ferocious attack on the FDR administration. In response to American Legion Commander Johnson's call for supporting the president, Means proclaimed, "I want to say to you I will never uphold the hand of the one who struck that cruel blow. We must not pussyfoot!" Means whipped the veterans into thunderous applause, exclaiming, "This economy act was conceived by income-tax dodgers. It was born of a result of ruthless, vicious propaganda. . . . It is a stain upon the honor of the United States." Major General Smedley D. Butler exhorted the crowd, "You've got to get mad. It's time you woke up—it's time you realized there's another war on."[43]

Even some ostensible administration allies urged VFW members to mobilize against the Economy Act. Recognizing the level of antagonism toward the administration, Senator Elmer Thomas, a Democrat, admitted that "a mistake was made" but pleaded with the veterans not to give up on Roosevelt. While the bulk of Thomas's address proposed to increase the purchasing power of ordinary Americans with an inflationary economic agenda including cash payment of the Bonus (positions FDR opposed), his comments drew the liveliest applause when he challenged the VFW members to continued political activism. Thomas exhorted the nominally apolitical, nonpartisan VFW, "My friends, when everyone else in is in politics, this organization and no other can afford not to be in politics." He continued, "I do not mean partisan politics. . . . I mean patriotic politics. I mean economic politics." Thomas concluded with the reason veterans needed to remain active: "So long as the [National] Economy League stays in politics, I want you to get in politics and stay there." With good reason, Thomas failed to mention FDR's fundamental agreement with the National Economy League on veterans' issues.[44]

The VFW furthered its standing as a center of New Deal dissent by inviting one of the most outspoken and controversial critics of the "first" New Deal to address the encampment: Senator Huey P. Long. Although the reasons are unclear as to why the VFW invited Long, his support for the Bonus and his opposition to the Economy Act made him a prized speaker for the more populist VFW. Long obliged by denigrating the Roosevelt administration in a rancorous ninety-minute address.[45] He repeated an oft-cited claim that he was responsible for FDR's nomination at the 1932 Democratic convention and expressed hope that Roosevelt would get "back on the right track." But he spent the majority of his speech rail-ing against the concentration of wealth and the Roosevelt administration's failure to honor campaign promises to address that issue. Long attacked the administration's missteps such as the Economy Act and mocked the New Deal as ineffective. In an allegory criticizing the New Deal for not addressing the concentration of wealth, Long described a poker game in which the winner walks away from the table with 95 percent of the money, prompting the remaining players to ask for a "new deal." Long responded, "Well, what are you going to deal with? It isn't going to do any good to break open a new deck of cards and deal another hand. The man has gone home with all the money!" Long proposed to redistribute wealth through sharply increased income and estate taxes and continued his calls for immediate payment of the Bonus—all as measures to increase the purchasing power of ordinary Americans. Long told the assembled veterans that the Bonus "would do ten times the good the 'sapling bill' and the Recovery Act put together are doing."[46]

Long's anti–New Deal diatribe found a receptive audience in the VFW members. They handed questions to the stage for Long to answer and begged him to continue with cries of "Go ahead!" when Long began his concluding remarks. *Foreign Service* reported to the VFW membership that Long's speech was "vociferously applauded" and his "wit" and "droll anecdotes" elicited "long laughter." Moreover, the VFW members in at-tendance provided Long with more physical measures of approval. Repre-sentative Everett Dirksen reminisced that after Long asked the VFW audi-ence, "Fellows, do I have to put up with this?," VFW Sergeants at Arms manhandled the reporters who were crowding in on the dais, smashing photographers' cameras as the newspapermen were bum-rushed from the stage apron in a "real scuffle." This brouhaha nearly forced the leadership to shut down the encampment. The *New York Times* summed up Long's appearance with the headline "Long Amid Bedlam Denounces Foes." The front page of the *Washington Post* read, "'Kingfish' Fans VFW Frenzy."[47]

Aside from applause and the donnybrook (no doubt intensified by the recently legalized beverage for which Milwaukee was famous), the VFW's frustration with the limitations of the New Deal and its agreement with Long's dissenting political agenda can be measured in more profound ways. The 1933 VFW national encampment went on record with a spate of resolutions concerning the political economy of the country. A resolu-tion calling for the total repeal of the Economy Act proved popular, with numerous state delegations offering versions for consideration. It passed unanimously. The encampment also endorsed the National Industrial Recovery Act and the National Recovery Administration (NRA) but in a rather backhanded way. In the resolution, the delegates declared their loyalty to the U.S. Government and made it veterans' patriotic duty to "respond to the national program" because of the severity of economic conditions. The bulk of the resolution, however, criticized the president and the NRA for failing to "establish a definite relationship between price increase and payroll increase." The VFW delegates, like many others who criticized the New Deal from the left, believed the NRA unjustly favored industry's welfare over workers'. The assembled delegates also passed resolutions reiterating their insistence on cash payment of the Bonus, calling for the reduction of interest on existing tax-exempt securities, and demanding the "universal draft" of industry and capital during times of war. However indirectly, these resolutions addressed the issue of concentrated wealth and its corollary, lack of purchasing power, and demonstrated a consistent critique of the existing political economy.[48]

Most notably, the encampment passed Resolution No. 64, stating the VFW's position "heartily endorsing" a proposed constitutional amendment providing for the limitation of wealth. The VFW pledged "every effort possible to secure [the] enactment . . . of this humanitarian proposal." According to the resolution, the amendment would "benefit the entire Nation and all out people [*sic*] by distributing wealth, limiting income, and making spending power more equitable than is possible at present." Seamlessly, the VFW delegates wove the problems of the Depression, the concentration of wealth, and popular veteran understandings of the causes of wars into the language of the resolution. According to the veteran delegates, the amendment would "through the elimination of huge fortunes, with their attending greed and selfishness, serve to limit the possibilities of future wars."[49]

The debate on and the passage of this resolution proved contentious and demonstrated the controversial nature of such a declaration. The Committee on Resolutions initially rejected the resolution after a sharp exchange among the delegates. The exchange underscored the tensions felt by veterans committed to "stamping out" Communism but nonetheless considering a constitutional amendment to limit wealth. Comrade Cullen from Prairie Du Chien, Wisconsin, pointed out the VFW members' oath to uphold the Constitution, including the protection of "life, liberty, and property." Cullen continued, "Whenever this Government undertakes to limit anything of that kind, it is the first step toward bolshevism." Cullen contended that the resolution should be thrown out, even though he was "in favor of the poor man all the way through." In defense of the resolution, Comrade Thomson exhibited a fervor that showed the effects of Long's address to the encampment. At times employing Long's rhetoric and even his exact phrases, Thomson exhorted the committee, "Let's get organized; let's get hot; let's go places; let's can this idea of 2 percent of the country owning 95 percent of the wealth!" Thomson concluded that with the limitation of wealth, the "fellow who lost his leg in France gets $100 and no 10 percent cut from now on." Despite Thomson's spirit, the committee voted down the resolution on technical considerations. The encampment delegates, however, called for a floor vote and passed the measure over the Resolutions Committee's objections. Despite the VFW leaderships' claims that there was "little or no tendency toward radical thought or action" and that "a spirit of conservatism, coupled with aggressive determination, seemed to prevail" during the encampment, the set of resolutions situated the VFW as a leading critic of the "first" New Deal.[50]

On September 22, 1933, James E. Van Zandt, the newly elected VFW commander, brought the VFW's agenda directly to the White House. In a brief meeting with FDR, Van Zandt described "the wide-spread suffering that has been caused among disabled veterans," including the "plight of more than 400,000 disabled World War veterans . . . thrust upon local community charities" after losing their pensions for nonservice-related injuries. Van Zandt issued an "emphatic plea for the President's cooperation and tolerant consideration of policies" adopted by the Milwaukee encampment. Reiterating the encampment's mandate—opposition to the Economy Act and continued support for immediate cash payment of the Bonus—Van Zandt garnered little sympathy from FDR on either issue. He probably received even less when he described the organization's expansive view of the federal responsibility for veterans, enumerating three "fundamental" principles of veteran legislation: adequate relief for veterans with service-connected disabilities, relief to veterans "suffering from disabilities due either to injury, disease, or old age, who are unable to carry on," and relief to widows and orphans "regardless of the cause of the veteran's death." Van Zandt's articulation of these principles, in direct opposition to the very basis of the Economy Act, possibly crystallized plans for FDR to address the upcoming American Legion national convention in Chicago.[51]

Much like Herbert Hoover during the Bonus battle, FDR chose to address the convention of the more hospitable, and still more powerful,

Legion as a way to undermine unrest among World War veterans. A *Washington Post* report quoted unnamed Legion leaders as saying that the president would attend because "resentment against congressional cuts in disability pensions has been mounting steadily in veterans' ranks." An internal White House memorandum describing why FDR should attend this gathering of veterans indicated the depth of veteran resentment and the political stakes at risk. The writer, John C. Fischer of the Board of Veteran Appeals, described the political calculations of the veteran situation. He argued, "Someone must speak" to pacify the angry veterans, and only the president, with his "magnificent personality," could "escape unscathed." The political clout associated with the voting bloc of veterans and their relatives represented "one sixth of our citizenry," he noted, and this was a necessary engagement to insure the future "success of the Administration's programs." Fischer also pointed to the short-term legislative concerns, noting that only FDR's presence could "forestall legislation calculated to emasculate the Economy Act and will mollify the radicals and disarm a thoroughly aroused and recalcitrant Congress . . . deluged with veterans' appeals." Legion Commander Johnson wrote to the president, obsequiously explaining that his "presence and example will ensure that we keep the Legion on the right road of conservatism and patriotism." He painted a rosy picture, promising FDR "the greatest reception of your life."[52]

On October 2, 1933, FDR addressed the Legion national convention in Chicago. He acknowledged the government's responsibility to care for veterans with service-connected disabilities and the dependents of those killed in action. Yet, FDR bluntly rebuffed further demands by veterans—and specifically the VFW—proclaiming that "no person, because he wore a uniform must thereafter be placed in a special class of beneficiaries over and above all other citizens." He continued, "The fact of wearing a uniform does not mean that he can demand and receive from his Government a benefit which no other citizen receives." In this frank refutation, a *Washington Post* reporter explained, "Facing the blue-clad soldiers of 1918, who felt the swing of the Administration's economy ax in the drive to assure National credit, the President dramatically pointed his finger at them and backed up his program."[53]

FDR's address helped win over the Legion convention. Commander Johnson tried on his own to get the delegates to abandon the "road to recklessness and extravagance." But he wrote to FDR and assured him that only his presence had allowed Legion leaders to reverse the mandate of the 1932 Legion convention supporting immediate payment of the Bonus and to quiet the clamor to rescind all of the Economy Act. To be sure, the Legion still adopted resolutions dedicating a "four point program" to redress the Economy Act's excesses regarding reductions in benefits for those with service-connected disabilities. Nonetheless, the *New York Times* called the convention "a victory for the conservative element," leaving "little doubt of the ability of the Legion's leadership to hold its members in line . . . with the Administration." Despite FDR's success in pacifying the Legion delegates, his words further inflamed the more militant VFW. [54]

VFW leaders and members issued sharp rebuttals to FDR's remarks. Many VFW members agreed that the wearing of a uniform did not entitle all veterans to benefits but found it incomprehensible that this would apply to overseas and combat veterans. Frank O. Gangwisch, commander of Post 12 in Pittsburgh, informed FDR, "We are writing you, Mr. President, to let you know that we do not agree with you. We believe that the

President Franklin D. Roosevelt addresses the American Legion national convention in Chicago, October 2, 1933. Seated next to him is Louis Johnson, the Legion's national commander and FDR's friend. Courtesy of the American Legion.

Herbert Lake, "Old Ideals vs. 'New Deals,'" *VFW (Foreign Service)* Magazine, December 1933. Courtesy of the Veterans of Foreign Wars.

man who donned a uniform in time of war is entitled to special benefits not enjoyed by the man who stayed home and earned from fifteen to fifty dollars a day while we were fighting at the front." Commander Van Zandt issued a statement contradicting the president and reiterating the VFW's liberal position on veteran benefits, claiming that the veteran's "welfare today is exclusively a federal responsibility." The VFW's *Foreign Service* editorial page assaulted FDR's speech as an abrupt departure from long-held American views concerning veterans. In an editorial entitled "Ideals Ignored," the VFW pointed out "the radicalism of the 'new deal' Administration on veteran issues." Moreover, the VFW leadership predicted, "If Franklin D. Roosevelt believes for one moment that his drastic theories on the problem of veteran welfare reflect the wishes of the American people, he is indeed due for a sad awakening at the hands of an aroused Congress." Herbert E. Lake, the VFW artist, penned the scornful accompanying drawing. In "Old Ideals vs. 'New Deals,'" statements from Abraham Lincoln and Theodore Roosevelt concerning the federal obligation to veterans contrasted with FDR's "new deal" departure. The imagery rendered the drawing an especially harsh condemnation of FDR. Lincoln and Teddy Roosevelt stood sternly and statesman-like while FDR was drawn with a whimsical, mocking countenance.[55]

In October 1933, the VFW initiated an intense publicity drive to bring attention to the plight of veterans and to galvanize opposition to the Economy Act. As VFW leaders continually found themselves frozen out by the Legion on veterans' policy matters, the only way they could wield political power was to build up the membership by appealing to veterans disillusioned with the Legion and to work outside the conventional political and legislative processes to mold public opinion. George Brobeck, the VFW's legislative chairman, instituted a "nine point program" to utilize the network of VFW local posts, radio broadcasts, and VFW national publications in the effort. Commander Van Zandt was a dynamo. Speaking almost weekly on radio programs on the NBC and CBS national networks, giving addresses with titles like "The VFW Legislative Policy for the Coming Year," Van Zandt called for the total repeal of the Economy Act and immediate cash payment of the Bonus. Moreover, throughout the winter of 1933–1934, Van Zandt continually traveled the country to address and recruit veterans for the VFW and to win public support for the VFW agenda.[56]

In December 1933, a national speaking tour headed by Van Zandt and the extremely popular Marine major general Smedley D. Butler drew national media attention to the VFW's mobilization efforts. Butler, recently retired to the lecture circuit, commanded huge veteran audiences everywhere he spoke. For recruiting purposes, the VFW published Butler's "You Got to Get Mad" address to the 1933 encampment in *Foreign Service*. The VFW also realized that Butler was a real asset in its effort to obtain national media attention. Van Zandt and Butler's tour, hitting ten cities across the Midwest and the South in eleven days, garnered reporting from the *New York Times* even when they were in the Deep South. A Roosevelt supporter in 1932, Butler now decried the administration's cozy alliance with "Big Business." His animated harangues against "Wall Street" and his calls for veteran political activism energized veteran audiences. Veterans—and reporters—loved Butler's salty language and colorful analogies. In Omaha, Nebraska, Butler "launched a stormy attack against capitalists, blaming them for the National Economy Act." In New Orleans, Butler shared the dais with Huey Long at a VFW rally and told the veterans, "I believe in making Wall Street pay for it—taking Wall Street by the throat and shaking it up." In Atlanta, he explained, "Jimmie [Van Zandt] and I are going around the country trying to educate the soldiers out of the sucker class."[57]

In advance of the 1934 congressional session, the American Legion likewise began its lobbying efforts. Rather than arousing veterans with spirited attacks against the president, Legion leaders sought to implement the "four point program" by working the levers of power and calmly convincing the American public that the Economy Act went too far. The four points enumerated in the program included a return to World War Veterans Act disability standards. Not only would this return the rates for service-connected disabilities to pre-1930 levels; it would ipso facto maintain the elimination of the 1930 pensions for nonservice-related disabilities. The Legion also argued for free hospitalization for indigent veterans, the restoration of many of the service presumptions outlined in the 1920s, and a small widow's and children's pension. Around Christmas, the new Legion commander, Edward A. Hayes, and John Thomas Taylor discussed the Legion program with White House officials. Hayes then traveled the country trying to convince the public of the injustices done veterans with service-related disabilities. At the opening of the session, Legion allies in the Senate introduced language into appropriations legislation that would implement the Legion's program.[58]

In contrast to to the Legion's maneuvering in the corridors of power, the VFW leadership continued to encourage militant grassroots activism. At the start of the congressional session, the VFW's mobilization efforts picked up intensity. In the January 1934 issue of *Foreign Service*, George Brobeck, the VFW's legislative representative, notified members that "'Fire at Will' is the command to veterans as Congress convenes." Brobeck explained to VFW members that the organization's militancy was the only way to affect the repeal of the Economy Act. He proclaimed that "the time has passed when the veterans of this country should come with their hands outstretched, humbly begging their pittance." Brobeck announced that "all over the country former service men under the leadership of the VFW are awakening to their responsibility as 'soldier-citizens.'" With this inversion, "soldier-citizen" from "citizen-soldier," Brobeck stressed the level of veteran militancy encouraged by the VFW leadership. Commander Van Zandt reaffirmed the organization's stance: "The time for politeness and modesty is past. We have reached the stage where fighting—and fighting only—will convince our enemies that we mean business." Major-General Butler advised the VFW members, "What you've got to do now, beginning this minute, is to make this battle a *personal* battle. You've got to tell your Senators and Congressmen what you want and why you want it." The February *Foreign Service* issue ran a special announcement from the VFW leadership urging members and nonveterans alike to "Write Those Letters!" Even though the announcement said veterans should write in their "own words," it also included detailed instructions on how to address their representatives and senators: "Make your letters firm and militant. Let them know you and your relatives and your friends are prepared to vote against them at the next election if they play traitor to the veteran cause."[59]

Once again, the editorial artist Herbert E. Lake graphically depicted the VFW viewpoint, this time on the power of veteran political activism. As the drawing "Happy New Year(?)" showed, the veterans' protest against the Economy Act would be the basis for a congressional revolt. Lake characterized the growing clamor for the repeal of the Economy Act as a tornado, with "veteran protest" kicking up the funnel cloud of an "Approaching Session of Congress." As the twister heads toward the White House, tiny administration officials scurry inside for safety, powerless to avert the coming tempest. This message conveyed by this image became prophetic as Congress undertook the dismantling of the Economy Act in the 1934 session.[60]

In March 1934, the passage of a second Independent Offices bill reversed most of the Economy Act as the power of veteran politics over a Congress facing reelection proved too much for the administration to suppress. In late January, the Roosevelt administration recognized the certainty of revisions to the Economy Act and developed two strategies to undermine congressional support for such measures. First, FDR issued four more executive orders liberalizing the 1933 terms yet again. Then, the administration's congressional allies such as Senator James F. Byrnes (D, SC) attempted to reduce the size of the restorations by warning of a certain presidential veto. The strategies partially worked as a more expensive bill supported by the VFW that would have essentially repealed the Economy Act went down to defeat after FDR announced his intentions of vetoing it. The version of the bill that emerged from Congress after heated debate hewed closely to the Legion's plan by not reinstating nonservice-connected pensions. Only the Legion's widows' pension provision did not make it into the legislation. Despite this rather conservative alternative, it restored much more than the administration could stomach. FDR vetoed the bill, but, on March 29, 1934, both houses of Congress voted to override the President—handily in the House (310–72), more narrowly in the Senate (63–27). Secretary of the Interior Harold Ickes complained in his diary that the members of the House "man after man, like so many scared rabbits, ran to cover out of fear of the soldier vote."[61]

In the end, the 1934 Independent Offices Act handed FDR his first significant congressional defeat. Ickes confided that the veto override dealt

FDR "his first serious political setback" and was "a serious blow to his economy program." Arthur Krock of the *New York Times* called the veto override "the President's first Manassas," pointing out that FDR's "supreme control of the parliamentary arm lasted a year and twenty-four days." The *Boston Herald* noted that the veto override offered "a grim warning that the veterans are in the saddle again and they have always ridden hard." According to Senator James F. Byrnes, an administration ally, the "resounding defeat" of the Economy Act also profoundly altered Roosevelt. Byrnes explained in his memoirs that "it entirely changed the President's attitude toward economy measures." He argued that the Independent Offices Act convinced Roosevelt that Congress would no longer countenance attempts at economy in government, and, as a direct result, FDR "became the leader of those advocating liberal spending." Not surprisingly, Budget Director Lewis Douglas eventually became a casualty of the economy program's demise, too. In September, after months of increasing dismay over FDR's political reversal on spending, Douglas resigned from the administration.[62]

While both claimed victory, the VFW and the Legion came away from the Economy Act drama with different perspectives. Commander Van Zandt of the VFW brashly issued a statement claiming, "Congress has demonstrated it will no longer tolerate dictatorship." The VFW leadership gloated in *Foreign Service* that "the potency of organized veteran pressure was ably demonstrated . . . when Congress rode roughshod over a Presidential veto." But VFW leaders, keenly aware that the pension cuts for nonservice-related disabilities remained in place, reiterated the organization's support for some form of nonservice pensions and promised to fight for them in the future. They also rededicated their energies to the immediate cash payment of the Bonus and, in doing so, continued to voice dissent with the Roosevelt administration. At the American Legion's National Executive Committee meeting in May, Raymond J. Kelly, chairman of the National Legislative Committee, praised the Legion's handling of the Economy Act controversy. Kelly proclaimed, "Thank God the American Legion kept its head, and with grim determination set out to rectify this grave injustice." He then gratuitously derided the Legion's new rival for Great War veterans' affiliation, the VFW, as "vicious and bitter in their attacks," spending a large portion of his report harping on the upstart VFW's unwarranted chutzpah. Chief lobbyist John Thomas Taylor proudly proclaimed the Legion's decisive maneuvering in the Economy Act episode as "our most successful yet," but Legion officials looked to regroup after a very difficult string of years in which they no longer seemed in control of World War veterans' policy, much less of World War veterans.[63]

Roosevelt's Economy Act, as much a reaction to the 1930 expansion of the veterans' pension system as to the Great Depression, precipitated an angry political mobilization by veterans. The Economy Act emerged as a unifying theme for veterans who issued very clear renunciations of the Roosevelt administration and decried the New Deal's failures to keep the federal government's contract with its citizens and, by extension, to reshape the political economy as many had hoped. When the Legion adopted conciliatory tones and tactics in its dealings with the administration, the VFW's energized national leadership, national publications and meetings, and high-profile spokesmen provided the early organizational structure and the means of national conveyance for New Deal dissent. Predating both Long's and Coughlin's organizations, veterans became founding members, and the VFW national organization an early meeting ground, of an otherwise loosely organized Depression-era protest movement. Veteran politics produced the original "voices of protest."

Even after the overturning of the Economy Act, veteran politics remained at the epicenter of New Deal dissent. Indeed, the hullabaloo surrounding the second Independent Offices Act obscured two significant developments in New Deal politics. On February 23, 1934, Huey Long delivered a nationally broadcast speech touting his new political organization, the Share Our Wealth Society. In this speech outlining the organization's platform and purpose, Long appealed to disaffected veterans, "We ought to take care of the veterans of the wars in this program. . . . *Every man that wore the uniform* of this country is entitled to be taken care of." On February 25, 1934, Father Coughlin, who in 1933 had endorsed FDR's positions on both the Economy Act and the Bonus, reversed course by calling for the immediate payment of the Bonus on his weekly broadcast. The renewed battle for the Bonus would keep veterans and the VFW in the vanguard of New Deal dissent.[64]

4

The Bonus Re-emerges

A showdown between veterans and the Administration in the near future seems inevitable.

—VFW editorial, *Foreign Service*, March 1934

Although the spotlight shifted away from the Bonus after its Senate defeat in 1932, veterans and their congressional allies continued to call for the immediate cash payment of adjusted service certificates. From the start of the 73rd Congress in 1933 until the spring of 1934, however, the rearguard battle to restore veterans' benefits cut by the Economy Act preoccupied supporters of the Patman Bonus bill. Moreover, FDR's adamant opposition to the Bonus and the concerted efforts of the administration's powerful congressional allies succeeded in scuttling any attempted Bonus legislation. In February 1934, however, concurrent with the dismantling of the Economy Act, the Bonus re-emerged on the national political scene with a vengeance, becoming one of the most emotionally charged issues of the era. The Bonus provoked contentious debate because the issue developed into a political litmus test, transcending the limited aims of a cash disbursement to veterans. Bonus opponents feared that prepayment would be the final nail in the coffin of fiscal responsibility and would prove that governmental largesse had reached pathological proportions. Bonus supporters argued that immediate payment to suffering veterans and their families would provide an economic stimulus in every community and would help lift the nation out of the Depression. Considering the array of conservatives and business groups allied against them, supporters believed that the fight over the Bonus was a zero-sum contest pitting Wall Street against Main Street.[1]

The American Legion and the VFW once again took different approaches toward the Bonus. For the Legion, the 1933 encampment's disavowal of pre-payment turned the powerful organization into a by-stander during the ensuing debate. Legion leaders continually failed to reach a consensus among the rank and file over the merits of Bonus payment. A unified VFW, however, resumed its high-profile political activities in the renewed battle for the Bonus and continued its lead role in New Deal dissenting politics. Facing significant obstacles, the VFW championed the drive for Bonus payment to a successful House vote and gained prominent allies in national political figures Senator Huey P. Long and Father Charles E. Coughlin. For the VFW, this was a pragmatic decision as much as an ideological commitment; the organizational strides made in the previous years convinced VFW officials that militancy on Great War veterans' issues translated into increased membership and status. The same could be said of Long's and Coughlin's courtship of veterans with their Bonus support: an ideological affinity converged with calculated opportunism. Regardless of the reasons, veterans, led by the VFW, criticized the Roosevelt administration's refusal to stand up for ordinary citizens against Wall Street in the Bonus fight and continued in the vanguard of New Deal dissent.

Within weeks of Roosevelt's inauguration, the Bonus briefly threatened to re-emerge as a national political issue when another Bonus March descended on Washington. Despite admonitions from the national offices of both the Legion and the VFW, in early May veterans began arriving in the District. Unlike in the 1932 march, Communist veterans' groups played a significant role in the planning of this trek. Even with the Communist tinge to it, Roosevelt gently handled the much smaller group (estimated at around 3,000, less than a tenth the number who attended the 1932 march) and defused the situation. FDR ordered the government to provide shelter and plentiful food for the men at nearby Fort Hunt, Virginia. Eleanor Roosevelt visited the marchers' encampment, leading them in old camp songs and sharing her antiwar convictions with them in a brief speech. One veteran camper quipped, "Hoover sent the Army; Roosevelt sent his wife." A few days later, FDR met with a small delegation in the White House. Following the advice of VA Director Hines, Roosevelt issued executive orders altering age and marital restrictions and allowing up to 25,000 veterans to join the newly created Civilian Conservation Corps (CCC). When the marchers finally dispersed, on May 22, 2,657 veterans took the CCC offer; the remaining 400 or so took a free ride home. In short order, FDR turned the potentially distracting event into a symbolic victory. Although a rancorous veteran revolt was under way over the Economy Act, many veteran marchers and political commentators hailed Roosevelt's handling of the episode as a signature New Deal departure from the Hoover regime's treatment of veterans. Ever since, historians writing the New Deal narrative have continued to employ the 1932 and 1933 Bonus Marches in this contrasting manner.[2]

More important—though less poignant—than the diplomatic resolution of the second Bonus March was the way the Roosevelt administration successfully bottled up the Bonus in Congress for almost a year. FDR made it very clear that too much important work was waiting to be accomplished to allow another Bonus battle to sidetrack the 1933 congressional session. In the Hundred Days, therefore, Democrats controlling Congress kept the screws on any Bonus legislation. Indeed, throughout 1933, the Patman Bonus bill (H.R. 1) wallowed in the Ways and Means Committee, stifled by the administration's powerful congressional allies who served on the committee. By December 1933, however, veterans pinned their hopes on a discharge petition started by their Farm-Laborite and Spanish-American War veteran ally, Representative Ernest Lundeen (Farm-Labor, MN). Lundeen needed to obtain 145 signatures on his petition to bypass the recalcitrant Ways and Means committee and send the Patman Bonus bill to the House floor for a vote. Ironically, Wright Patman, the bill's author, did not sign the petition in deference to the Democratic administration. In fact, signing the petition proved no small matter for tempted Democrats, as it rested on the desk of House Speaker (and staunch FDR ally) Henry T. Rainey (D, IL), an obvious but effective form of political intimidation.[3]

In the winter of 1933–1934, the VFW orchestrated veteran protests in support of the Bonus and led the lobbying effort against administration policy. The American Legion's refusal to endorse cash payment of the Bonus at its 1933 national gathering hampered the campaign but did not deter it. Foremost, VFW officials threw the organization's weight behind the discharge petition drive, working side by side with Lundeen to collect signatures. Even during the VFW's efforts for repeal of the Economy Act, the VFW leadership explained that the pension saga would not derail the organization's demands for the Bonus. A *Foreign Service* editorial proclaimed, "With Congress about to convene, the demand for an increased amount of currency in circulation will be pushed more vigorously than ever by the VFW in its fight for cash payment." As the new congressional session began, VFW leaders pledged to veterans, "Although this cause has been definitely deserted by other veteran groups, the VFW is clinging to this objective in its program with characteristic tenacity."[4]

At the beginning of the session, an energized insurgent faction in Congress also stood poised to challenge the Roosevelt administration on veterans' issues. The insurgents, described by one national periodical as "the veterans' bloc," clamored for the resolution of two issues in direct and open opposition to administration policy: the dismantling of the Economy Act and the immediate cash payment of the Bonus. Indeed, in the early months of 1934, these two veterans' issues dominated national political debate. For the purpose of analysis, here the two issues are disentangled. In early 1934, however, the congressional revolt against the Economy Act and the re-emergence of the Bonus were inextricably linked. Political reporting on the congressional revolt always connected the issues, attributing the success of veterans' lobbying to the upcoming midterm elections. Arthur Krock, the *New York Times* political columnist, called the veteran protests "skillful and forceful" and observed that the importance of "the activity of the veterans' lobbies in the nominating primaries" had "frightened many Representatives and a large percentage of the Senate into voting against the White House."[5]

By February 1934, the Bonus battle erupted on the Hill. The previous December, fewer than sixty signatures had adorned the Lundeen petition. In January and February, however, with the congressional revolt on veteran issues well under way, Lundeen's petition quickly filled with names. On February 18, the Lundeen petition had 113 signatures. Two days later, Lundeen and the VFW picked up the signature of the Patman bill's author, quickly followed by the remainder of the necessary signatures. Just before the last signature was collected, Speaker of the House Rainey returned from a White House meeting and proclaimed, "I am authorized by the President to say this is not the time to pay the bonus and he cannot approve any legislation to that effect." The threat failed. The *New York Times* noted that "advocates of the bonus broke loose in the House today in the face of a warning of a veto by President Roosevelt." In all, ninety-seven Democrats split with the White House in signing the petition. Forty-three Republicans and the entire Farm-Laborite delegation joined them. By discharging the Patman Bonus bill, Bonus supporters secured a House vote on the measure scheduled for March 12, 1934.[6]

The VFW instantly mobilized to lobby Congress on the Bonus vote, challenging the White House's opposition to immediate payment. Commander Van Zandt quickly issued a statement to the press claiming sole credit for the organization in the successful petition campaign. Van Zandt recognized that the VFW stood alone, with no aid from the Legion, but noted, "we know that we have the support of the rank and file of all ex-servicemen and all clear thinking citizens." He explained that the Bonus would be an important additional measure in the president's economic recovery plan and predicted that the Bonus bill would pass both the House and the Senate. Van Zandt expressed hope that it would pass by a wide enough margin to discourage the "defiant challenge" of a White House veto. Yet, the VFW leadership bluntly predicted, "a showdown between veterans and the Administration in the near future seems inevitable."[7]

Van Zandt badgered the administration over the Bonus. On February 28, hours after yet another FDR threat of veto, Van Zandt fired off a sharply worded telegram to Roosevelt, demanding that he "make public [his] objections to immediate cash payment." After listing the litany of reasons for supporting the Bonus in the telegram, Van Zandt told FDR, "we are honestly convinced that our recommendations are justified by your desire to increase the purchasing power of the masses." The commander requested an explanation to the veterans of the nation, since, "in asking [them] to abandon all hope of your favor on this issue, [they are] at least entitled to a statement that will make clear your views on this subject and why it fails to warrant your approval." A handwritten margin note from the president's clerical secretary to his personal assistant, Marvin H. McIntyre revealed the frustration elicited by this telegram, "Mac: President says 'How — do you answer it?'" VFW headquarters released a copy of the telegram to the national press wires to pressure the administration, but the administration ultimately ignored it rather than cave in to such an antagonistic demand.[8]

In the weeks between the discharge and the vote on the Bonus, Van Zandt rallied veterans in multiple radio addresses and countless personal appearances across the country. On March 9, 1934, Van Zandt and Lundeen, the discharge petition sponsor, spoke on a nationwide VFW program broadcast over the NBC network. They emphasized the importance of swamping Congress with personal letters demanding a favorable vote on the Patman Bonus bill. The national headquarters also issued "battle orders" to all post commanders and individual members for "a bombardment of both the House and Senate with continued demands for support of pending legislation." The VFW leadership instructed veterans to warn House members that the vote "will be watched back home by thousands of voters." The leadership hoped that, with enough lobbying pressure, a decisive victory in Congress might change the administration's attitude. Van Zandt exhorted members, "Let's get wise and mobilize!" The Legion, meanwhile, committed to staying out of the Bonus battle in accord with the 1933 convention's mandate and remained deafeningly silent.[9]

Even before the Bonus measure came to a vote, the VFW continued to garner the rewards of its position as Great War veterans rushed to the banner. From November 1933 to March 1934, the VFW mustered in 164 new posts. In February and March alone, the organization added well over a post a day, including four in Chicago, three in Cleveland, and four in the Los Angeles metropolitan area. Posts also formed in the more rural locales of Oklahoma, Montana, and Nebraska—even one in Centralia, Washington, a town made notorious for a battle between Legionnaires and Wobblies that took place in 1919. In the spring of 1934, VFW leadership gloated over these institutional gains. R. B. Handy, Jr., the national adjutant general, issued an announcement in a national veteran publication proclaiming that "the Veterans of Foreign Wars is still the fastest growing veterans organization in the country." Handy emphasized the VFW's fight for the Bonus as the key to the organization's growth, noting that "the majority of veterans agree with us and wish to cooperate in our efforts" as proved by the "large numbers by which they are joining the VFW." On the gains in membership, Commander Van Zandt wryly observed, "All over the country the overseas men are flocking to our standard. I guess they like the way we fight."[10]

In spite of the growth, with the Legion out of this campaign VFW leaders felt compelled to defend their standing as representatives of World War veterans. Opponents in the National Economy League seized on the VFW's secondary status and attempted to minimize the organization's importance in veteran affairs. In a letter sent to all congressional members, the National Economy League highlighted the VFW's role in procuring the discharge petition by noting that "the 'bonus act' does not even come from a representative group of veterans . . . it comes from a single organization whose membership only represents an insignificant percentage of the veterans of the World War." In a letter to the editor of the *New York Times*, Van Zandt blasted the idea that the VFW represented only a minority view of World War veterans as "absurd," pointing out that 3 million of the 3.5 million veterans holding adjusted service certificates had already borrowed up to 50 percent against them. Van Zandt claimed that these veterans were "naturally in favor of immediate cash payment of the balance due." Whether or not the majority of veterans supported immediate payment, the VFW and Bonus supporters soon picked up key endorsements from two of the most recognizable and controversial political figures of the era.[11]

After the re-emergence of the Patman Bonus bill, Senator Huey P. Long joined with the VFW in the battle for both ideological and opportunistic reasons. In fact, Long's unqualified support for veterans became an important plank in the agenda of his new national political organization. On February 23, 1934, just three days after the Patman Bonus bill discharge, Long addressed a national radio audience on the creation of his Share Our Wealth Society (SOWS). In this speech outlining the organization's platform and purpose, Long asserted, "We ought to take care of the veterans of the wars in this program. . . . Every man that wore the uniform of this country is entitled to be taken care of." Of course, the limitation of wealth formed the centerpiece of the SOWS, a measure the VFW national organization had already endorsed in the 1933 encampment. Long's cooperation with the VFW extended to the Senate floor. In the debate over the Independent Offices Bill, Long offered an amendment that would pay the Bonus in terms identical to the VFW-endorsed Patman Bonus bill. In the cantankerous debate, the administration's Senate allies read aloud a message from FDR to Speaker of the House Rainey that put FDR's opposition to the bill in unmistakable terms. FDR's message read, "I [will] veto the bill, and I don't care who you tell this to." The Long amendment fell in a 64–24 vote. During this battle, Long took to wearing a VFW lapel pin while on the Senate floor, even though he was not a veteran, much less an overseas veteran. Long's display of the VFW lapel pin drew contemptuous jeers from other Senators, particularly Bennett "Champ" Clark (D, MO), a founding member of the American Legion. When pressed on the matter, Long jauntily responded that he had received honorary membership in the organization for being a "friend of the veteran" through the good wishes of Van Zandt and a New Orleans post. In public and behind closed doors, Legion officials ridiculed the union of the radical Long and the upstart VFW. [12]

The re-emergence of the Bonus issue also elicited pointed comments from the "Radio Priest," Father Charles E. Coughlin. In one of the first public signs of strains in the Coughlin-Roosevelt relationship, Coughlin returned to the issue that he had promoted throughout the Hoover administration but had been silent on in deference to the president. On February 25, 1934, the first Sunday following the Bonus discharge, Coughlin used his weekly radio address to advance his banking and monetary policies. In the address, however, Coughlin turned to the "vexed question" of the Bonus and reversed course significantly from his initial cooperation with the administration.[13]

Noting that the Bonus "comes again to our national attention," Coughlin emphatically placed himself in favor of immediate payment and, therefore, in open opposition to the Roosevelt administration's policy. He asserted that he supported the payment but not if it was to be paid in "banker's money." "Banker's money," to Coughlin, referred to the issuing of governmental bonds to pay the Bonus, bonds that would end up in the hands of bankers collecting tax-exempt interest. Coughlin also viewed the Patman bill's method of payment, the printing of money against revaluated gold, with suspicion, asking, "Why should we help to restore a bankers' prosperity employing this method of payment?" Instead, Coughlin called on ex-soldiers to support an ambiguous "nationalization of credit" as the means to secure immediate payment of the Bonus. He exhorted, "Veterans—your bonus must be paid not with borrowed money, not with banker's money—but with nationalized credit money. Get this first—the bonus will follow!" Coughlin addressed ex-soldiers directly in his radio talk: "Do you realize that you did not fight in vain to save the world for democracy? I do not mean the political democracy. . . . I mean the financial democracy which now has the kings and princes of finance whining for mercy." Coughlin exhorted the veterans to political action: "Do you realize that if one or two million of you ex-servicemen raise your voices in unison you can finish this cruel capitalism that caused the war through its mad policy of production for profit?"[14]

The differences between the Patman Bonus bill and Coughlin's plan of national credit were minor. Both plans supported the Bonus as a means of inflation and as an economic stimulus, spreading more than $2 billion across the entire nation. Both Patman and Coughlin regarded the use of bonds to pay the Bonus as anathema. Indeed, Wright Patman and Coughlin had long shared common goals and a working relationship in support of their monetary plans. Both Patman and Senator Elmer Thomas of Oklahoma, the House and Senate sponsors of inflationary Bonus legislation, openly aligned themselves with the Radio Priest. Likewise, Patman and Thomas united with the VFW on the Bonus issue. In fact, the differences between the Patman bill and Coughlin's plan for the Bonus were so negligible that the VFW organization considered the Coughlin speech an important endorsement.[15]

Van Zandt, the VFW national commander, quickly seized upon Coughlin's renewed interest in Bonus payment. In a statement issued from VFW national headquarters, Van Zandt pointed out that Coughlin's call for immediate cash payment signaled a change of direction. Fully aware of Coughlin's vocal defense of the Administration's position on the Economy Act and the Bonus during the previous year, he used the speech as evidence that public opinion was beginning to shift on the issue. In the statement, Van Zandt repeatedly tied the organization to Coughlin's position and reputation as a monetary specialist. He noted, "The VFW agrees with Father Coughlin that to finance the payment of the payment of the bonus through bankers would retard recovery and neutralize the benefits that otherwise would be shared by industries and commerce." Van Zandt proclaimed that Coughlin "very ably describes the process by which all the benefits of inflation may be obtained without the usual aftermath of inflationary experiments by simply paying an acknowledged debt." Thus, the VFW had gained another important, albeit controversial, ally in the Bonus battle.[16]

On March 12, 1934, the House took up the Patman Bonus bill. First, the House voted on whether to discharge the bill from the Ways and Means Committee. Then, the Patman bill came under consideration. With the galleries filled beyond capacity, Bonus supporters routed the opposition by tallies of 313–104 and 295–125 on the respective votes. Two hundred and thirty-five Democrats defied their party leadership by voting for the Bonus, enabling the vote to reach the two-thirds threshold necessary to override an all-but-certain veto. The House debate over these votes bordered on bedlam. In a scene described as "disorder at point of chaos," Bonus supporters shouted down Democratic administration allies and conservative Republicans with equal disregard. Long-serving House members called the episode "the most disorderly" they had ever witnessed. The *New York Times* editorial page ridiculed the congressional revolt against the administration, noting a grave error in political calculus. The editors scoffed at the "scattered, intangible, and largely non-existent 'soldier vote'" courted by representatives. The *Times'* columnist Arthur Krock blamed the "wild and unseasoned quality" of some of the Democrats and the "radicals of all stripes" that were voted into the House in 1932. *Time* dismissed the vote as "only a political gesture for home consumption since no one expected the bonus bill to become law." Regardless, the congressional revolt against the administration over the Bonus dominated the news. Moreover, the revolt succeeded with no support from the American Legion; among veteran organizations, only the VFW could take credit for the House victory. With the president still adamantly opposed to the legislation, the House sent the Patman Bonus bill to the Senate for consideration.[17]

After the House Bonus vote, the VFW kicked the mobilization efforts into high gear. The VFW aggressively challenged FDR in the organization's publications and in veterans' periodicals, augmenting the organization's reputation as a leading voice of New Deal dissent. The issue of *Foreign Service* released after the House vote contained numerous examples of direct confrontation. The editorial page, in reference to Van Zandt's telegram to FDR, claimed that FDR had "failed to justify his threat of a veto with a logical explanation." The VFW editors regarded the "vast expenditures" and budget deficits of the New Deal as proof that the administration did not take fiscal responsibility too seriously. The editorial sardonically noted that FDR "is hardly in a position to charge that [Bonus] payment . . . will bring financial ruin." The editorials suggested that FDR might be poorly served by his advisers on the issue. Regardless of whether FDR received poor advice or stuck to principle, the VFW leadership threw down the gauntlet. The editorial warned, "If the VFW is unable to convert President Roosevelt, then this organization will do everything in its power to override his veto." Commander Van Zandt added, with typical bravado, "The VFW refuses to lay down its arms. Vetoes have been overridden by Congress in the past." An editorial drawing by Herbert E. Lake accompanied the challenging rhetoric. Lake's "A 'New Deal' Decoration" [cover image] resembled his earlier drawings of FDR in which he portrayed the president as an affable, effeminate opponent. In this drawing, a laughing FDR pins a military decoration on the Bonus bill that reads simply, "No." Even though the Patman Bonus bill sat in the Senate Finance Committee awaiting action, VFW leaders did not flinch from challenging the critical source of Bonus opposition, neither congressional conservatives nor anti-Bonus business groups but FDR himself.[18]

In 1934, the VFW leadership made one significant exception when it came to political activism: yet another Bonus March. Much as they had during the 1933 Bonus March, the national leadership informed all VFW posts that the organization was "vigorously opposed" to members' participation. Commander Van Zandt and the organization's leadership believed that another march on Washington would ruin any chance that the Bonus had of passing the Senate. Van Zandt objected to the 1934 Bonus March for a number of reasons. First, the Communist Party's leadership of the proposed march made it untouchable to the staunchly anti-Communist VFW. Second, the VFW believed that it would undermine the extensive groundwork already laid by the legislative committee. Last, Van Zandt claimed—without providing any evidence—that the VFW leadership had reason to believe that the proposed Bonus March was "a deliberate attempt to discredit the veteran . . . financed by anti-bonus forces who feel certain that such an undertaking will prove a fatal boomerang to the cause itself." Fewer than 1,500 veterans participated in this march, which took place between May 12 and May 27, 1934. Once again Roosevelt provided generously for the group and then whisked even more of the veterans into the CCC.[19]

From March 12, 1934, into June, Democratic allies of the administration mired the Patman Bonus bill in the Senate Finance Committee. The White House drafted a lengthy veto speech on March 27 just in case the Senate crossed the administration. But, under the able direction of Senator Pat Harrison (D, MS), the bill languished in committee until Bonus supporter Senator Henrik Shipstead (Farm-Labor, MN) threatened to initiate a discharge movement. Fearing this loss of control, Harrison arranged a committee vote on the measure for June 5. The Senate Finance Committee returned an unfavorable report on the bill by a large majority. In response, Bonus supporters in the Senate such as Shipstead, Robert LaFollette, Jr. (Progressive, WI), Bronson Cutting (R, NM), Arthur Robinson (R, IN), and Huey Long, repeatedly tried to bring up the bill under a unanimous consent rule, only to be continually thwarted by the administration's floor leader, Joseph T. Robinson (D, AR). Bonus supporters finally succeeded in making senators go on the record with a vote by proposing an amendment that called for paying the Bonus to a bill remonetizing silver. The hastily arranged Shipstead Silver Bill amendment lost without debate, 51–31, with many Bonus supporters casting a confused vote against it. Thus, on June 18, the second session of the 73rd Congress adjourned with no action on the Bonus. FDR's prepared veto message went undelivered. The VFW served notice, however, that the organization considered this only a temporary setback. Commander Van Zandt warned the administration and its Democratic allies that "the representatives of the VFW will again be on the firing line demanding immediate cash payment of the adjusted service certificates on the first day of the next session of Congress."[20]

From September 30 to October 5, 1934, VFW members convened at their annual encampment in Louisville, Kentucky, to elect national officers and to discuss the organization's agenda for the coming year. In a validation of the VFW's controversial and aggressive fight for the Bonus and the repeal of the Economy Act, VFW delegates unanimously reelected James Van Zandt as national commander. The delegates included representatives from the 340 new posts gained since the 1933 encampment, a vibrant growth rate. The 1934 national encampment endorsed a legislative agenda called the "Seven Point Program," reiterating many longstanding VFW demands such as the conscription of wealth in time of war and the immediate payment of the Bonus. The encampment also endorsed the nationalization of munitions manufacture, a series of veteran pension reforms, sharp rises in inheritance taxes, and the recall of tax-exempt securities. On the Bonus, the VFW delegates ignored the thinly veiled request by FDR in his perfunctory opening message to the encampment urging them to focus on the "welfare of the country" rather than on "lesser things." Significantly, though, the VFW's renewed demand for the Bonus neither named the Patman bill specifically nor listed a preferred method of paying it. Although Representative Wright Patman spoke to the encampment, garnering overwhelmingly enthusiastic applause, the VFW's refusal to endorse any particular method of payment raised the possibility that the organization would consider less controversial proposals than currency inflation as a means to pay the Bonus.[21]

In a highly charged political atmosphere, the delegates also became embroiled in a heated debate as they considered a change in the organization's prohibition against direct political involvement. The Nebraska delegation proposed changes in the "political code" that would allow the organization, at the national level, to become in involved in the 1934 election. Although the Committee on Resolutions disapproved of the proposal, the debate carried onto the encampment floor. Van Zandt explained that the resolution originated in the leadership's confusion over the politics issue during the primary season. The VFW judge advocate general had rendered an opinion that VFW endorsements were acceptable at the national level because the by-laws allowed participation in "legislation for veteran welfare." This ruling did nothing but throw the national leadership into further confusion. Van Zandt refused to break the prohibition against direct political involvement until the national encampment could vote on the issue.[22]

In the debate, Van Zandt explained his support for the measure. He told the delegates, "Our participation in politics should be in national politics, and the national organization should say whether a Member of Congress has been a friend of ours; and if you want to endorse him, that is your privilege." Van Zandt provided examples as to why the VFW should leap into the political fray. He cited the cases of Representatives William Connery (D, MA) and Gerald Boileau (R, WI), who, after voting against the president and with the VFW, suffered from the lash of the administration and administration allies through lost patronage and reduced committee assignments. Van Zandt explained that the VFW should be able to help these veteran supporters in more concrete ways.[23]

The floor debate over the issue grew tense. Supporters of the measure ridiculed those who opposed it as naïve. Skillman, a member of the National Council, roared, "Who in hell gave you what you have? Politics." He admonished the delegates, "[W]e haven't had the guts to get out and support the men that have supported you and me." Skillman "hoped and prayed" that the delegates would override the committee's recommendation because "How in hell are you going to get anywhere unless you endorse your friends?" The Department Commander of North and South Carolina, A. W. Hamilton, declared that his department already endorsed candidates with a great deal of success despite the prohibition. He proclaimed that "the whole veteran body of the States of North and South Carolina is determined that we shall act in unison and in harmony in endorsing specific political candidates for national office." Another delegate, Bowe, announced that if the encampment refused to change the by-law, "we hamstring ourselves in our fight." Bowe followed this by conjuring the image of the veteran's enemies, noting that if the VFW did not explicitly get into politics, "[t]hose national racketeers, the National Economy League, who try to disrupt us, will laugh from now until election day."[24]

Opponents of political involvement relied on tradition and the logistical difficulties of political involvement. Many opponents worried that political participation would be a dangerous precedent, leading down a slippery slope to total cooptation by the political parties. Delegate Cohen of Illinois commented, "Politics, without question is the dirtiest game in the world. I know; I'm in it." He added, "[Y]ou can't play dirty politics without getting dirtied up by it." Cohen pleaded with his fellow veterans to reject the idea, noting that "we have come along all these years because . . . we were not political, because we have been able to keep our skirts clean." Delegate Haley agreed with Cohen, citing the logistical problem of getting the six VFW posts in his congressional district to agree on a candidate. A delegate named Smith, from Albany, New York—FDR's home state— voiced his opposition to the proposal, caustically noting that, "if we want to form a political organization like the American Legion, let us get out and join the American Legion and to hell with the VFW!"[25]

The dispute over the overt politicization of the VFW reflected ambivalence on the part of VFW members over what such a move might mean. The VFW's political mobilization in 1933 and 1934 placed the organization not only in the vanguard of New Deal dissent but also on the brink of open partisan political participation. VFW members ultimately decided that this irreversible step would place them in unknown and potentially hostile waters. The political code measure failed on two floor votes. Delegate Hamilton, who had supported the resolution, proclaimed that the VFW had just "furnished the occasion for a hallelujah dinner for the National Economy League." The prohibition, however, did not stop veterans from actively participating in the 1934 election. It simply prohibited the organization from giving institutional approval. The national leadership reiterated the call for veteran political activism in the 1934 election, calling the veteran vote "the only solution."[26]

Regardless of the VFW's positions, the upcoming American Legion convention in Miami held the key to how far the Bonus might go in the next congressional session. The Legion, although still bitterly divided, appeared to be heading in the direction of supporting Bonus payment again. In August, well prior to the Miami convention, Louis Johnson, the former Legion commander, wrote frantic telegrams to administration officials begging them for a statement against the Bonus to strike at the Legion's budding Bonus movement. He informed Steve Early that he believed this new Bonus push was merely a Republican attempt to "embarrass our President" and that things were "getting pretty hot" in the Legion. Then, in October, Johnson suggested that FDR make a speech "without direct mention of the Bonus" that would stress the government's responsibility for economic recovery for all citizens over a Bonus for some. Three days later, on October 19, 1934, FDR made an address at a Veterans' Administration hospital dedication ceremony in Roanoke, Virginia, in which he told veterans that they were "today in the prime of life . . . (and) better off, on the average, from the point of view of employment and of annual income than the average of any other great group of our citizens." Roosevelt hoped veterans would "put first things first" and wait patiently while federal money improved the lot of all needy Americans. *Time* observed that, while FDR was officially in Roanoke for the opening of the new psychiatric hospital, "actually he was there to serve notice to the American Legion." "Not once during his eight minute talk did he mention the Bonus by name," the article continued, "but the President made it quite clear that the nation's destitute had first call on the nation's purse."[27]

Although the president's comments were designed specifically for the Legion convention, they still accomplished little with the militant VFW. Three days after the Roanoke speech and just two days before the Legion convention, Commander Van Zandt continued his confrontational jousting with the administration. He presented the platform of the encampment to the White House in a gesture described as "a challenge" to President Roosevelt. Van Zandt couched the Bonus in progressive economic terms. He explained, "We feel that payment of this debt is in line with the President's recovery program," since it would "place in circulation much needed purchasing power." The occasion also gave Van Zandt a forum to express what he thought of the Roanoke speech. In interviews with reporters outside of the White House, Van Zandt claimed that he did not mention the speech in his conversation with FDR but scoffed at its message to veterans. He reminded the reporters that 62 percent of World War veterans were unemployed or underemployed and hardly better off than average citizens. Van Zandt repeated claims made the day after the Roanoke speech that FDR's opposition to the Bonus would be "futile" in the upcoming congressional session. A day later, he wired Edwin A. Hayes, commander of the Legion, urging the Legion to join the VFW in the struggle by passing a favorable Bonus resolution and agreeing to conference together to coordinate strategies.[28]

FDR's remarks from Roanoke also drew the ire of Legionnaires. Commander Edwin A. Hayes rebutted the president on the Roanoke speech. He countered sharply, "The experience of those of us who have been devoting the past fifteen years to the problems of the World War veterans has supplied us with ample proof to show that a vast majority are in a class of handicap because of their service in the war." Hayes further defended the special concern for veterans, proclaiming that "certainly these men are in a class by themselves, separate and apart from ordinary citizens and are entitled to every protection a grateful government can give them." Opponents of the Bonus recognized that FDR's effort to sway the Legion would probably be in vain. The *New York Times* editorialized that "the Veterans' Lobby will undoubtedly prepare again to exert pressure upon Congress, despite all of the President's noble sentiments." While the editors encouraged "the stiffest and most unyielding Presidential opposition" to the Bonus, all eyes turned to Miami.[29]

From October 21 through October 25, 1934, the Legion conducted a spirited convention in Miami. The VFW's nearly successful political mobilization in the face of administration, congressional, and Legion opposition and the liberal spending record of the New Deal convinced veterans that the Bonus might yet be won and forced the Legion to contend with the issue once again. What is more, the 1,186 delegates and 50,000 members in attendance were "in a peppery mood." Roosevelt's Roanoke speech rankled, with members "smarting" and "on record as resenting the President's remarks." F. Raymond Daniell's reporting for the *New York Times* described the surly mood of Legionnaires, explaining that the Roanoke speech "stiffened the drive of bonus advocates." Moreover, the barely concealed partisan political maneuvering that so worried Louis Johnson led the convention to adopt a resolution proposed by the Illinois Department demanding that the Legion "reaffirm its political neutrality." The headlines from the convention, however, focused on the Bonus battle that dominated the proceedings. Louis Johnson spoke against payment in a keynote address arranged by conservative Legion officials, pleading with Legionnaires to not "rock the boat" of national recovery by demanding the Bonus. Commander Hayes read aloud a message from Roosevelt reiterating the least objectionable reasoning from the Roanoke address, proclaiming that "our national interest is paramount. I urge you to carry such a spirit into your convention." Senator Frederick Steiwer and Representative Wright Patman delivered impassioned speeches in favor of payment. Hayes informed the delegates that no interference to a full discussion would be brooked. And, indeed, Legionnaires aired their differences in a lengthy and vibrant debate.[30]

On October 25, the Bonus cause gained an important convert when the Legion national convention passed a resolution in favor of the Bonus by an overwhelming 987–183 vote. When the New York, Arizona, Vermont, and Connecticut delegates opposed the resolution, they were booed lustily. Morris A. Beale, publisher of *Plain Talk* magazine and a well-connected Legionnaire, told FDR's assistant Louis Howe that none of "the most potent leaders of the Legion put together . . . could have stopped the 'Bonus' resolution from passing the Miami convention any more than they could have single-handedly stopped the Johnstown flood." F. Raymond Daniell reported that "nothing, it appeared could have stopped the stampede." The wording of the Bonus resolution proved significant. Legionnaires opted to "recommend" rather than "demand" the Bonus and couched their support in the New Deal's economic terms. The resolution explained that the Bonus "will increase purchasing power of the consuming public . . . and will lighten immeasurably the burden which cities, counties, and States are now required to carry for relief." Moreover, the Legion attributed its change of heart to the fact that "the Government of the United States is now definitely committed to the policy of spending additional sums of money for the purpose of national recovery from the present crisis." A compromise, the resolution contained no language on how the Bonus was to be paid. A flyer distributed at the close of the convention proclaimed, "Three Cheers For the Legion!" and "The Legion is now definitely in politics."[31]

Questions remained about how strongly the Legion would rally around the Bonus. Hines, the director of the VA, suggested that the American Legion would place it on the back burner for patriotic reasons. But the Legion's newly elected commander, Frank N. Belgrano, Jr., rebutted this notion, seeing no escape from the convention's overwhelming mandate. He cautioned that the National Executive Committee would have the final say on how to prepare the legislative agenda, but he believed that "no action taken by the convention will be relegated to the background, and certainly not one on which the Legion expressed itself so emphatically." In an official ceremonial meeting with President Roosevelt, the new commander claimed that no specific discussion of the Bonus had taken place but cautioned reporters that the conversation was not a measure of the Legion's interest in passing the Bonus during the next session of Congress. In late November, the National Executive Committee meeting reiterated that the Bonus would be priority legislative business. On November 28, Commander Belgrano issued a news release proclaiming, "There is no compromise to make." He added that he would follow the mandate of the convention "to the letter" because "it is a question of common sense business which I believe the country will support and the government will adopt." Although the VFW had lost the Bonus battle in 1934, with the Legion joining the fray, Great War veterans looked to the 1935 congressional session with hope. A new Congress and a new pressure group added to their sense of optimism.[32]

In the 1934 midterm election, significant Democratic gains presumably changed the political landscape favorably for the FDR administration. But Democrats had already exhibited a willingness to cross the administration on veterans' issues. Indeed, voters returned 75 percent of the 235 House Democrats who had defied the administration and supported the Bonus bill. *Time* offered an ominous assessment, describing the new Congress as divided between conservatives and radicals of two types: "inflationist-bonuseers and social innovators." It warned, "Because there are more of them, the former group will be harder for the President to handle." Associated Press surveys of the incoming Congress and the results of VFW congressional candidate questionnaires, while incomplete, also suggested that the 74th Congress would be more amenable to the immediate payment than its predecessor. As a result, the VFW leadership proclaimed, "Although the Democratic landslide eliminated from Congress a few loyal champions of veteran welfare legislation, a larger number of those who represent our bitterest foes were emphatically repudiated by the voters." VFW leaders insisted that the 1934 election "be recognized by the Administration as a protest against the anti-veteran policies that have been invoked during the past two years" rather than as a great partisan victory. Undaunted, the VFW leadership announced that the election gave the organization "new impetus to fight for cash payment of the so-called Bonus." Shortly after the 1934 election, Father Coughlin also offered his interpretation of the election and, in announcing the creation of a new political organization, openly courted disaffected veterans.[33]

On Armistice Day, November 11, 1934, in his first radio address following the midterm elections, Coughlin added an institutional player to the New Deal political arena: the National Union for Social Justice (NUSJ). Coughlin first acknowledged "the signal political victory of the New Deal." He cautioned, however, that despite the apparent success of the Democrats, the party stood "on trial." Coughlin warned, "Two years hence it will leave the courtroom of public opinion vindicated . . . or it will be condemned to political death if it fails to answer the question of why there is want in the midst of plenty." Then Coughlin announced the formation of the NUSJ as a pressure group to keep the newly elected Congress and the administration on the right track toward social justice. He enumerated sixteen principles that the new organization would promote and called upon "every one of you who is weary of drinking the bitter vinegar of sordid capitalism and . . . fearsome of being nailed to the cross of communism to join this Union." Coughlin exhorted his listening audience to transform into "a vibrant, united, active organization, superior to politics and politicians in principle, and independent of them in power."[34]

In politics, like good comedy, timing is everything. For both pragmatic and ideological reasons, an address on Armistice Day offered Coughlin a marvelous opportunity to parlay veteran political unrest into support for his nascent organization. By choosing Armistice Day, Coughlin clearly maximized the veteran audience for his announcement. On November 11, 1934, veteran-oriented programming literally filled the radio airwaves. Just prior to Coughlin's afternoon homily, both the VFW and the American Legion national organizations aired hour-long Armistice Day programs on the NBC national network. As important, Coughlin articulated the shared central premise of dissenting veterans' political ideology: the Great

War, "instead of making the world safe for democracy," was "fought to make the world safe for Wall Street and for the international bankers."[35]

Coughlin courted veterans with rhetoric ubiquitous in veterans' political struggles. He laid out the ostensible purposes of the war and the patriotic and democratic principles of those who fought, and then he moved to the bitter reality. Coughlin pointed to the gains in productive capacity made during the war years as the watershed in American economic life. He proclaimed that Armistice Day was "the day when there was born from the womb of war, the new problem of distribution." He explained how the 4.5 million returning soldiers bore the brunt of this new economic system first, returning to find "young girls and married women occupying positions in office and in factory" and facing chronic unemployment. While the Bonus did not make the list of sixteen principles outlined by Coughlin, by proposing a new organization premised on an interpretation of World War I shared by many veterans and launching it on Armistice Day, Coughlin attempted to tap into the existing structures of veteran political activism. He ended the address with a fairly explicit appeal to veterans: "This is a new call to arms—not to become cannon fodder for the greedy system of an outworn capitalism nor factory fodder for the slave whip of communism. This is the new call to arms for the establishment of social justice!" With the formation of the National Union, veterans added yet another important ally in the Bonus fight that loomed over the upcoming congressional session.[36]

With Coughlin's appeal to veterans and the American Legion's changed position on immediate Bonus payment, the administration recognized that public support for the Bonus was growing in quarters that it had recently influenced or controlled. Prior to the start of the 1935 congressional session, therefore, the Roosevelt administration attempted to undercut the new drive for the Bonus before it could even get under way. First, the White House arranged a private meeting with Louis Johnson and Frank Belgrano, Jr., the new Legion commander, to try to figure out a strategy on the Bonus. Roosevelt expressed the wish that they come in "without the knowledge of the newspaper men," a wise decision since a public meeting would signal to the national press either the administration's capitulation on the Bonus or the Legion commander's undermining of the national encampment mandate. Then an opportunity arose to combat the Bonus movement publicly in the guise of a letter to the president from Garland R. Farmer, the editor and publisher of the *Henderson* (Texas) *Times* and commander of the local American Legion post. In a letter dated October

31 (days after the Legion convention voted for the Bonus), Farmer appealed to FDR for information to find his way out of the "dilemma over the Bonus question." Although personally he "believed the time was not ripe" for payment, Farmer enumerated Bonus supporters' claims as to why it should and could be paid. The Legionnaire requested FDR's "side of the question, for I'm confident you have what you believe is justifiable reasons [*sic*] for your opposition to the present payment of the bonus." Nearly two months lapsed before the administration responded.[37]

On December 27, just days prior to his State of the Union address and the beginning of the 74th Congress, FDR replied to the Farmer letter. Roosevelt thanked him for the occasion to educate veterans, noting that Farmer's confusion "confirms an impression that I have had for some time . . . that the bonus question is not well understood even among veterans themselves." The president explained to Farmer that he was opposed to any payment at face value of the adjusted service certificates since that figure included interest through 1945. Moreover, FDR rejected the Bonus supporters' key claim that payment would spur economic recovery, noting that the loans given to veterans on their certificates in 1931 had failed to yield any appreciable results. On this point, Roosevelt betrayed a fundamentally flawed understanding of the central role consumer spending played in the American economy. He told Farmer that "indebtedness created by the veterans prior to the payment was liquidated, and the money advanced to clear that indebtedness rather than to create new business." FDR also added a curious rationale as to why veterans should wait for payment, noting that "of the veterans who die, approximately 85% of them leave no other asset to their family but the Adjusted Service Certificates or the balance due on the Certificates." In other words, veterans and their families were too impoverished to warrant immediate Bonus payment.[38]

By enumerating his objections to Farmer, FDR sought to accomplish more than convince a Texas Legionnaire of the reasonableness of the administration's position. Roosevelt exploited the opportunity offered by the Farmer letter to impress both veterans and congressional supporters with his resolve on the Bonus issue at a critical juncture. FDR's secretary, Stephen Early, mailed FDR's letter and telegrammed Farmer that he "wished very much you would wire me when the President's letter is received so that with your permission I may release it here to the press." Early's eagerness for Farmer's confirmation telegram betrayed the administration's plan: it wanted to publicize the exchange prior to the State of the Union address and the start of the congressional session in order to maximize its impact. On December 31, the press received a copy of FDR's response to Farmer, but not of the original letter, which would have revealed the amount of time passed since its receipt. On New Year's Day, the story and the text of the president's letter ran on the front page of all of the major U.S. newspapers. The *Washington Post* described the president's letter as an attempt "to dispel the storm clouds gathering on Capitol Hill" over the Bonus. Calling attention to the timing of the president's response, the *Post* accounts and analysis explained that the letter's release was "shrewdly timed to rally sentiment against the bonus on the eve of Congress' convening," a time "when it might do the most good." Moreover, the reporting noted that the letter reflected a continued "militant attitude at the White House" concerning the Bonus and that FDR's letter effectively "carried the fight to the proponents of bonus inflation." Indeed, the evidence suggests that the administration contrived this entire episode for just these reasons. On January 18, Farmer wrote an intimate letter to Steve Early, addressing him as "My Dear Steve." He sent samples of letters that he had received about the well-publicized incident, including one that told him, "your KING in the White House is just making a CATSPAW out of you." More important, though, Farmer told Early he was "very happy to have again been able to be of some little service." Whether contrived or merely adroitly manipulated, the Farmer exchange drew quick and dismissive responses from both the VFW and the Legion.[39]

The VFW leadership responded to the president's letter and its release to the press with withering comments. Commander Van Zandt, who had publicly predicted just prior to the release of the Farmer letter that the president would sign a Bonus bill, skewered FDR's reasoning in the letter in a press statement. Calling the president's message a "keen disappointment to the vast majority of World War veterans," Van Zandt refuted the president's grounds for opposing the Bonus. He began by stating, "There is no lack of understanding of this issue among the 3,700,000 veterans who hold adjusted service certificates. . . . There seems to be some misunderstanding of it on the part of the President." Van Zandt pointed to the Veterans' Administration numbers showing that 3,038,500 veterans had borrowed on their certificates, more than 80 percent of holders. Ninety percent of those veterans borrowing against their Bonus used the money for "absolute necessities," and 62 percent were unemployed. He thought this sufficient proof of the "dire need of these men and their families." In reference to FDR's understanding of the Bonus as a life insurance policy, Van Zandt reiterated the organization's opposition to the "tombstone bonus." Citing VA estimates, he claimed that the approximately 500,000 World War veterans would be dead by 1945, when the certificates matured, and thus "cheated out of their adjusted service pay."[40]

Van Zandt candidly questioned the authenticity of the Farmer exchange and downplayed the potential political impact. He voiced his suspicions about the letter while denigrating Farmer as an atypical veteran. Van Zandt coolly noted, "It is unfortunate that President Roosevelt, either by accident *or design*, should have selected Garland R. Farmer as the addressee of a letter in opposition to the immediate payment of the adjusted service certificates." The commander explained, "Mr. Farmer may hold an official position in a veterans' organization, but he is by no means representative of the World War veterans," noting that Farmer's military service consisted of less than two months in training camp, making him ineligible for an adjusted service certificate. Emphasizing the VFW's position as the representative of "true" veterans, he added, "It is this type of stay-at-home 'soldier' who always has attempted to embarrass the men who faced the enemy guns, thousands of whom are disabled and many other thousands are destitute and need money now to feed, clothe, and shelter their families." Van Zandt downplayed the ultimate political importance of the episode, explaining, "While we respect the views of the President, Congress will be the final arbiter of this issue."[41]

With the Farmer episode, the administration also failed to diminish the resolve of the American Legion's national leadership. The Legion's national commander, Frank N. Belgrano, Jr., issued a statement that the president's letter would not sway the organization from its mandate for immediate payment as established by the 1934 convention. Belgrano, a vice president of Bank of America, also pointed out the weakness of FDR's economic thinking, stating that payment of debts by veterans in arrears would be a tremendous economic stimulus. He noted that bonus payment would "benefit that very element of business men who are most in need of help—the average citizen, the vast bulk of merchants, and middle-class business and professional people." The president's Farmer letter fell short in restraining the gathering momentum for the Bonus issue. And, for the moment, the VFW and the American Legion stood unified. As the 1935 congressional session approached, it promised to be a lively one.[42]

Heading into the congressional session, the 1935 drive for the Bonus would feature an alignment of veteran organizations, Huey Long, Father Coughlin, and their new organizations, united in opposition to the FDR administration—a far cry from January 1934, when the VFW was the lone voice of dissent. When the most ardent of congressional supporters could muster only sixty signatures for the Bonus discharge position, the VFW's militant lobbying campaign resulted in the re-emergence of the Bonus as a national political issue. Despite administration and congressional opposition and a lack of support from the American Legion national organization, the Patman bill championed by the VFW resurrected the legislation in what amounted to a revolt against an extremely popular president. While the VFW lost this fight and struggled with what political mobilization might ultimately mean for the organization, the campaign convinced Legionnaires that the Bonus could be won. The VFW-Legion accord made those prospects much brighter in 1935. But the VFW's alliance with the nascent Long and Coughlin organizations became even more pronounced, too. Indeed, the VFW and the veterans it led joined with the two movements to form the structural core of the New Deal Dissidents, a coalition that would fundamentally shape New Deal politics. And at the center of this coalition lay the Bonus.

5

"The Pro-Bonus Party"

> You Sir, seem to have a perverted genius for thinking up ways and means of harming and discrediting in the eyes of the public the former soldier of this country.
>
> —Lawrence A. Brown, National Adjutant of the Bonus Expeditionary Force organization, to FDR in response to the Patman Bonus bill veto message, May 23, 1935

In 1935, the legislative drive for the Bonus turned into the most contentious issue in American politics. While Senator Huey P. Long and Father Coughlin had advocated Bonus payment in 1934, and while both had appealed to veterans' support for their newly formed organizations, a coalition consisting of Long, Coughlin, and VFW-led veterans took shape in earnest when the controversy over two competing plans for payment intensified the ideological dimensions of the Bonus issue. Long, Coughlin, and the VFW supported the openly inflationary Patman bill, while attacking the American Legion-sponsored Vinson bill as a boon to "the Bankers" for its reliance on conventional governmental borrowing to fund the measure. The eventual legislative victory of the Patman bill over the Vinson bill resulted from astute parliamentary maneuvering on the part of Patman bill supporters and the groundswell of grassroots activism by veterans and followers of Coughlin and Long. In fact, between February and May 1935, these dissident forces converged around the Bonus, becoming a potent political movement in the process, with the VFW, the Share Our Wealth Society, and the National Union for Social Justice all reaching the zenith of their organizational strength. FDR's persistent opposition to the Bonus spurred this New Deal dissent by signaling to critics that the administration planned to continue its veteran policies in agreement with "Wall Street" and "the Bankers." Indeed, by the late spring of

1935, the battle over the Bonus had created a political crisis for the Roosevelt administration, raising the specter of a new party consisting of Long and Coughlin supporters and buttressed by the veteran vote. More than any other single issue, the Bonus supplied the point of convergence for the New Deal Dissidents and fueled their rise to political prominence. As the movement built to a crescendo and dominated the national political arena, Roosevelt's veto of the Patman Bonus bill became a watershed of his presidency: the opening salvo of the "Second" New Deal.[1]

At the start of the 74th Congress, the Bonus dominated a legislative agenda that included the most far-reaching social legislation in U.S. history. Bills for social security, unemployment insurance, public works, and the rights of labor drew the attention of progressives and the president. FDR's State of Union address, on January 4, urged Congress to take up these measures expeditiously, as full recovery remained elusive. But when a scruffy veteran, a former Bonus marcher bearing a Huey Long guest badge, accosted FDR on his way into the Capitol to deliver the address and demanded the Bonus, the incident served as a metaphor for the 1935 congressional session. Despite all of the momentous pending legislation, the Bonus and its supporters simply would not keep their place. For this reason, new House Speaker, Joseph W. Byrnes (D, TN), declared that the Bonus would be taken up immediately to get the issue "behind him" as soon as possible. The Patman bill resumed its position at the top of the House docket (H.R.1), but the 1935 version of the bill varied from previous versions by linking the payment of the Bonus to commodity prices instead of relying on gold revaluation as the means to achieve currency expansion. Yet, currency inflation, and Patman's method for attaining it, drew criticism from the American Legion leadership.[2]

Following the mandate of the 1934 convention for Bonus legislation, the Legion promoted a measure less controversial than the Patman bill. After Patman refused to remove the inflationary aspects from his bill, the Legion asked Representative Fred Vinson (D, KY) to sponsor "darkhorse" legislation written by John Thomas Taylor that would pay the Bonus without stipulating any method of payment. By leaving the question of funding open, in all likelihood Bonus financing would be accomplished through traditional negotiable bonds. Although in 1934 Vinson had supported the Patman bill, he agreed for pragmatic reasons to sponsor the Legion bill. By divorcing the Bonus from the inflationary agenda, it stood a better chance of passing with a veto-proof majority. Vinson's influence on the House Ways and Means Committee would not hurt the bill's chances, either. An American Legion press release explained the rationale behind the Vinson plan: "to take the adjusted service certificate issue out of the dangerous realm of financial and political fantasies, the American Legion has introduced in Congress its own bill." Vinson railed against the ideological nature of the Patman bill, claiming, "I am not willing for the World War Veterans to be made a pack horse for the inflationists."[3]

The united front formed in 1934 between the Legion and the VFW on Bonus legislation showed immediate strain. The VFW leadership initially refused to endorse either of the Bonus plans because the 1934 encampment had mandated that the organization support the immediate payment of the Bonus regardless of the method of payment. VFW officials claimed they would not be dragged into that fight again, leaving the organization "free to support the piece of legislation . . . that has the best prospects of surviving White House opposition." However, both the VFW and Patman voiced suspicions that the Legion had pushed the Vinson bill to divide the veteran bloc in Congress and to undermine the Bonus's ultimate passage. In an editorial on the competing bills, the VFW leadership commented, "It would not be the first time that members of Congress have avoided direct responsibility for defeat of this proposal through clever maneuvers designed to place the blame elsewhere." The editorial archly noted, "There are those who suspect this apparent split was deliberately created as a loophole of escape." Meanwhile, the VFW's longstanding ally, Wright Patman, blasted the Vinson bill as the "Banker's Bonus," a reference to the inevitable use of bonds that it would entail. He accused the Legion's Commander Belgrano, who happened to be a vice president of the Bank of America, of financial self-interest. Patman insisted his method alone was in accord with the Legion's convention mandate to retire an existing debt and asked Belgrano to resign from the national commander position if he could not stomach support of Patman's version. Moreover, Patman suspected that the Legion, backed by New York bankers and by Wall Street, offered the Vinson countermeasure as an obstructionist ruse. Patman declared, "This thing will smell to high Heaven when it is exposed."[4]

A month into the congressional session, the shaky united front of veteran organizations cracked over the Bonus. When the divisions among Bonus supporters left House members confused and delayed action on the Bonus, the VFW came out for the Patman version. On February 8, 1935, pressed by congressional Bonus supporters and the rank and file of the organization to take a definitive stand, the VFW leadership announced the organization's endorsement of the Patman Bonus bill. The VFW leadership made the declaration after polling state commanders on whether the organization should take a position or stay neutral. When all forty-eight commanders decided to "Stand Pat with Patman," Van Zandt issued a statement from VFW headquarters announcing the organization's intentions. Van Zandt called the Patman bill "the soundest method of paying the bill" and denounced the Vinson bill as the "bankers' bonus bill to give bankers millions of dollars in interest profits." He scoffed at the "bankers' bugaboo of inflation" raised against the Patman bill. Indeed, the VFW leadership considered statements from the U.S. Chamber of Commerce, the American Liberty League, and the National Economy League deriding the Patman bill as inflationary and calling the Vinson bill "the lesser of two evils," concrete proof of the Patman bill's merits. Had pure economic self-interest been the prevailing concern, the VFW would have either supported the less controversial Vinson bill or stayed on the sidelines until a method of payment emerged from House debate. By jumping into the ideological contest over the Bonus, the VFW joined with the core of New Deal Dissidents in promoting the measure and criticizing FDR for opposing it. Indeed, as the Bonus emerged as a central issue in the spring of 1935, both veteran political activism and New Deal dissent rose to a crescendo.[5]

In the spring of 1935, the congressional battles over the Bonus raged. A three-way donnybrook among Vinson supporters, Patman forces, and Bonus opponents took place first in the House, where there existed broad support for some form of Bonus payment. On March 6, the Ways and Means Committee, after intense infighting, recommended the Vinson bill to the House over the Patman version in a very close 16–14 vote. The committee left the door open for the Patman version, however, by voting 14–9 to request that the House Rules Committee allow the Patman bill be offered to the whole House membership as an alternative. On March 14, as a result of some virtuoso lobbying by the Bonus Steering Committee, led by Wright Patman and the VFW canvassers, the House Rules Committee allowed both bills to be brought to the floor instead of opting for only an up-or-down vote on the Vinson bill. Influential American Legion lobbyist John Thomas Taylor fought this measure tooth and nail, trying to make the Legion version of the Bonus the only one brought up for consideration. However, broad support among progressives and inflationists in the House gave the "Patmanites" a victory in this first round, despite the official committee recommendation and spirited Legion opposition.[6]

Over a two-day period, a tense House battle over the Vinson and Patman plans enthralled political observers. On March 21, after ten hours of bitter debate and the beating back of various compromise measures, the House voted 204–201 to replace the Vinson bill with the Patman version. News reports that FDR would certainly veto the measure or demand that Congress raise taxes to pay the Bonus carried little weight in the deliberations. According to the *Washington Post*, "party lines were smashed" in the voting. Once the Patman bill had prevailed, Patman supporters shouted for a final vote in order to kill the Vinson version once and for all, but House leaders delayed the vote until the following day. On March 22, 1935, the Patman Bonus bill passed the House over Legion and administration opposition. The House passed the Patman Bonus bill 318–90 despite the efforts of the Vinson supporters to recommit the Patman bill and return to the Vinson plan. Vinson harangued the Patman forces, "I say to you, that unless you divorce currency expansion from cash payment you will have to go back and tell the boys, 'Well we fought a good fight, we did the best we could, but you haven't got the money yet.'" As the House "thundered defiance to the President," the administration suffered a blow in prestige as the veto threats proved ineffective even among members of its own party. Yet, arguably, the administration favored the Patman bill over the Vinson bill. Indeed, some administration stalwarts voted for the Patman version with the understanding that it would be easier to sustain a presidential veto of this measure. The administration, while opposed to the Bonus, preferred its chances of defeating the "greenback" Patman Bonus bill. Nonetheless, the House voted overwhelmingly for the Patman Bonus bill and sent the matter to the Senate.[7]

Cash payments to veterans clearly merged with inflationist and progressive politics in the 74th Congress. The Patman-Vinson debate in the House revealed what an ideologically freighted issue the Bonus had become. *Washington Post* political commentator Raymond Clapper observed after the Patman bill's substitution that "If paying the veterans were the only object, the Vinson Bill would do just as well. . . . But inflationist sentiment tipped the balance in favor of Patman's greenback plan." As a measure of the Bonus's ideological nature, the vote to enact the Patman Bonus bill was the only vote in the 74th Congress in which *every* member of both the Liberal Bloc and the Wisconsin-Minnesota Progressive Group caucuses voted in complete unanimity. According to one analysis, the Progressive Group became "most visible" in the Bonus fight and joined with the Liberal Bloc to become "decisive factors" in the victory of the Patman over the Vinson plan. *New York Times* analyst Duncan Aikman claimed that "disturbed elders" in the House viewed the "leftist" "mavericks" with alarm after their successful squashing of the Legion-backed plan.[8]

In late April, the Senate took up the Bonus issue with equal vigor. The Senate Patman forces, led again by Huey Long, Fred Steiwer, and Elmer Thomas, fought back a compromise measure introduced by Senator Pat Harrison (D, MS), chair of the Senate Finance Committee, that would pay the veterans in bonds but without the accrued interest through 1945. The ideas incorporated in the "Harrison plan" came directly from administration officials. In the previous year, Secretary of the Treasury Henry Morgenthau, Jr., sent a detailed recommendation to the president outlining the benefits of exactly such a compromise. The Patman forces in the Senate also derailed the drive spearheaded by the American Legion and sponsored by ex-Legion national commander Sen. Bennett Champ Clark to substitute some version of the Vinson plan for what Clark called derisively the "Patman-Coughlin bill." In the final hours of the Senate debate, Patman supporters gained an important convert when Senate lion William G. McAdoo (D, CA), a former Treasury secretary in the Wilson administration, dismissed concerns about the inflationary features of the bill. In announcing his support for the Patman version, McAdoo proclaimed, "Here is a chance to blaze something of a new trail without the slightest injury to the credit of the country and without bringing upon ourselves any of the dangers or any of the evil consequences of so-called 'inflation.'" Conservatives of both parties, however, heaped scorn on all of the Bonus versions and gleefully welcomed the promised FDR veto.[9]

Thanks to the parliamentary efforts of Long, Thomas, and Steiwer, the Senate passed the Patman bill on May 7, 1935 by a vote of 55–33. The importance of Long and Coughlin ally Thomas to the victory cannot be overemphasized. The *Washington Post* declared, "Louisiana's 'Kingfish,' Huey Long, assumed the four stars of the Patman floor plan general in the march toward passage, working hand-in-hand with Senator Elmer Thomas of Oklahoma, Senate inflationist leader." In this, however, they received assistance from ten administration allies, including Senators Harrison and Robinson, who had their own reasons for favoring the Patman plan. Their objective became "to pass a Bonus Bill against which a veto could be made to stick." While the Patman forces emerged victorious, they lacked the crucial two-thirds majority. A showdown over the Bonus loomed. [10]

In early May, Patman supporters mobilized an all-out campaign to pass the Bonus over the expected presidential veto. Senate Bonus supporters managed to keep the bill from being delivered to the White House for more than a week as they attempted to persuade enough senators to ensure an override victory. Huey Long, James Van Zandt, and Father Charles Coughlin all took to the airwaves, begging their followers to send senators and the president urgent letters and telegrams demanding support of the Patman Bonus bill. Finally, on May 14, Congress sent the Patman Bonus bill to the White House. The Patman bill already commanded a veto-proof majority in the House and appeared on the verge of attaining the same in the Senate. The passage of the Bonus bill despite immense White House opposition suggested the movement of Congress into much more radical waters. But the significance of the Bonus transcended this. Between February and May, as the supporters of the competing bills battled in Congress and in the national political arena, three proponents of the Patman Bonus bill rose to the forefront of New Deal politics.[11]

The forces of VFW-led veterans, Huey Long, and Father Coughlin converged around the Bonus, in the process becoming a potent oppositional political force. Among the veteran organizations, the VFW led the fight for the Patman bill. After the split with the American Legion, the VFW sponsored the legislation and resumed the aggressive lobbying tactics that had propelled the Bonus into the legislative arena the previous year. VFW officials such as James Van Zandt, George Brobeck, and former Commander Paul Wolman participated in the Patman Bonus Steering Committee. The *New York Times* called the VFW "the extreme bonus-seekers" and the "real fighters in the Bonus movement . . . the infantry, so to speak." *Time* described the Patman bill's passing as representing a defeat of the Legion by the VFW, "an older, smaller organization, which in recent years has found that the most headway is gained by always outbidding the Legion by longer and more radical demands upon the Government."[12]

Van Zandt, the VFW commander, continued to be a highly visible New Deal Dissident. He made innumerable appearances at state and local VFW gatherings across the nation, touting the organization's support for the Patman bill. Van Zandt debated with Bonus opponents on the radio and delivered radio addresses to national audiences and countless local communities. His testimony before the House Ways and Means and the Senate Finance Committees in support of the Patman bill always proved lively. Before the Senate Finance Committee, Van Zandt called the worries over the Patman bill financing "tommyrot." As part of Patman's steering group, Van Zandt prowled the congressional hallways and chambers applying pressure to legislators. The *New York Times* described Van Zandt as the "generalissimo of the huge 'lobby' that fought the Patman Bill through." *Literary Digest* depicted him as "chockfull of energy, obviously sincere and highly vocal." After the Patman bill passed the Senate, Van Zandt appealed to the American people, asking them to send a million messages to FDR urging him to sign the measure. When the Bonus bill passed the Senate, the front pages of major newspapers ran a photograph of the bill's most noteworthy advocates shaking hands in victory: Van Zandt, Patman, and Elmer Thomas.[13]

With its prominent place among the Patman bill supporters, the VFW eclipsed the American Legion in the spring Bonus struggle. The Legion, while on the record for immediate payment "as a relief and recovery measure and as a matter of long delayed justice," never warmed up to supporting the Patman bill. Legion Commander Belgrano explained the organization's support of the Vinson plan—and its rejection of the Patman bill—in an *American Legion Monthly* article entitled "Let's Have the Truth!" Belgrano contended that a new set of forces were blocking passage of the Bonus. In the past, business had opposed payment. This time, Belgrano argued, "the vast majority of business men are now with us." The obstacle now was "a small but active group *within our own ranks* . . . [whose tactics] play squarely into the hands of the selfish interests who want to defeat us." Legion allies in Congress, national officers, and lobbyists fought the Patman bill at every stage of the legislative process. Former commander Johnson informed FDR's White House assistant, Steve Early, after House passage of the Patman bill, that the Legion's National Executive Committee stood firmly against the bill in a special April meeting. Johnson went to the meeting "fearful," but "the Committee refused to have anything to do with the Patman bill or with inflation" and "approved of the conservative actions of the National Commander." Even after the Patman bill passed the Senate, the Legion only halfheartedly gave the Bonus its support. Belgrano sulked out of the Senate gallery after the vote and then issued a subdued request that Legionnaires lobby the president and senators to pass the bill.[14]

As in 1932 and 1934, the Legion's and VFW's respective positions on the Bonus carried institutional ramifications. For the Legion, membership stagnated. Conversely, the VFW found that its outspoken support for the Bonus paid dividends for the organization. In the heat of the Bonus push, the VFW gained well over a post a day. In its fourth annual "Hello America" broadcast, the VFW added another 20,000 new members. By May, the VFW extended to more than 3,300 posts across the nation and had approximately 300,000 members. The VFW leadership continually linked new member recruitment and post growth to increased national prestige accumulated in the Bonus fight. In the Depression era's notoriously toxic environment for voluntary associations, two other organizations supportive of the Bonus matched the VFW's rapid growth during the 1935 Bonus campaign: Father Coughlin's National Union for Social Justice and Huey Long's Share Our Wealth Society.[15]

From February until May 1935, Father Coughlin dedicated frequent Sunday sermons and National Union for Social Justice rallies to trumpeting the virtues of the Patman Bonus bill, making support of the bill a cornerstone of the organization's agenda. On February 3, 1935, Coughlin used his weekly forum to promote the National Union, an organization that existed in name only at this time. He urged his listeners to join the organization and contribute money to further its cause. The Radio Priest derided the Vinson plan, reminding his listeners of his opposition to any Bonus bill paid through bonds. Coughlin explained that bonds merely "permit the favored few to profit while the veterans who served in the World War are denied the pittance of a just debt we recognize as their due." In the following months, as Coughlin touted the Patman Bonus as a primary issue in the fight for social justice, the National Union grew to a reported 8.5 million members. In the process, Coughlin found himself more and more at odds with the Roosevelt Administration.[16]

On April 25, Coughlin opened a membership drive for the National Union that highlighted the importance of the Bonus to the organization's agenda. The Radio Priest's push for ten million members coincided with his renewed efforts on behalf of the Patman Bonus bill. It served both as an ideological touchstone for his followers and an excellent opportunity to bring veterans into the NUSJ fold. In Detroit, 17,000 people crowded into Olympia Auditorium to attend a rally initiating the Michigan chapter of the NUSJ. Coughlin invited Senator Elmer Thomas, the Patman Bill sponsor in the Senate, and a number of congressmen (including William Lemke, future Union Party presidential candidate) to join him on the dais. All championed the Patman Bonus bill. On May 8, in Cleveland, 30,000 members gathered to hear their leader speak. Coughlin thrilled the crowd, spreading the message of the National Union and threatening Roosevelt's "banker-minded" administration and Ohio Senator Robert J.

Bulkley (D, OH), who had opposed the Patman Bonus bill in the previous day's vote. He exclaimed, "The New Deal Administration will commit suicide if it follows through with a veto of the Patman soldiers' bonus." Commentators viewed this as a threat against FDR should he go ahead and veto the Bonus bill and a signal that Coughlin "would walk off the Roosevelt Reservation, taking the members of the huge National Union for Social Justice with him." While holding the membership rallies, Coughlin continued to address his radio followers on the merits of the Patman Bonus bill.[17]

The organizational buildup of the National Union became inextricably linked with the Bonus issue. Coughlin's triumphant Cleveland meeting came between two of his most passionate radio addresses concerning the Patman bill. Once the Bonus moved into Senate deliberations, he gave two national addresses almost entirely devoted to the importance of the Patman Bonus to the goals of social justice. On May 5, 1935, the night before the Senate was to deliberate and vote on the Bonus question, the Radio Priest used the issue as the first "lesson on solidarity" for his fledgling NUSJ. In a lecture entitled "Solidarity and Justice," he appealed to his weekly listeners to initiate an intense lobbying campaign aimed at the Senate in support of the Patman Bonus bill. Once again, Coughlin outlined the ideological differences that lay at the heart of the competing versions of the Bonus bills, focusing on World War I as the great watershed moment in the concentration of wealth and rise of plutocracy. He ridiculed the stated war aims, claiming that the conflict "to keep the world safe for democracy" had produced "a democracy out of which was born the red Bolshevism of Russia, the dictatorships of Germany and Italy, and want amidst plenty in America." Moreover, Coughlin reiterated the view that the war "created the billions of bloody bonds to make millionaires out of the stay-at-home profiteers and paupers out of the American laborer and farmer." As for the veterans, he explained, the "heroes returned home to find wealth concentrated in the hands of a few . . . and stood in factory lines seeking their old jobs only to discover that mass production machinery had forced them into the bread lines."[18]

Coughlin argued that the Vinson proposal merely perpetuated the concentration of wealth, since any Bonus payment funded by bonds would further aggrandize the bankers and Wall Street. He explained, "The banker waxed fat on war bonds; tomorrow he wishes to wax fatter on veteran bonds." Coughlin summed up the differences between the two bills succinctly, "The Patman Plan wants Justice. The Vinson Plan wants graft—graft for the banker . . . still racketeering on the broken limbs and broken hearts of the American public." He described the National Union's interest in the Bonus as an easy means for the expansion of purchasing power. Therefore, in this first lesson on solidarity, Coughlin summoned his supporters to lobby their senators in support of the Patman plan. He issued a "call to arms," beseeching his listeners: "[I]n the name of social justice, I ask everyone in the audience to cast aside all lethargy, all selfishness and stand shoulder to shoulder tonight and tomorrow behind the Patman Plan." He ended with the question, "Here is a sudden call to arms. . . . Is it solidarity or individualism?" After the Radio Priest's address, a *Washington Post* political commentator reported that the telegraph companies handled "the heaviest floods in their history," with 97,000 telegrams pouring into the Senate chambers from one telegraph office alone.[19]

After the Senate passed the Patman bill, Coughlin directly challenged the president to sign the Bonus. On May 12, he dedicated the conclusion of his weekly broadcast to a personal appeal to the president. After assigning credit to the National Union and his listeners for the Senate passage of the Patman Bill, he addressed FDR, explaining the reasons he should not veto the Bonus. Coughlin implored FDR to sign the bill, pointing to the 1934 elections as a gauge of the people's wishes. He proclaimed, "The responsive House of Representatives, freshly elected by the people in 1934, has passed the bonus by a tremendous majority." He continued, "I cannot believe you will prevent the soldier from receiving his just dollar of dues simply because the banker is not to receive his unjust 81 cents of bonus." In an emotional appeal, Coughlin beseeched FDR to sign the Bonus in reminiscent terms: "You have told the people you would drive the money-changers from the temple. You have told them of a new deal, a new deal for the forgotten man. May I ask you then, Mr. President, in the name of the millions who joined the National Union . . . in the name of social justice, to pay fully the soldiers according to the provisions of the Patman Bill." The Radio Priest concluded his address by pleading to his former ally, "Before your God and your country, sign on the side of justice! You cannot forget the common man!"[20]

Coughlin's appropriation of the Bonus as a symbol of New Deal dissent matched that of the other main dissenter, Senator Huey P. Long. For both ideological and politically opportunistic reasons, Long continued his support for the Bonus, publicly joining with the VFW in the process. He initiated a broad offensive against the Roosevelt administration when he agreed to be one of the floor managers for the VFW-sponsored Patman bill. He led the Patman Bonus bill through hostile territory in the Senate. Long, with Elmer Thomas, beat back the parliamentary maneuvers of supporters of the Vinson and Harrison plans. Moreover, in the Senate debate on the three competing Bonus measures, Long attacked the president with impunity. The Louisiana senator used the Patman bill to symbolize the failed promise of the Roosevelt administration to address the distribution of wealth. He derided the president's promised veto as "a political monstrosity that no party can defend, and no man can defend, either in his own conscience or in a political campaign." On May 10, Long nearly came to blows with administration ally Senator Millard E. Tydings (D, MD) when he took to the Senate floor to denounce Roosevelt over the threatened veto of the Bonus. Long deplored the president's position, saying, "somebody ought to go down to the White House and advise this man" because he was "leading the Democratic Party to slaughter with these contradictory measures."[21]

Recognizing both Long's contributions to the Patman bill on the Senate floor and his rising political influence, the VFW national organization enlisted him to help sway national public opinion on the issue. On May 11, 1935, Long and the VFW publicly joined forces to push the Bonus. Long delivered a radio address entitled "A Fair Deal for the Veterans" on the NBC national network, with VFW sponsorship. The VFW and Long, attempting to drum up enough extra votes to salvage the Patman Bonus bill from the looming presidential veto, intended to instigate a massive public lobbying campaign aimed at the U.S. Senate. The senator explained his position on the Bonus very carefully: the adjusted service certificates paid back "wages," not a "Bonus"; payment of the Bonus would stimulate business everywhere; and inflationary means of paying for it were financially sound. Long recognized that the lobbying campaign aimed at the president would not change his mind on the veto. He explained to his listeners, "We hear the President is being urged to turn a deaf ear to the people's plea." Therefore, Long exhorted, "Wire your United States Senators now. . . . Ask them to do the same justice by the soldiers as has been done by the captains of finance."[22]

Long used the Bonus address to advance a line of attack on FDR as out of touch with veterans and common people. He assailed Roosevelt for opposing "this obligation which the Government now owes the soldiers" while "the bankers have been given everything for which they have asked." Long ridiculed the president's claims of being a veteran, a status that played an important role in his objections to the Bonus. As Long described it, FDR asserted his veteran status to tell veterans that "he understands [the Bonus issue] somewhat better than we may think." He admitted that FDR was a veteran but noted that as assistant secretary of the navy, FDR "stayed up here on Pennsylvania Avenue in the daytime, and in a very fine home during the nighttime, and drew $10,000 a year for his services . . . 3,000 miles from the gunfire." Long criticized Roosevelt for not understanding the real veteran, "the man that did not stay on Pennsylvania Avenue, who did not stay in a luxurious home . . . and who not only went through the fourteen kinds of carnage worse than the fires of hell itself but who, when he came back, found his occupation destroyed, and the job which he had held gone." The Kingfish, who had been criticized by Legion allies in the Senate for opposing the war and not volunteering his services, admitted that he, too, had escaped service in the war and was in the same position as FDR. But, Long wryly commented, "the only difference is that I didn't receive $10,000 a year not to go."[23]

The Senator contended that the president's lack of shared perspective with veterans matched his lack of sympathy for the common people. He claimed he understood why FDR might have these misconceptions of popular opinion on the Bonus, blasting the president for a remark that when he needed to "get a better conception of the American people," he went fishing. Referring to Roosevelt's recent fishing trip on Vincent Astor's yacht, Long snorted, "I am afraid that his sailing that $5,000,000 yacht into the British waters with the Duke and Duchess of Kent . . . has distorted the viewpoint of the President, rather than giving him the common perspective of the common people of this country." He remarked, "I hope he will pay attention to the letters and telegrams [in support of the Bonus] he is receiving and judge that as being nearer the impression of the American people." To Long, supporting the veterans in the Bonus struggle was supporting the common people against the Banks and Wall Street.[24]

Like Coughlin's National Union, the Share Our Wealth Society enjoyed its first great wave of recruits in the spring of 1935, when Long's political movement and influence spread nationally. The best estimates placed the membership at between seven and eight million. Between January and March, Long made six national radio addresses and planned personal appearances across the nation, most notably an appearance in Des Moines at Milo Reno's National Farmers' Holiday Association convention, where third-party politics filled the air. At every chance, the central tenets of Share Our Wealth were read, including point six, which called on the government to "pay the veterans of our wars what we owe them and to care for their disabled." Indeed, anecdotal evidence suggests that veterans played an important part in the growth of the Share the Wealth movement. In some areas, Share Our Wealth clubs became, according to historian Alan Brinkley, "little more than extensions of existing veterans' organizations." In Philadelphia, a Share Our Wealth club publicity drive consisted of two veterans handing out flyers touting Long's Bonus position. In Washington, Emil Hurja, the Democratic pollster and aide to DNC chair Farley, asked D.C. officials to investigate a local institution for destitute veterans because it had become "a 'sounding board' for the political philosophies of Huey Long" and "a distribution center for a newspaper advocating Senator Long's 'share-the-wealth' views." As the Long movement spread outside the South and among veterans, Long and Coughlin began to merge in the public mind in the late spring of 1935.[25]

The Bonus, the symbolically freighted issue revealing the failures of the New Deal, provided the point of convergence for the Long, Coughlin, and veteran coalition. The fusion of the Long and Coughlin movements with VFW-led veteran political activism took place in April and May, as the intensity of the debates over the Patman bill reached its zenith. Simultaneously, critics and countless political commentators conflated the Long and Coughlin phenomena, remarking on the melding of their followers into a protean third-party movement. Political columnist Frank R. Kent wrote of the importance of Father Coughlin to the 1936 election. He posed a series of questions: "Will he join with Huey Long? Is he working toward a third party with a candidate of his own? Where is he going?" Van Zandt warned that the "threat of a third political party in the field for the next election, makes the friendship of the veteran vote a definite asset." To be sure, in 1935, Long and Coughlin moved closer to each other's central economic proposals. Likewise, they shared the same cast of villains and what Alan Brinkley calls the "broader set of symbols, images, and values" of "the dissident ideology." But it was the Bonus issue that gave the men and their followers the clearest, most direct expression of that ideology. It also instilled in a disparate, inchoate cluster of dissidents a common political purpose—so much so that, on May 14, while the Bonus awaited FDR's veto, political analyst Arthur Krock discussed the possibility that a "pro-bonus party" would form out of this insurgent landscape to challenge FDR in the next election.[26]

More shrill commentators suggested that something worse might be afoot. From March 1935 through May 1935, Long and Coughlin began to

At the height of the Bonus struggle, Senator Huey P. Long addresses a crowd of 10,000 during the national convention of the Farm Holiday Association in Des Moines, Iowa, April 28, 1935. Courtesy of Bettmann/CORBIS.

be lumped together as an emerging threat to constitutional government. On March 4, 1935, the former director of the National Recovery Administration, General Hugh S. Johnson, told an audience, "You can laugh at Father Coughlin, you can snort at Huey Long—but this country was never under a greater menace." On May 12, 1935, the day after a Coughlin Bonus address, the Reverend Norman Vincent Peale warned in a well-publicized sermon that "unless something is done to stop it, this country will become a dictatorship. The dictator will be either Coughlin or Long or a combination of the two." Peale, no friend to FDR, placed the specter of this "sinister power" in the context of the Bonus. Peale continued his sermon: "[T]he President is right should he veto the Patman Bonus bill and sensible citizens should support him against this mad priest and his attempts to coerce the lawful government of the United States by threats and intimidation." In 1935, Raymond Gram Swing released a book, a collection of *Nation* articles describing Long and Coughlin, entitled *The Forerunners of American Fascism.*[27]

Also in 1935, Sinclair Lewis published the best-selling *It Can't Happen Here*. In Lewis's novel, figures based on Long and Coughlin create a dictatorship supported by a paramilitary organization called "the Minute Men," a thinly veiled reference to the uniform-wearing veteran organizations. Lewis's dictator, Buzz Windrip, promises that veterans' Bonuses will be paid in cash and in full and that for those making less than $5,000, the amount will be doubled. Lewis's narrative arc seemed less fanciful to Americans of 1935 than to historians since. In fact, it followed the contours of a bizarre story that emerged on November 20, 1934. At a House Un-American Activities Committee (HUAC) meeting, General Smedley D. Butler, the VFW stalwart, testified that he had been approached by agents of Wall Street to lead an army of 500,000 ex-soldiers that would over throw Roosevelt and establish a fascist dictatorship. Everyone mentioned by Butler as possibly connected to the plot, including NRA Director General Hugh Johnson and General Douglas MacArthur, denied it vehemently. HUAC eventually published a noncommittal report, with segments of Butler's testimony suppressed even though Van Zandt, the VFW commander, corroborated Butler's story and HUAC investigators deemed much of it to be accurate. Regardless of the authenticity of Butler's claims, whispers of a dictatorship backed by veterans swirled about the political world, helping to make Lewis's novel an instant sensation.[28]

In April 1935, administration leaders, too, became concerned about this coalition of forces. As early as February, FDR was assessing the possibilities of an oppositional progressive "third ticket" and a "'Share the Wealth' ticket" with Woodrow Wilson's right-hand man, Colonel Edward House. By April, these possibilities became the subject of more than musings. In one of the earliest uses of political polling, James Farley, the chairman of the Democratic National Committee, asked Emil Hurja to conduct a secret poll measuring Long's strength. On April 30, in the middle of Senate debate on the Bonus, Hurja mailed out 150,000 ballots from the fabricated periodical the *National Inquirer*, asking for voters' preferences among

FDR, Long, and a hypothetical Republican candidate. The DNC received almost 31,000 returned ballots, ballots containing some troubling results. While Roosevelt garnered the plurality of votes, Long received 10.9 percent and Coughlin received nearly 1 percent in write-in votes. Most worrisome, Long's strength in a number of key electoral states such as New York, Minnesota, and Michigan might throw the election to a Republican candidate. As Jim Farley later explained the startling results to the administration in a cabinet meeting on May 10, Long's and Coughlin's popularity posed no small threat to the administration. Farley warned, "[Long's] third party might constitute a balance of power in the 1936 election." At the same time the administration digested the poll numbers, the White House received confirmation of the significant oppositional coalition under formation in a deluge of correspondence concerning the Patman Bonus bill.[29]

Following the passage of the Bonus bill, the political activism of veterans and of Long and Coughlin followers who supported the Bonus reached a fever pitch as all focused their attention on persuading FDR. Long, Coughlin, and the VFW urged veterans and the ordinary citizens who made up the NUSJ and SOWS constituencies to flood the White House with letters and telegrams voicing their support for the Bonus. In May 1935, the correspondence to the White House over the Bonus reached massive proportions, becoming a roar of New Deal dissent. Fifteen thousand letters flooded the White House on one day alone; telegrams came in at 250 an hour. The collected correspondence on the proposed Bonus bill veto formed one of the largest outpourings of correspondence received by FDR on any single issue. While the majority of letters by veterans described the desperation of their circumstances and their hopes that FDR would sign the Patman bill, the letters also exposed the centrality of the Bonus issue to the New Deal Dissident movement.[30]

In letter after letter, veterans chastised the president for his position on the Bonus. Richard Demmary of Englewood, New Jersey, asked the president, "What have you got against the veterans that makes you discriminate against them?" Frank Anderson warned FDR that "if you want to stay where you are I would at least give us what you gave the bankers and the railroad," adding, "I thought the President was the head of the U.S.A. and not the Wall St. Bankers." Edwin A. Lake of Brooklyn also expressed his disdain for the president. Lake rhetorically asked FDR, "May I take the liberty as an overseas veteran . . . to express my contempt for your attitude on the Soldiers' Bonus Bill." He continued, "[T]he people of this land will prove their resentment at the coming election." Not to be outdone, Joseph Eugene Dash opened his letter to the president with scorn. Dash told FDR that, "in the eyes of the ex-serviceman, his family, and his friends, you are pictured not [as] the man we thought you would be when you entered the White House; but a low-flung coyote." He added, "yes, dear President, we will fight you in every possible manner and to the last breath if you veto the Patman Bill."[31]

The White House received many letters, from veterans and nonveterans alike, proclaiming support for Coughlin and Long and urging FDR to allow the Bonus to pass. Joseph Nash of Cleveland began his letter urging FDR to pay the Bonus this way: "As a member of the National Union of Social Justice and as an ex-serviceman, I appeal to you." Winfield Phelps of Minneapolis explained to FDR that only the bankers were opposed to the Patman bill. Phelps, a VFW member, also gave his reasons for supporting Coughlin: "I joined the National Union for Social Justice because we have been fed up with the banking group of this country." Robert L. Turner fired off a letter to FDR that blasted Bonus opponents in Congress and the president's position. Turner called it "plain un-American for anyone who directs attacks upon the War veterans, as the present national Administration has practiced." Turner boldly claimed that he could "whip" certain congressional Bonus opponents "any day in the week for Senator Huey P. Long," with his right hand tied behind him, no less. John O'Connell wrote FDR a letter approving of the Bonus on "Huey P. Long for President Club" stationery.[32]

The correspondence that reached the White House on the Bonus revealed the confluence of veteran activism and the Long and Coughlin movements during the spring of 1935. Veteran James O. Sabin wrote a letter to Wright Patman, with a copy sent to the White House, proclaiming that, "with men like Father Coughlin, Huey P. Long, and yourself [Patman], the American people are awakening." The political strength of the veterans and the convergence of Long, Coughlin, and veteran supporters featured prominently in the Bonus letter deluge. R. S. Appleton warned FDR, "If you are the shrewd politician they credit you with being, you will think twice before you go against the veterans and the National Union for Social Justice." Another veteran and NUSJ member reminded FDR that "there are more votes in middle class than there are in Wall Street class" and that his five family members were "against you if you vote against the Vets bonus bill." A self-proclaimed "Democrat, veteran, and a great admirer of Father Coughlin" informed FDR that a veto of the Patman bill might thwart his reelection since the "Republican party will surely line up the veteran like they did with G.A.R."[33]

Those who corresponded with FDR put the possibility of a third-party development—or worse—involving Long, Coughlin, and veterans in explicit terms. E. J. Hawes wired FDR: "Remember it was the service vote and Father Coughlin that put your party in." Hawes warned the president that "veto of the Patman Bill means only one thing, Huey Long next." John Allen of Jersey City alerted FDR to the possibility of more ominous developments: "[I]f this [Patman] bill is beaten, this country will see a dictator in the White House in 1936, [a] veteran of the World War, backed by the veteran vote, Father Coughlin, and Huey Long." An insurance broker from Englewood, New Jersey, Frederick E. Rieger, compared the situation to that of Germany "a few years back," casting the blame for the present circumstances on "Father Coughlin, Huey Long, the American Legion, the Veterans of Foreign Wars, and other payroll patriots."[34]

Even letters from Roosevelt supporters depicted the turbulent political climate that rendered the Bonus coalition of Long, Coughlin, and veterans a gathering political threat. Roosevelt supporters in favor of the Bonus, veterans and nonveterans alike, felt the need to distance themselves from the Long and Coughlin movement. Harry Bowen from Troup, Texas, pleaded with FDR not to veto the Bonus bill. Yet, Bowen told Roosevelt, "*I am your friend* and not a friend of Huey P. Long or the Radio Priest." E. L. Westbrook from Meridian, Mississippi, lectured Roosevelt on the economic stimulus the Bonus would provide across the country and put that economic gain in stark political terms. Westbrook claimed, "It will tend to turn many 'deaf ears' to those preaching 'Share Our Wealth societies' and other Bolsheviki Demagogism [sic] which I am afraid is going to cause plenty of trouble in 1936 in spite of all our efforts to subdue them." New York's E. Harry Schiome felt obliged to postscript a respectful letter asking FDR not to veto the Bonus, saying, "Please do not misunderstand me as being a follower of the Rev. Charles E. Coughlin, I am not." Writing from a ritzier Manhattan address, E. F. Hackett begged the president's secretary, Marvin McIntyre, to pass along his advice regarding the Bonus. Hackett explained that FDR, by allowing the Bonus to pass, had an opportunity "for scuttling the work by Long Talmadge Coughlin [sic]."[35]

All spring, Roosevelt wrestled with what to do with the Bonus. Following the pleading of Secretary of the Treasury Henry Morgenthau, Jr., and his own fiscally conservative economic principles, FDR instinctively wanted to kill the Bonus drive. And he found a close ally when Eleanor Roosevelt weighed in on the matter in a memo early in 1935. She began with the assertion that "the people who want the bonus frequently do not need it." Then she proclaimed that both veterans' existing privileges and the expense of the Bonus made prepayment unwise. The First Lady inveighed, "The veterans as a class are already more or less privileged in that they have special consideration under Civil Service, and special consideration under PWA [Public Works Administration]. By giving them [the Bonus] we will accentuate the fact that they are a privileged class." She cautioned that the national credit might suffer, invoking the example of Germany's runaway inflation and its political consequences. "Those of us who have seen what has happened to Germany," she wrote, "can hardly think that our veterans want to see their country and their families put through the same experiences or to be a party in any way to action which might bring us to the verge of such an experience." The cautionary example of Germany's "printing press" money—cautionary both economically and politically—informed FDR and Morgenthau's thinking, too.[36]

Despite the advice from Morgenthau and Eleanor, FDR vacillated on the how to approach the veto. For the president's political team, the electoral calculations on the Bonus proved more important than ones of principle. At a May 3 cabinet meeting, Vice President John Nance Garner suggested a best-case scenario in which FDR would veto the Bonus only to see it overridden. Garner argued this was the only way to take the issue out of the 1936 election and yet keep FDR clear of responsibility and to stymie potential conservative criticism. According to the Democratic Party chairman, Jim Farley, while the Bonus sat in the Senate on May 11, FDR discussed his options with Garner and Farley in a late-night car ride. Garner urged FDR to veto the Bonus in "temperate language" so that he would not once again provoke veterans. But Farley and Garner believed the party would benefit most at the polling booth from a successful override. According to Farley, "The President agreed that if the bill were passed over his veto, it would not affect the credit of the country and would not have the inflationary effect which many feared." Farley and Garner went further, claiming that payment of the Bonus would "do much toward bringing about recovery." They both left that evening assuming that their suggestions would become the administration's plan.[37]

By May 17, however, Roosevelt had made both a political and a principled decision to veto the Bonus decisively. Farley found a new set of circumstances when he was called back to the White House to discuss the

Bonus situation. An angry FDR told Farley, "Jack Garner has been talking too much. He's got me in a spot where I can be accused of bad faith if the bonus is passed over my veto." FDR sent Farley off to work: "I want you to contact Robinson [the Senate majority leader and the administration's floor leader] and work with him to get enough Senators to uphold my veto." Farley described the president as jumpy; the Democratic National Committee's secret polling had found his public approval rating at an all-time low. During a press conference that afternoon, FDR stunned many Washington insiders by announcing that the veto would be given in person to a joint session of Congress. When questioned by a reporter about the possibility of the Garner strategy, he forcefully attempted to quell the rumors. Roosevelt answered, "The bill is going to be vetoed. That is number one. It is going to be vetoed as strongly as I can veto it. And number three, I hope with all of my heart that the veto will be sustained. Now is that clear?" At Roosevelt's behest, Secretary of the Treasury Morgenthau began a campaign blitz of newspaper editors to try to build a "bonfire of support" for the veto message. On May 20, Morgenthau called an editor, explaining, "I'm not leaving a stone unturned to lick the bonus—any kind of Bonus, see?" The editor asked, "[T]his stuff of a veto with the tongue and cheek [*sic*] is all off?" "All off," replied Morgenthau. The editor remarked again about rumors that were circulating about a "veto with a wink"; Morgenthau squashed them once more. Roosevelt summoned crack speech writer Samuel Rosenman to help him craft a powerful veto message. Shaking two fists in the air, he exclaimed in a late-night meeting with Morgenthau, "My God! If I win I would be on the crest of the wave." The stage was set for one of the era's most remarkable political dramas.[38]

On May 22, 1935, FDR challenged the Bonus coalition and took the political initiative that marked the beginning of the "second" New Deal. He took the unprecedented step of delivering a veto message in person before a joint session of Congress. Never before had a president presented objections before a joint session (and never since), nor had a president done so on a live radio hookup. (Huey Long unsuccessfully filibustered the Senate for five hours, attempting to disallow the speech and blasting the president's effort to give "a White House Bull" to the chamber.) The veto of the Patman Bonus bill became a Washington spectacle. The radio networks transmitted the speech live, and newsreel crews filmed the address. Five thousand people rushed to obtain 553 gallery seats. Newspaper photographers hung backwards over the balcony rails in the Capitol to snap photographs of Eleanor and Administration cabinet members and staffers. The *Washington Post* style editor analyzed the fashion wear of the prominent women in the audience, including the First Lady and the wives of congressmen, senators, and diplomats. The event dominated the newspapers the following day with mammoth headlines.[39]

Speaking to Congress, described by the *Washington Post* as "a grim-faced cold audience" and a "hostile atmosphere," FDR presented a forceful and thorough refutation of all of the Bonus supporters' claims. While he offered no new objections, FDR restated the objections to bonus legislation he had been voicing since coming to office. Roosevelt first laid out the benefits veterans already received from the federal government, such as health care, civil service preference, employment services through the Department of Labor, and pensions. He then argued that veterans also received extra consideration as part of the New Deal's public works projects. After explaining the diligent care the federal government already provided veterans, Roosevelt attacked the central premises of the Patman bill. Roosevelt conceded that immediate payment might slightly stimulate retail trade, but he argued that it would have no effect on the expansion of industry. He also rejected the call for extra veteran relief, noting that the existing New Deal programs and others under congressional consideration, such as Social Security, already addressed the issue of relief and unemployment. Roosevelt claimed that the Bonus supporters' argument that the Bonus would spur economic recovery was "so ill considered that little comment is necessary."[40]

After attacking the central premises of the argument for immediate payment, FDR moved to the bill's specifics. Here, Roosevelt argued that the details of the bill, even disregarding the larger goals sought by Bonus supporters, made it impossible to sign. Roosevelt claimed that, since the bill called for cash payment at the Bonus certificates' face value, it included interest on the certificates through 1945. The extra ten years of interest meant that veterans would receive much more than the additional $1.00 or $1.25 a day for services rendered. FDR claimed the 1945 provision made the certificates worth "two and one-half times the original grant" and amounted to "a new straight gratuity or bounty to the amount of one billion six hundred million dollars." Moreover, FDR claimed that the extra expenditure of $2.2 billion without any additional taxes or bonds to pay for it rendered the bill indefensible. FDR maintained that "solely from the point of view of the good credit of the United States, the failure of the Congress to provide additional taxes for an additional expenditure of this magnitude would in itself and by itself alone warrant disapproval of

FDR reads Bonus bill veto message to a joint session of Congress, May 22, 1935. Courtesy of the Franklin D. Roosevelt Library.

this measure." With no apparent irony, FDR continued to hold fiscal austerity in high regard despite the New Deal's burgeoning deficits. Indeed, the American Liberty League, a conservative organization created in 1934 to oppose the New Deal's spending programs, referred to the veto as a "strong, sound document."[41]

FDR employed the Bonus bill veto to reiterate his position against broadly defined veteran prerogatives. First, he contended that currency expansion and inflation would disproportionately harm those disabled veterans on a fixed income, in effect pitting veterans against one another. As Roosevelt explained, the Patman Bonus bill would favor "the able-bodied veteran at the expense of the disabled veteran." He also restated his principles from the 1933 Chicago Legion speech that able-bodied veterans held no special claims over the rest of the citizenry. FDR argued that the "great majority [of veterans] are today in the prime of life, are today in full bodily vigor," and needed no additional help outside the New Deal programs. Notably, in giving his address, FDR omitted an almost verbatim line from the Legion speech that had created such a stir among veterans opposed to FDR. His written text, published in the next-day's newspapers, stated that "the able-bodied citizen, because he wore a uniform and for no other reason, should be accorded no treatment different from that accorded to other citizens who did not wear a uniform during the World War." The omission of this passage suggests that the earlier outcry over this politically sensitive issue made FDR slightly more circumspect about unnecessarily alienating veterans.[42]

FDR also used the Bonus bill veto to initiate a spirited offensive against those who argued for currency inflation and the redistribution of wealth, namely the coalition of New Deal Dissidents. The conservative *Los Angeles Times* editors rejoiced in the veto because "behind the Patman Bill was every advocate of immediate and undisguised inflation, from Huey Long's share-the-wealthers to the silver raiders [Coughlin and Thomas]." *Literary Digest* proclaimed, "in the popular mind . . . the Patman bill got through the Senate, not merely because it was supported by many veterans, but because it was supported by the Hearst press, by senator Huey P. Long, and most notably, by the Rev. Charles E. Coughlin of Detroit." FDR addressed the distribution of wealth, claiming that, with the inflationary Bonus, "wealth is not created nor is it more equitably distributed by this method." The *Washington Post* reported that Roosevelt made the comment "in response to the Huey Long school of thought." Coughlin's insistent call to his listeners to apply pressure for the Patman Bonus in the weeks leading up to the veto made him an undeniable presence in the episode. As one prominent political analyst observed about the veto message spectacle, "Floating around in the shadow like a fish in the sea was the spirit of Father Coughlin intoning, 'What a mighty thing am I.'" Although Coughlin was not named in any way, FDR's speech refuted Coughlin's arguments in a systematic way. FDR's veto ultimately changed few minds in Congress, but it was impressively delivered to the captivated national radio audience and signaled FDR's vigorous return to the political fray following a long dormant period. *Time* claimed that Roosevelt's "mood had changed" and that "the President of the two years past, taking the political initiative, breaking precedent with verve and satisfaction," had returned. FDR's veto fired the opening salvo of what became the "second" New Deal.[43]

FDR's veto message did little to suppress congressional enthusiasm for the Bonus. Before FDR had even left the Capitol, rowdier members of the House began to chant, "Vote! Vote!" Within forty-five minutes, with what one analyst deemed "contemptuous celerity," the House delivered an overwhelming rebuke to the president's message, voting 322–98 to override. It is worth reiterating that this came from the Democratic "pro-New Deal" Congress voted into office the previous November. James Van Zandt explained to the press that the House had given the president a "decisive answer." He pointed to the override as "conclusive proof" that "80 percent of the American people favored enactment of the Patman Bill." The Senate chose to take up the veto the following day. Before the Senate met, however, the New Deal Dissident coalition would experience one of its defining moments in response to the Roosevelt veto.[44]

On the evening of May 22, in the high point of Father Charles E. Coughlin's political career, the National Union for Social Justice held a raucous rally at New York's Madison Square Garden that emphasized the importance of the Bonus to the organization. The Bonus veto served as the subtext for the entire spectacle, which took place just hours after FDR vetoed the Patman bill. In his "most stunning triumph," Coughlin delivered a speech to the 23,000 people assembled that many compared to William Jennings Bryan's "Cross of Gold" speech. Coughlin denounced "plutocratic capitalism" in all its manifestations, including opposition to the Bonus. Regarding those opposed to the Bonus, Coughlin declared that "they who regarded money as their god and their fellow beings as their cannon fodder still hold sway." Coughlin rejected FDR's veto message: "No later than this afternoon, you heard the President of the United States condemn class legislation, as he called it, while for years he and his

Father Charles E. Coughlin addresses the crowd at Madison Square Garden in New York City following FDR's veto of the Bonus bill, May 22, 1935. New York World-Telegram & Sun Collection, courtesy of the Library of Congress.

predecessors in office have been upholding this very class legislation for the benefit of the bankers, the money creators." He decried FDR's veto as a "money-changer's feeble argument, pronounced by the same person who promised to drive the money-changers from the temple." Each time Coughlin mentioned FDR, the crowd booed. The New York congressional members who voted to override the veto shared in the glory on the dais.[45]

Demonstrating the foundations of the dissident coalition, veterans and especially the VFW played conspicuous roles in Coughlin's NUSJ rally. Coughlin entered the jammed arena surrounded by uniformed veteran flag-bearers. Van Zandt, the VFW's national commander and the most visible veteran activist in the Bonus saga, addressed the crowd immediately prior to Coughlin's speech. The *New York Times* reported that Van Zandt's address was "frequently punctuated with cheers for his assault on the Bonus veto message of President Roosevelt or boos for points made by the President in his address." Van Zandt called FDR's arguments against the Bonus "familiar and overworked" and exhorted the crowd to write or wire their senators to urge them to override the veto, claiming that Bonus advocates were "standing on the threshold of success." The reporter remarked that, "at the close of his address, Mr. Van Zandt aroused the crowd to howling enthusiasm." This event at the Garden demonstrated most clearly the primacy of the Bonus as a galvanizing force in the convergence of veteran political activism and the Coughlin movement. While the VFW national organization and Coughlin agreed on many issues, the Patman Bonus fused them together politically.[46]

On May 23, in a testy five-hour session, the Senate deliberated on the veto override. Progressive Senate lions William G. McAdoo and William Borah (R, ID) threw their considerable weight behind the override effort. Senate Bonus leaders Thomas, Long, and Steiwer took to the floor, condemning the veto and the president's strident message. Thomas called a vote against the Bonus "political suicide," noting that 50 percent of the senators who had voted against the Bonus in 1932, not to mention the then-president, no longer maintained Washington addresses. Long complained that the administration felt no compunction about granting banks currency in exchange for bonds, as called for by the Glass-Borah Amendment of the Home Owner Loan Bill. Long asked, "If it's fair for the Bankers, why isn't it fair for veterans to give them currency on the obligation they hold?" At the close of his speech, Long warned that the sustaining of the veto "will be a source of deep regret to all who wish to do the President and the Democratic Party a favor" and asked to have a transcript of his "A Fair Deal for the Veterans" May 11 VFW radio address and a pamphlet touting the "Share Our Wealth Principles" entered into the *Congressional Record*. Steiwer found the president's assertions that veterans were on the same plane as other citizens impossible to accept. He also argued that to deny the Bonus translated into a victory for the war profiteers. Steiwer asserted, "We can never win back the affections of the common people if we accord privilege to this class, and deny the debt due to the veterans." Nonetheless, the Senate override vote came up nine votes short. In defeat, however, forty-one Democrats voted to override the president, joining eleven Republicans and each Progressive and Farm-Laborite senator. With the final vote tallying 54-40, one wag claimed that the Bonus bloc would revise the rallying cry from the 1844 election, "Fifty-four forty and fight!" Indeed, syndicated political columnist Frank R. Kent contended that the narrowness of Roosevelt's victory over the Bonus in a nonelection year should give opponents pause. Kent explained, "No one . . . who analyzes bonus-inflation strength today, and who knows the history of veteran legislation, will doubt the result next year, veto or no veto." Roosevelt's veto had survived, but no one believed the issue permanently dead.[47]

Acknowledging the setback, the VFW vowed to keep fighting for the Bonus. James E. Van Zandt stood outside the Senate chambers with a sheath of typewritten statements, declaiming with typical bravado that "the fight for full and immediate payment of the adjusted claims certificates will be renewed at once with redoubled vigor." Van Zandt also wired the American Legion Commander Belgrano, "The Veterans of Foreign Wars has just begun to fight. What is the American Legion going to do?" After the defeat, however, it became clear that no successful action could be taken on the Bonus in what remained of the legislative session. Instead, Van Zandt and the VFW national leadership carried the fight to the president immediately and ferociously in the VFW's monthly publication.[48]

The official VFW reaction to the defeat of the Bonus proved fierce and more directly confrontational than ever before. In *Foreign Service,* the VFW published a two-page editorial on the Bonus veto excoriating FDR. The VFW editorial began, "Defeat of the Patman Bill . . . as a direct result of the Presidential veto, proves conclusively that America is now in the same class with Germany and Italy. Franklin D. Roosevelt has plainly taken unto himself the same dictatorship powers that characterize the regimes of Hitler and Mussolini." Regarding the message itself, the VFW leadership declared it "a masterpiece of evasion—a symphony of sophistry—an opus of discordant notes." The VFW detested most thoroughly the abandonment of the longstanding philosophy toward veterans "that service to the flag of our country, in time of war, endows a citizen with an honor and distinction." By rejecting this principle, FDR placed veterans on equal footing with "stay-at-home profiteers, draft dodgers, weak-kneed slackers, the mentally unfit, and the morally incapable."[49]

According to the VFW leadership, the Roosevelt administration's command of the newly created Works Progress Administration budget rendered opposition particularly difficult. The editorial explained that "Roosevelt, Farley, & Co." controlled an enormous source of patronage through the WPA and did not want federal funds to leave their control. The accompanying drawing, "You Can't Lick Five Billion Dollars," depicted this charge in stark imagery. The Bonus bill lost out to FDR, "Kid Patronage," and plutocrats in top hats. The VFW leadership summarized the conclusions reached on the nature of the New Deal very succinctly: "[I]n no uncertain terms, Franklin D. Roosevelt has told the veteran that patriotic service to the nation, in time of war, carries no significance as far as his Administration is concerned . . . and public monies will be spent only to win elections and build up political machines."[50]

After the Patman bill's defeat, the American Legion leadership continued to support payment but felt vindicated in its promotion of the Vinson plan over the Patman bill. Leaders blamed "the bull-headedness of the VFW" in demanding the Patman version for the Bonus's ultimate defeat. Although the Legion called for Bonus supporters to wire their senators and the president as the bill sat on FDR's desk, Commander Frank Belgrano chose to spend the day of the Senate override vote at a luncheon for veterans in Utah rather than in the Senate gallery. After the veto was sustained, Belgrano reaffirmed the Legion's support for Bonus prepayment in a terse comment. He announced that "it is high time that men of all veterans' organizations point their fingers at their Congressmen and force passage of some kind of bonus." A day later, Belgrano complained that on the Bonus fight he was "tired of being taken up blind alleys by Congressmen and Senators who are interested in something else." The Legion's implicit disavowal of the Patman bill also betrayed more mundane reasoning. Most in the Legion leadership viewed the Patman bill as dangerous for the country, and many saw it as dangerous for the Legion, too. In 1936, a flyer in support of FDR's reelection secretly circulated among Legionnaires; it touted FDR's Bonus veto as an organizational boon for the American Legion. The flyer described the veto of the Patman Bill as a relief since the VFW would have become the most important political player among veteran organizations if its advocacy of the Patman bill had paid dividends. Legion leaders looked to 1936 for Bonus payment on their terms: with conservative financial practices, with the Legion's respectable guidance, and untainted by the controversial Dissident movement.[51]

Public reaction to the veto message as revealed by newspaper editorials and letters to the White House was generally positive. Nevertheless, correspondence sent to FDR confirmed that the Bonus had been the most important issue in the Long and Coughlin coalition. Mrs. Alice V. McCoy in Windsor Locks, Connecticut, expressed her disappointment with FDR's veto of the Bonus. She scolded the president, "We understand Father Coughlin and I think it is your duty to the people of the United States either to come out publicly and uphold Father Coughlin who wants to uphold you, or explain why the things Father Coughlin wants done cannot be done." Howard H. Banker of Cincinnati praised the veto speech as "a real answer to the rantings of Father Coughlin, Huey Long, and others who are constantly picturing half-truths to the American people." R. H. Baker from Houston commended FDR's "courageous stand in opposition to the Veterans' Bloc in Congress and its powerful lobby." He added that the 'American Legion, and the Father Coughlins and Huey Longs are very vocal, but they do not represent the American people." Dr. Rodney D. Block informed the president that he felt compelled to write "so that our officials will not get the idea that the Longs and Coughlins and army lobbyists [opinions] . . . are the opinions of *all* the citizens of the United States." In an attached letter to his congressman, Book warned "when it comes to vote there are other 'armies' in America who can cast just as emphatic a ballot as any of the Big Noise Coughlins and Longs." P. A. Rishberger lauded the president's message and hoped Congress would sustain the veto. He added, "If they do not then Father Coughlin will say he did it and Huey might do that, too. If Father gets so he can control Congress that is not so good even though he [is] true to you."[52]

Much of the mail sent in reaction to the veto once again put the Bonus battle in the electoral terms that so worried the administration. A group of "Michigan World War Veterans" wrote of the veto, "You met your 'Waterloo,' and our prediction is that you will be defeated in the 1936 presidential campaign . . . [for] your attitude against the soldier." John W. Marshall respectfully disagreed with Roosevelt's stand on the Bonus. He explained, "I am not an ex-soldier and don't look for any benefits but I sure think that the boys sure got the worst of a rotten deal and if there is not something done to even up the score Mr. Huey Long will be your successor." A veteran in Minnesota rejected the president's message and lashed out at the administration's treatment of veterans even as he wrote from a CCC camp. He explained that he would follow the advice of Smedley Butler and vote for a third party because he wanted "to see the present

Administration defeated as badly as the former were (*sic*) in the Democratic landslide of 1932." George C. Post sent a telegram deriding the veto speech and warning of veterans' electoral strength. He proclaimed, "You are on your way out, Huey Long has your number." While the Roosevelt administration won the Bonus clash of 1935, it had many political fences to mend before the 1936 election.[53]

By examining the political mobilization for the Bonus in 1935, the political origins of the "second" New Deal come more clearly into focus. The Bonus explains how disparate, disgruntled political actors with wildly different agendas merged in public perception into a singular oppositional political force against the Roosevelt Administration. Of course, the unsuccessful battle over the Bonus aroused veterans against the FDR Administration and precipitated wide-spread veteran political activism. More than that, though, in the late spring of 1935 the Bonus battle fused together a politically threatening coalition of Long, Coughlin, and VFW-led veterans. FDR's veto of the Patman Bonus Bill capped a political season like no other. But it also launched another of enormous magnitude. During the "second hundred days," Congress passed the landmark legislation of the "second" New Deal that all political commentators then (and since) framed as Roosevelt's response to the New Deal Dissidents. For their part, Bonus backers relented after the veto, allowing Congress to take up the important list of sidetracked legislation. The Bonus and the political forces aligned with it, however, did not vanish. All onlookers assumed that the Bonus would come up again in the next congressional session; most assumed it would finally be paid since it was an election year. Veteran politics continued to shape to the politics of the New Deal.

6

Veteran Politics and the New Deal's Political Triumph of 1936

Actual shipment of the first soldiers' bonus bonds to Federal Reserve banks preparatory to their delivery to ex-servicemen in July, August, and September has revived speculation as to the political and economic effect of the bonus payment. . . . The Administration does few things without an eye to their political effect and may be expected to work every dodge this summer.
—*Los Angeles Times*, "Bonus and Business" editorial, March 30, 1936

In the presidential election of 1936, Franklin D. Roosevelt cruised to an electoral landslide over his Republican opponent, Kansas governor Alf Landon. The Union Party candidate, Representative William Lemke of North Dakota, received fewer than a million votes nationally, dashing the hopes of the third party's dissident founders—Father Charles E. Coughlin, Dr. Francis Townsend, and Huey Long's successor at the Share Our Wealth Society, Reverend Gerald L. K. Smith— of having a tangible impact on the election. The reported millions of supporters of the Union Party leaders simply failed to materialize as voters. Viewed from the vantage point of the spring of 1935, the political triumph of the New Deal in 1936 seemed an uncertain proposition. In 1935, the economy continued to languish, unemployment hovered around 20 percent, and Roosevelt appeared besieged by political forces both to his left and right. How, then, did this historic election landslide come to pass?

While others point to the political and economic impact of the landmark legislation of the "second" New Deal, the death by assassination of Roosevelt's most dangerous political adversary, Huey Long, and FDR's adoption of a more anticapitalist, populist posture to explain the election results, this chapter continues to place veteran politics at the center of the New Deal political narrative. The politics of the Bonus, so essential to the rise of the New Deal Dissidents, finally climaxed with passage and payment of the Bonus in 1936. With that, the glue that held the dissident coalition together in 1935 dissolved. As for the veteran members of the coalition, the Roosevelt administration left nothing to chance, aggressively courting veterans disaffected by nearly three years of antagonistic federal policies. Perhaps most important, however, the disbursements of Bonus payments provided a massive economic stimulus in June 1936, turning that summer and fall of the election season into a period of banner economic growth. In the short term (and all politics is measured at the polls in the short term), the passing of the Bonus in 1936 may have been the most successful piece of "second" New Deal legislation—even if it passed over FDR's veto. Veteran politics, therefore, proved crucial to the political triumph of the New Deal.

The month of May 1935 marked a decisive shift for the Roosevelt administration. FDR retooled his administration's agenda, emphasis, and tone and wrested the political initiative both from the New Deal Dissidents and from a conservative opposition energized by the Supreme Court's overturning of the National Industrial Recovery Act. As the extended congressional summer of 1935 unfolded, the economic and social legislation of the "second" New Deal finally emerged from a Congress long distracted by the Bonus drama. The Social Security Act, the National Labor Relations Act, the Revenue Act, the Banking Act, and the Public Utilities Act all followed the earlier creation of the Works Progress Administration, in April. With this legislation, the federal government created the outlines of a welfare state, guaranteed the rights of labor, initiated progressive reform of the tax code, increased federal regulation of the financial and utilities industries, and put millions of Americans to work in $5 billion public work projects. In the process and in the results, the administration staked an increasingly aggressive anticapitalist position as a means of coopting the mobilization of dissenters on the left. Historians have judged FDR's political "turn to the left" a success for undermining the New Deal Dissidents' support, effectively "stealing Long's thunder," as Roosevelt phrased it to aide Raymond Moley. Long's death, on September 10, 1935, undercut further any momentum that a third-party movement had gathered in the spring. But the Bonus, the issue that had forged the New Deal Dissident coalition, remained unsettled.[1]

The Bonus battle reverberated throughout the summer of 1935. The Bonus had been a significant factor in the legislative course of the "second" New Deal beyond supplying the point of convergence for the New Deal Dissidents. It preoccupied Congress to such an extent in the spring of 1935 that it bottled up the vast array of progressive initiatives until after the issue had run its course. Only after the May 22 veto could legislators concentrate on the legislation that ultimately passed in the extended session of the "second hundred days." After the frustrating spring Bonus defeat, Legion officials looked to regroup for the next session, certain that a Congress facing reelection would want to settle the issue once and for all. Undaunted, Wright Patman and the VFW attempted to reintroduce the Bonus in a number of different bills and as riders to others, including the "Soak the Rich" revenue bill. All summer, Patman and Commander Van Zandt of the VFW denounced the Legion, especially Commander Belgrano, for not supporting these measures. Yet, with the president's plan under way and the Democratic congressional leadership focused on finishing the program that summer, the majority of progressive Bonus advocates ultimately opted to forgo attempted Bonus legislation until January in what the *Washington Post* called an "informal agreement between Administration forces and strong veteran factions." As the 1935 session finally came to a close, in late August, Bonus backers made their intentions clear by securing enough discharge petition signatures to send the Patman bill to the floor in the first weeks of the 1936 session.[2]

Some suggested that the administration had settled for the Bonus agreement with a wink and a nod, signaling an intention to let the measure pass in 1936 in exchange for removing the Bonus irritant from the crucial summer session. A "personal and confidential" letter from Secretary of the Treasury Henry Morgenthau to FDR dated September 4, 1935, suggested that FDR indeed now was seeking compromise on the Bonus. Morgenthau wrote the letter because FDR had mentioned to him in passing that he was "considering announcing some plan to pay the bonus." The horrified Morgenthau explained his reaction: "I almost literally 'passed out.'" He pleaded with FDR, "I most strongly urge you, first as your Secretary of the Treasury and, second, as one of your true and tried friends, to do nothing about the bonus for the balance of this year." But even Morgenthau, who bitterly opposed the Bonus, could see the potential political ramifications of the issue if it remained unsettled. He wrote that "if you feel that politically it is necessary to do something about the bonus, then it seems that the time and place for you to make a statement . . . would be in your message to Congress when it meets in January." Clearly, FDR now wanted to resolve the Bonus impasse quickly, preferably before the upcoming election season so that veterans and veteran politics would not haunt his campaign. But he also wanted to turn the tide of veteran politics in his favor. As congressional Bonus supporters waited for the new year to take up the issue yet again, FDR and his surrogates began to work on transforming veterans and veterans' organizations from adversaries into allies.[3]

In September 1935, remembrances of Huey Long cast a shadow over the VFW national encampment held in New Orleans less than a week after his death. Long's assassination in the Baton Rouge state capitol building by a physician seeking vengeance for a smear against his father-in-law still reverberated throughout the state. Before the start of the encampment, Commander Van Zandt represented the VFW at Long's funeral services in Baton Rouge. Careful to distance the VFW from any overt partisanship, *Foreign Service* described the offering of condolences to the Long family as a token of respect for the departed Senator's "100 percent record in the upper house on veteran legislation, and in appreciation of his loyalty to the veteran cause." Groups of VFW members, including two hundred officers and delegates of the VFW's fun-loving "Cooties" community service club, made the pilgrimage to Baton Rouge to pay their respects and to place wreaths at Long's tomb.[4]

During the New Orleans encampment meetings, the Kingfish's presence remained keenly felt. The presumed new leader of the Share Our Wealth movement, Reverend Gerald L. K. Smith, delivered a five-minute eulogy of Long to the veteran delegates. Although Smith had initially been asked to take Long's place as an invited guest speaker, administration allies succeeded in scuttling a formal address by Smith. According to the *New York Times*, "foes had tipped off James E. Van Zandt that he might be involving his organization in some rather controversial matters if he turned his convention into a forum for the Share Our Wealth Crusade." Within the constraints of a eulogy, however, Smith unleashed a stirring political tribute to the fallen Long. He also gave the VFW delegates his assurances that Long's followers would continue to support the veteran cause. The melodramatic Smith went so far as to communicate Long's alleged deathbed words, claiming that Long had told him that "there is only one thing that we must commit ourselves to without any opposition, and that is the honest compensation due the men who defended the United States in that

one hellish conflict of the World War." The supposedly nonpolitical eulogy concluded, "May no surrender ever be offered you . . . until the total
wealth of this great Nation has been put at the disposal of all of its total
population."[5]

While Van Zandt bowed to the pressure within the organization by
limiting Smith to a short eulogy, a chief VFW spokesperson and other
invited guests explicitly invoked Long's name and causes. General Smedley Butler, still the VFW's most popular speaker and recruiter, commented on the senator's death in his address to the encampment. Butler
bemoaned the fact that Long "could have put a spike in [FDR's] wheel."
Instead, Butler explained to the assembled veterans, Long's death made
a second Roosevelt term inevitable. Butler proclaimed, "Roosevelt is going to be reelected, and you can't help it for the simple reason that the
best friend the soldier ever had, and the one magnificent human being
in America, Huey Long, is dead." Butler also pointed out that Roosevelt controlled $5 billion in WPA funding, a key source of patronage
and political support. As Butler described it, "You can elect a Chinaman
President of the United States for $5,000,000,000!" Eugene Talmadge,
governor of Georgia and no friend of the New Deal, also expressed re-
grets that Long, the man he "learned to love," would no longer be with
them. Talmadge called the "share our wealth" plan Long's "great idea"
and hoped Reverend Smith would explain it to the veterans in his then-
scheduled address.[6]

The VFW's encampment demonstrated the organization's position in
the forefront of New Deal dissent. The 2500 delegates voted to support "the
Coughlin bill providing establishment of a government controlled bank
to issue and have supreme control over all monetary and banking mat
ters." Wright Patman commended the VFW for its work on behalf of the
Bonus, claiming "no other organization has so persistently, consistently,
and effectively sponsored this cause as the Veterans of Foreign Wars." Additional resolutions continued to voice the VFW's support for controversial issues: the taxation of all "federal, state, and municipal bonds, current
and future," the conscription of capital and labor in time of war, and an
amendment to the Constitution requiring a "permanent neutrality policy."
The VFW also expressed outrage at the deaths of 256 veterans—ex-bonus
marchers—in the Labor Day hurricane that decimated several FERA work
camps in the Florida Keys. The VFW delegates demanded a congressional
investigation despite White House statements exculpating the federal officials in charge of the annihilated veteran camps.[7]

The 1935 VFW encampment was mostly notable for what did not happen: the delegates avoided an endorsement of the Patman Bonus bill and pulled back from official criticism of FDR. In its resolution on the Bonus, the VFW vowed to "work militantly, aggressively, and uncompromisingly" for immediate payment. But the VFW delegates now chose to remain flexible regarding method of payment instead of "standing pat with Patman" as had been done the previous spring. In reverting to the position of the 1934 encampment, the organization tacitly acknowledged that its advocacy of the Patman bill's inflationary agenda had reached a point of diminishing returns. The Legion's denunciations of the VFW for stubbornly yoking the Bonus to currency expansion had gained traction in veterans' circles. With the Legion now squarely behind Bonus payment, VFW leaders knew they risked being blamed more widely if veterans did not get their Bonus money because they continued down the inflation path. The Bonus now needed to be paid—not just fought for—if the VFW organization was to continue to profit from its longstanding support of the measure. As important, official criticism of FDR failed to materialize from the convention proceedings. This was not for lack of opportunity. Outrage lingered over the Bonus veto as many VFW delegates pushed for resolutions censuring or condemning FDR. Minnesota delegate David Lundeen even cited FDR's veto as the direct cause of the Keys hurricane deaths in his proposed censure resolution. Yet, no such resolution emerged from the convention, and the president avoided political embarrassment.[8]

The possibility for antagonistic resolutions so concerned the Roosevelt administration, however, that it sent a key Democratic veteran operative to the encampment in New Orleans to undermine any such activity and to rebuild the fractious relation between the VFW leadership and the president. On September 10, 1935, the White House received an urgent message from Frank M. Kirwin, a Democrat and state VFW officer from Ohio. Kirwin telegrammed Steve Early requesting that Joe Heffernan, an attorney working in the Federal Communications Commission on the ATT trust case, accompany the Ohio delegation on the trip to the 1935 VFW encampment in New Orleans. Kirwin told Early that he had "an important assignment for Joe Heffernan" and that Heffernan's presence "would be of mutual benefit to Administration and to our organization." Kirwin asked Early to "prevail upon Communications Commission to permit his going." The next day, Early called Anning Prall, the chairman of the FCC and told him he thought this should be done. On September 14, the secretary to Anning Prall sent a memorandum to the White House stating, "Mr. Heffernan called on Mr. Prall and has started for the national convention of the Veterans of Foreign Wars in New Orleans."[9]

On September 18, 1935, writing from the Roosevelt Hotel— ironically, Huey Long's old headquarters—in New Orleans, Joe Heffernan informed Steve Early of his actions at the VFW encampment. In a letter marked "confidential," Heffernan, who had worked with Early on *Stars and Stripes* in France, detailed the proceedings of the Americanism and Resolutions Committees. Heffernan relayed to Early the strong feelings against the administration that had emerged in the Resolution Committee's meetings. Heffernan noted that "there were at least fifty proposals clearly of political import." Heffernan then proceeded to enumerate the openly hostile resolutions. "One of these was intended to provide for the adoption of a slogan: 'Remember the Veto!' Another was headed: 'Broken Political Promises.' A third was 'Unconstitutional Usurpation by the President.' A fourth demanded that the organization go on record as opposed to the reelection of the President and that support be offered to any opponent." Heffernan informed Early that "All such clearly antagonistic resolutions I was able to have disapproved." He did not explain further, though in committee sessions he and Democratic allies probably pointed to the VFW's prohibition against partisan politics and played to the VFW members' patriotism to defuse the explosive and potentially politically costly situation. Heffernan told Early that "it was prudent in you to have me come here."[10]

Heffernan proved immediately useful to the administration by undermining some of the more hostile expressions against FDR, but his letter also very ably explained the current situation with the Bonus and the VFW's position as a leading voice of New Deal dissent. Heffernan attempted to convince Commander Van Zandt that there was a good chance that the Bonus would be passed in the January congressional session, which meant that "veterans now have nothing to gain by a provocative utterance which would only arouse the President." Heffernan correctly speculated that the VFW would back off its inflationary demands in the Patman bill and withhold support for any particular bill, choosing instead to put immediate payment over the ideological demands inherent in the Patman bill. Heffernan also related to Early why the VFW had become such an embittered critic of the New Deal. Heffernan explained, "There is a feeling that in his [1933] Chicago speech, [FDR] went further than any other President in rebuffing the veterans." He added that, "in insisting that veterans, no matter what their service, are entitled to no special consideration, he went contrary to our school book stories and thus disturbed the underlying sentiment of the people." Heffernan gave this reason special weight since even the "more thoughtful and deliberative men" expressed this view. In a telling ending, Heffernan described the difficult position he and his "personal friends and political allies" were in. Although all were diehard Democrats and would support the president in the 1936 election, they were "somewhat saddened by what appears to be his broad philosophy and in their hearts wish that he could see his way clear to reassert the historic outlook on veterans."[11]

Heffernan's work for the administration attempted to do more than just undermine critical expressions. Heffernan acted to mend the rift between the administration and Commander Van Zandt. Van Zandt's outspoken criticism of the administration had been unending from the time of his first appointment, in September 1933. Moreover, his tireless recruiting work and speaking tours promoting cash payment of the Bonus and the alliance with the Long and Coughlin forces made him a highly visible New Deal Dissident in his own right. After the convention, however, Heffernan wired Early that "Everything personally critical of the President has been stopped. Van Zandt gave us personal support. I promised appreciation and suggest that you arrange social contact." Heffernan enthused, "foresee prospect of better feeling if we handle situation adroitly." Kirwin, the Ohio VFW leader who had requested Heffernan's attendance, also wired Early "a thousand thanks for sending Joe Heffernan. . . . Am confident his actions will bring Van Zandt and Administration closer."[12]

One of Heffernan's actions involved personally nominating Van Zandt for his third term as commander-in-chief, a move that Kirwin claimed "threw [the] convention into panic." Given the battles between the VFW and the Roosevelt administration during Van Zandt's leadership and the widespread knowledge of Heffernan's ties to the administration, Kirwin probably did not exaggerate in his description. Heffernan's rousing and, by VFW standards, lengthy nominating speech for Van Zandt masterfully alluded to FDR's principled position vis-à-vis the veterans on the Bonus. In a passage ostensibly referring to Van Zandt, Heffernan told the encampment, "The Nation of ours today is in a great crisis. . . . In this crisis we must look for a man who is firm in his purpose and resolved in his principle, and a man who will not hedge from momentary rebuff or retreat in the face of vilification and misrepresentation." Heffernan added, "We must have a man who will stand like a pillar in the temple of state." The VFW encampment unanimously elected Van Zandt for a third term and looked to the 1936 congressional session as the final chapter in the Bonus saga.[13]

The American Legion presented the Roosevelt administration with a seemingly less intractable problem than did the VFW. The Legion's opposition to the Patman bill and its advocacy of the noninflationary Vinson bill played a substantial role in the sustaining of the veto. Moreover, Commander Belgrano, while in favor of the Bonus, in no way sympathized with the New Deal Dissidents as the VFW's Van Zandt did. In fact, quiet efforts by the Legion to smooth over the relationship with the president began just days after the veto when FDR received an invitation to address an American Legion church service at the Washington Cathedral. An American Legion official in Washington explained the reasoning behind the invitation to FDR's secretary: "We want to break it all over the country simultaneously to off-set anything coming out of the Bonus veto. It is Commander Belgrano's idea of healing the breach, so to speak." Roosevelt declined the invitation for reasons that are unclear, instead sending a message to be read to the gathering. After the long summer of legislation, however, administration officials sought ways to address this matter of "healing the breach."[14]

Much like their view of the VFW, administration officials and allies worried that the Legion's annual convention, in St. Louis, might turn into a political humiliation for the president. On the eve of the convention, the politicizing effects of the Bonus battle left even Legion officials concerned about the continued nonpartisan nature of the organization. "Shall the Legion Remain Non-Political?" asked the chairman of the National Legislative Committee in a cautionary essay written for the preconvention issue of *The American Legion Monthly*. To defuse the potentially volatile environment, Legion officials, including Commander Belgrano, decided to invite FDR to speak at the convention, as had been done in 1933 to calm Legionnaires after the Economy Act. On September 9 and 15, Belgrano and other Legion officials traveled to Hyde Park to see if FDR might include an address to the convention in his upcoming western trip. As Roosevelt mulled it over, presidential adviser Steve Early and Monroe Johnson, a Legion national officer and Assistant Secretary of Commerce, warned him about the risks of such an appearance. Evidently, FDR had mentioned to them that he might go and not bring up the Bonus. Early and Johnson argued that he could not simply ignore the issue because "Not to mention the bonus would cause every newspaperman covering the story, and every editor to say that you evaded the issue." Early concluded, "This sort of press reaction, in my opinion, would be worse than if you did not go to the Legion meeting." Roosevelt agreed but left room for a change of heart;

he announced that his work schedule made it quite nearly impossible to get to St. Louis in time for the convention. Later, travel plans for his western swing were altered to preclude a St. Louis appearance. Despite FDR's avoidance of the convention, the administration still found it prudent to mend fences with veterans and to avoid further bad feelings from emanating within the Legion.[15]

In the days after the Legion's invitation to the convention, administration allies in communication with the president and his staff orchestrated a convention offensive to turn Legionnaires back toward a friendlier relationship with the administration. On September 12, Senator William G. McAdoo (D, CA) wrote the president a personal letter about the upcoming convention. McAdoo's note came with an enclosure, a letter from his law partner William H. Neblett suggesting action on behalf of the president at the St. Louis meeting. Neblett explained that Republican Legionnaires led by Representative Hamilton Fish (R, NY) and Hanford McNider, the former Assistant Secretary of War under Coolidge, sought a resolution explicitly condemning the president for his attitude toward veterans. Neblett urged McAdoo both to send their other partner, Dean Warner, to "neutralize this movement" and to inform FDR of "this danger" immediately. In his letter to FDR, McAdoo informed "Frank" that he would send Warner to the convention to deal with the issue, but he also recommended that "your good friend, [DNC chairman] Farley," be advised of the situation so that other representatives might be brought to St. Louis to nip the potentially embarrassing situation in the bud. Indeed, less than a week later, ex-Legion Commander and Democratic operative Louis Johnson communicated with Steve Early, asking for the administration's blessing in sending Oswald Ryan, general counsel to the Federal Power Commission, to St. Louis. Johnson explained that this was imperative "in our fight to keep this certain organization on an even keel." Johnson said that Ryan, a "very prominent Legionnaire and past national officer," wanted to go but that his duties kept him in Washington. Johnson asked Early to call the Commission chairman, Frank R. McNinch, and press the case. Early jotted down the response in the memo's margin: "'We will do it', McNinch." With this, two different individuals with administration ties set out for St. Louis to do the administration's bidding. As predicted by many, the convention turned into a raucous event.[16]

At the convention in St. Louis, Legionnaires formulated their agenda for the next year in spirited meetings marked by two internecine disputes over the Bonus and the election of a new national commander. From

September 23 to September 26, some 250,000 of them took over the city with parades, the shooting off of fireworks, and multiple beer tents sponsored by the Anheuser Busch Brewing Company. In between the episodes of widespread frivolity, Legion delegates passed resolutions urging that the official diplomatic recognition of the Soviet Union be rescinded and seeking the compulsory fingerprinting of all U.S. citizens, the designation of November 11 as a national holiday, and the implementation of multiple efforts to stamp out subversion. No resolutions critical of the president made it out of committee. On September 26, however, the delegates passed a resolution in favor of the Bonus. In strong language, the resolution stated that the Legion did not want the Bonus issue "complicated or confused by other issues of government finance or theories of currencies, with which the Legion does not intend to become involved."[17]

In the deliberations over the Bonus, pandemonium broke out in the convention hall as Wright Patman once again sought to persuade the Legion to adopt his currency inflation method of payment. All summer, the animosity between Patman and Legion officials, especially Commander Belgrano, had been escalating, with each side blaming the other for the Bonus's failure in May. In July, Patman blasted Belgrano, claiming that "certain leaders of the American Legion have deliberately and willfully sold out to Wall Street interests and have become disloyal to the American Legion." Belgrano and Legion lobbyist John Thomas Taylor responded in kind, blaming Patman's fixation with currency expansion as the reason that veterans now did not have their Bonus money. At the convention, then, when Patman rose to speak against the proposed Bonus resolution, chaos enveloped the hall. Boos rained down on Patman and his fellow Texan Representative William D. MacFarlane (T, TX) until they finally gave up the floor because, according to the *New York Times*, "it seemed so probable trouble would ensue." Commander Belgrano wielded the gavel so furiously in his attempt to maintain order that he broke the stage table on which he pounded. After Patman was shouted down, the 1,207 delegates passed the Legion's Bonus resolution with "a deafening roar." The next day, the *Times* special correspondent, Charles McLean, reported that several foes of Patman surrounded him as he began to speak and that only with Patman's walking away from the microphone was "violence . . . averted."[18]

The delegates turned next to the election of their new national commander. During the convention, two candidates emerged from a pack of eleven: Ray Murphy of Iowa and Harry W. Colmery of Kansas. The *New*

York Times called the battle to replace Belgrano a "bitter contest," one that promised to be as fierce as the Bonus fight. A Legionnaire predicted that "It's going to be worse than the 1924 Democratic convention [where fist fights broke out in the hall] when they begin to call the roll." Murphy and Colmery, both Legionnaires of good standing and impeccable records, were staunch partisans of the Democratic and Republican parties, respectively. The floor fight for national commander turned into a proxy political battle between New Deal supporters and opponents. A tense second ballot settled the matter. Even though the largest department in the Legion, New York, twice cast eighty votes for Colmery, Murphy emerged victorious. With that, the convention came to a close, and St. Louis's residents finally got a decent night's sleep.[19]

At the St. Louis meeting, the Bonus bill veto, the incident in the Keys, and prominent Republican Legionnaires all blocked the path to better relations between FDR and the Legion. Administration allies, with the blessing of Democratic Party leadership and administration officials, effectively dealt with them all. Dean Warner returned from the convention with the insiders' version of events for Senator McAdoo, who promptly forwarded it to Roosevelt. In the confidential memo to McAdoo, Warner explained that there were "several dangerous movements under way" when he arrived in St. Louis. Resolutions to revoke the charter of the Legion post that had granted membership to FDR, to investigate the Keys hurricane and to censure the president's handling of the disaster, and to "tie together Patman, Belgrano, and the President as enemies of the veterans" threatened to turn the Legion convention against the president. Warner wrote that "all of these matters were taken care of" by a "good deal of work in all delegations and by carefully watching the various committees of the convention." He expressed his belief that the FDR had made the right choice in not attending because "the general feeling at the convention was such that it would have taken very little to have set off an unfavorable demonstration against the President." Warner also wrote that Patman, by bearing the brunt of the pent-up antagonism during the episode on the convention floor, effectively "segregated" himself from the unscathed president.[20]

Warner's recollection of the Legion's election of a new national commander showed how important the administration's covert efforts were. Harry Colmery's candidacy, according to Warner, was backed by the more conservative, anti–New Deal faction. Warner looked into the other candidates and found in Murphy "a lifelong Democrat" and a "loyal supporter of President Franklin D. Roosevelt and the Administration on all issues except the bonus." Warner then took a page out of McAdoo's book to get Murphy elected. Warner's position within the California delegation meant that the California votes could be manipulated to achieve the desired result exactly as McAdoo's orchestration of the California delegation at the 1932 Democratic Party convention had secured the nomination for FDR. To Warner, the adroit handling of floor votes had saved the day for a Democratic national commander—no small matter, as he believed that "the National Commandership of the American Legion during the coming election year should be in friendly hands." There was little doubt that Murphy's were friendly hands, but confirmation came anyway from George L. Berry, an administration official in the Department of Commerce, who wrote to Marvin McIntyre that "Ray Murphy . . . is just one hundred percent right. He is not only a Democrat, but is a friend of the president." Despite Murphy's promise to continue the drive for the Bonus, the administration now found the Legion's national commander squarely in its corner as it entered the 1936 election year. Both the Legion and the VFW had been politically neutralized by the administration's efforts as the fight for the Bonus geared up once again.[21]

Between October and January, the Legion and the VFW prepared individually and collectively for the 1936 congressional session. In November and December, the organizations' national commanders separately conferenced with the president, placing their respective organizations' agendas in his hands. On November 1–2, the Legion's National Executive Committee met in Indianapolis, where they deliberated Bonus strategy for the next session. The NEC concluded that the Legion would need to present a noninflationary bill to Congress before the Patman bill came up for a floor vote on January 13. Once again, ally Fred Vinson would champion the Legion's legislation. Also in November, Commander Murphy continued to try to "heal the breach" with the president by inviting FDR to cap off the Legion's Armistice Day ceremonies at Arlington National Cemetery with an address. More important, on the day before Roosevelt's speech, Commanders Murphy and Van Zandt met clandestinely in Washington and successfully reconciled their organizations' differences on the Bonus. The VFW commander sought compromise because he recognized that support for an inflationary Bonus had reached a point of diminishing returns for the organization. Legion leaders believed that, while the VFW had grown to the point that it now needed to be accommodated, the Legion would still get ample credit from veterans for bringing about Bonus payment, since it would be accomplished on the organization's more conservative terms. In December, after his conference with the president, Murphy made an elliptical reference to the results of the veteran summit when asked by reporters about the past differences between the Legion and the VFW. Murphy replied that he had "reason to believe the Legion and the VFW would be united on the Bonus Bill." On the final day of 1935, the spirit of veteran unity reached its zenith when the national commander of the much smaller Disabled American Veterans offered to join with the two larger groups to form a "united front." As the New Year rang in, congressional Bonus leaders could count on a unified veterans' lobby, unlike the fractured one of the discordant 1935 session.[22]

In the same period, both public and congressional momentum grew for Bonus payment. As early as October, Van Zandt brashly announced, "I predict with the utmost confidence that victory is at hand." In December, a survey conducted the previous month by the newly created Gallup public opinion poll found that 55 percent of Americans now supported the Bonus legislation. Even the flinty New England region approved by a slim 50.5-49.5 margin. Americans on relief favored payment by a four-to-one ratio. This suggests that, perhaps because of the expansion of New Deal relief, recovery, and social welfare programs, arguments against veterans' relief and deficit spending now failed to alarm most Americans. Another frequent comment, one made by Legion officials, was that if the government was already liberally spending money, why not immediately retire a debt already owed rather than waiting until 1945? Regardless of the reasons for this shift in public opinion, by the end of December, support for a compromise Bonus ran so high in Congress that even the more cautious Legion commander described it in optimistic terms. "The psychology of Congress now is favorable to the bonus," Ray Murphy explained to reporters. Indeed, when Democratic congressional leaders, including Speaker Joseph W. Byrnes (D, TN), convened to discuss parliamentary matters for the upcoming session, they predicted that the Bonus "would be paid despite all objections" and the matter settled no later than February. This sentiment reached the point that Murphy felt compelled to caution veterans that they might be getting too confident about the inevitability of Bonus payment. He told a Minnesota assembly that Legionnaires "must not . . . take too much for the [*sic*] granted." Likening the situation to a football game, Murphy warned, "We know what happens to an overconfident team even when it meets a weaker foe." He added, "The bonus is by no means in the bag. If we fumble a bit or stumble a bit, we may find at the end of the year that the adjusted service certificates are still unpaid." Despite this warning, veterans and all of Washington, including administration officials, believed that some form of the measure would pass quickly in the new session. The only question that remained was what version of the bill would win out.[23]

In January 1936, the matter of how the Bonus should be funded found surprisingly quick resolution. Representatives Fred Vinson (D, KY) and John McCormack (D, MA) offered the veteran organizations' version that did not specify the method of funding. Patman temporarily held out hope for his inflationary version of the Bonus. Father Coughlin, too, continued to support Patman's version of the bill, delivering a sermon on the eve of the congressional session railing against any compromise. Indeed, Patman kept Coughlin informed of the parliamentary maneuvering under way with telegram updates. With the VFW and the American Legion in agreement on a noninflationary compromise plan, however, even Patman finally caved on the currency inflation issue, now agreeing to pay for the Bonus without specifying a method of payment. Bonus supporters in Congress pointed to the unified veteran organizations as the impetus behind their concerted action. In fact, the preamble to the Vinson-McCormack-Patman Bonus bill did so explicitly, beginning, "Whereas, the American Legion, Veterans of Foreign Wars, and Disabled American Veterans of the World War . . . have united upon this measure. . . ." With currency inflation decoupled from immediate Bonus payment and all of the veteran organizations in accord, veterans and congressional supporters believed a veto-proof majority was ensured.[24]

As expected, the Bonus compromise easily passed both the House and the Senate. On January 10, the House voted 346–59 for the "united front" Vinson-McCormack-Patman Bonus bill. Ten days later, the Senate approved a similar bill drafted by Senate Finance Chairman Pat Harrison (D, MS) with a veto-proof majority, 74–16. The political momentum behind the measure proved so powerful that only four senators up for reelection in 1936 voted against it. Even more telling, staunch administration allies who had helped sustain the veto in 1935, such as Majority Leader Joseph Robinson (D, AR), Democratic Whip James Lewis (D, IL), and Finance Committee Chair Pat Harrison, now voted for the bill. The Senate version paid the Bonus in small-denomination bonds. These fifty-dollar "baby bonds" would be disbursed to veterans beginning June 15, 1936. If the bonds went unredeemed for at least one year, the holders would collect 3 percent annual interest until 1945. In addition, the Bonus bill forgave interest on all loans

Senate Bonus supporters and veteran leaders cheer Senate passage of Bonus bill. L-R: Sen. Pat McCarran; Ray Murphy, national commander of the American Legion; Sen. Frederick Steiwer; John Thomas Taylor, national legislative director of the American Legion: Sen. James F. Byrnes; James Van Zandt, national commander of the VFW; George Brobcck, legislative director of the VFW; M. A. Harlan, commander of Disabled American Veterans; and Sen. Robert R. Reynolds. January, 20, 1936. Hulton Archive, courtesy of Getty Images.

veterans had taken against the certificates since 1931, a stipulation that raised the cost by approximately $250 million to $1.9 billion. Rather than settle the differences between the bills in conference, the House hastily approved the Senate version on January 22 in another lopsided, veto-proof vote. The lone veteran organization leader in the Capitol for the final House vote, VFW Commander Van Zandt basked in spotlight. After the bill moved on to the White House, Van Zandt and Speaker of the House Byrnes, surrounded by newsreel cameras, performed a mock signing ceremony for the sound films. The jubilant Van Zandt announced, "Thank you, Mr. Speaker. By your actions, you have made 3,500,000 veterans very happy."[25]

During the legislative stampede for the Bonus, Roosevelt played coy with his staff over his intentions for the measure should it pass. In a

January 17 cabinet meeting, Vice President Garner addressed the president concerning the Bonus. He began, "I don't know what your attitude is going to be on the bonus bill, but it is sure to pass the Senate tomorrow and, in my judgment, will be passed even over your veto." At the behest of his friends in the Senate, he wanted to ask the president a question about the Bonus—most likely, whether it was politically safe to vote against the president. But FDR did not ask what the question was and promptly changed the subject. On January 24, after telling his staff that he had worked on a message to Congress on the Bonus bill until late in the night, he ordered his press secretary, Steve Early, to prepare both a veto press release and a signing press release, while not divulging to anyone what course he would take. Roosevelt's coyness masked a very subtle political maneuver. While the Bonus waited its fate in the Senate, Democratic Party chairman Jim Farley rode from New York City to Washington with FDR and "put in a few licks" for vetoing the Bonus again. Roosevelt shook Farley's hand and thanked him, noting that "most of the people I have talked to have urged me to sign it." He confided to Farley that he believed the Bonus would pass over his veto this time around. The sanguine president assured Farley that if that happened it would be a win-win-win political situation for the administration: veterans would get their money, the "party would not suffer and he could preserve his record" against the Bonus.[26]

On January 24, FDR once again vetoed the Bonus bill, expressing reservations identical to those espoused in his 1935 veto message. But the 1936 message, a two-hundred-word *handwritten* note, arrived at the Capitol without any of the hoopla that attended the 1935 version. FDR explained his veto in a perfunctory fashion, stating that "the circumstances, arguments and facts remain essentially the same as those fully covered and explained by me only eight months ago. I respectfully refer the members of the Senate and of the House of Representatives to every word of what I said then." Some administration officials lamented that the president's attitude concerning the Bonus seemed to have changed. Harold Ickes complained in his diary that the president's veto "was totally lacking in vigor or argument of any sort." He continued, "If the president was against it, he ought to have fought it. . . . I do not like this playful attitude on such an important measure." Political commentators agreed. The *Washington Post*'s Franklyn Waltman, Jr., called FDR's veto message "feeble resistance" and "a milk toast document," adding that "one can visualize Mr. Roosevelt winking one of his eyes at Congress as he solemnly asserted he meant every word he said on the bonus subject last May." Waltman concluded, "Instead of fighting for [his] convictions, he surrendered, it might almost be said abjectly surrendered, to political expediency." Indeed, the administration anticipated that the Bonus would pass and even allowed the Veterans' Administration to begin printing and distributing the necessary application forms before the bill had become law.[27]

On January 27, 1936, boisterous veterans in the Senate galleries rejoiced as the Bonus bill became law over FDR's veto. Four days before, 324 House members had defied the president by voting to override the veto. With only the late Huey Long's Senate seat vacant, seventy-six senators followed suit. Just twelve Democratic senators voted to sustain the president, while fifty-seven Democrats voted to override. That afternoon, the leaders of the Legion and the VFW, Murphy and Van Zandt, joined by Marvin A. Harlan, commander of Disabled American Veterans, called on the White House, where they issued a joint statement with FDR asking veterans to cash the "baby bonds" only if in dire need or "for some permanently useful purpose." The president and the commanders rather patronizingly explained what those purposes might be: "the protection of their families," "the paying off of indebtedness," and "something of permanent value such as a new home." Veterans were asked to refrain from "frittering away of cash" by seeking "temporary pleasure." FDR released a statement declaring that the congressional "mandate" would be carried out "as expeditiously as accuracy will permit" and announced that 3,000 new Civil Service employees would be needed to help expedite the Bonus application process to meet the June 15 payment date. With preferential treatment in civil service hiring, veterans would get many of these new jobs. (Veterans constituted nearly 25 percent of all federal employees hired since 1919.) *Baltimore Sun* columnist Frank R. Kent expressed dismay at the day's events. He fumed that senators "who have followed [FDR] blindly for three years, blithely voted against him on this issue entirely secure in the conviction that their vote in no way impaired their relations or would be held against them." Kent chalked this up to Roosevelt's graciously releasing his Democratic allies who were facing reelection because they were all "afraid of the soldier vote." But, as the machinations at the veteran organization conventions and the weak veto message made clear, Roosevelt and administration officials shared the concerns about the soldiers' vote. Indeed, both politically and economically, the Bonus became the last, albeit unsigned, piece of "second" New Deal legislation.[28]

• • •

After the passage of the Bonus, the VFW and the Legion reached an informal period of détente with the administration on policy matters. Explicitly rejecting any controversial veterans' policies such as general service pensions, both organizations began to focus more intently on foreign policy and national security issues, especially permanent neutrality and universal service legislation. Indeed, the day that the Senate overrode FDR's veto, the three major veteran organizations issued another statement under the title "No More Wars, No More Bonus," advocating "honest and realistic neutrality laws," universal service, and "adequate" defense spending. In the release, the veteran organizations challenged Bonus opponents, saying that if they "will join us in this [neutrality] fight they need fear no more bonuses." On these issues, the VFW, the Legion, and the Roosevelt administration ostensibly agreed.[29]

Despite the new cooperative relations with the veteran organizations on policy matters, administration officials and Democratic members of Congress continued their attempts to sway the VFW leadership into a more favorable attitude toward the president and his party. Thanks to the convention intrigue in the fall, Ray Murphy's tenure as commander kept the Legion in safe hands as far as the administration was concerned. But both the administration and Democrats in Congress tried to disarm the VFW further by giving special recognition to the organization and its confrontational three-term commander. On the day the Bonus passed, General Frank Hines, director of the VA, turned over the symbolic first batch of application forms to Commander Van Zandt, ending happily the VFW's nearly seven-year crusade. In May, Francis E. Walter in the House (D, PA) and Matthew M. Neely (D, WV) in the Senate sponsored legislation granting the VFW a congressional charter in recognition of its new stature gained in the Bonus battle. On May 28, FDR signed the bill, admitting the organization, as the VFW leadership saw it, into "the ranks of the great organizations of the country whose position and influence have been recognized by congressional charters." Thirty-seven years after its founding, the VFW finally received what the Legion had acquired in just months. Thanks to the Democratic Congress and president, there were now two recognized pillars of the veterans' lobby.[30]

Even with this new spirit of congeniality toward the veterans' organizations, administration and Democratic Party officials still worried about the political ramifications of Roosevelt's Bonus vetoes for the 1936 election. To be sure, having VFW and Legion commanders as allies or, at worst, neutralized substantially helped the administration's relationship with disaffected veterans. Individual veterans might rail against the president, but, without organizational structures of support and communication to focus the discontent, there was less to fear. Still, the "soldiers' vote" loomed large, since it was widely viewed as crucial to the outcome of the 1932 election. As early as January, Steve Early, Louis Johnson, and Jim Farley discussed options for handling the "veterans' matter." Johnson, with his ties within the Legion, kept his finger on the pulse of veterans' attitudes. He pleaded with Early to convince Farley of "the urgent necessity of plans being made and carried through" to convince veterans that the president was on their side. Johnson told Early that on the veterans' front, "there is a job to be done and we ought to be about the doing of it." When Farley dragged his heels, Johnson took the initiative.[31]

On January 30—just days after the Bonus passed—Johnson compiled a point-by-point comparison between Roosevelt's and Hoover's records on veteran issues and forwarded it to Monroe Johnson and Steve Early. Designed to be circulated among Legionnaires, Johnson's memo itemized Hoover's record against the Bonus and then ended with Hoover's culpability in the Bonus March rout. He summed up Hoover's achievements as a zero "batting average" because the former president had "helped the Legion to fulfill none of its mandates and principles." Turning to Roosevelt, Johnson highlighted the president's record of direct relief, CCC placement, and WPA jobs for veterans, along with his advocacy of hospital construction and neutrality legislation. He frankly admitted the "mistakes" of the Economy Act and the Bonus vetoes. Johnson pointed out, however, that Roosevelt had recognized the errors of the Economy Act and moved to amend them. And he explained that FDR could have mustered the votes to sustain his second Bonus veto but chose not to do so. Johnson wrote, "The president refused to compromise with his public conscience so far as his own duty was concerned; but with the same determination he permitted Congress to exercise its own judgment above his." Johnson also inserted a paragraph on why FDR's veto benefited the Legion's long-range vitality. He noted that had the Patman Bonus bill become law, "there can be no doubt that the VFW would have become the big veterans' organization and the Legion would have taken second place, at least for several years." (Johnson prudently asked that the VFW reference be omitted when Early used the memo for non-Legion audiences.) He summed up the president's batting average as a "900 plus." The Johnson circular would be just the start of concerted Democratic organizing for the veteran vote. More efforts would commence in the summer of 1936. But nothing was as effective in gaining the support of veterans as the disbursement of the Bonus, which began on June 15, 1936.[32]

With the Bonus battle, veteran politics had exerted a tremendous influence on national political affairs from 1929 to 1936. Now, in the summer of 1936, the immediate payment of the Bonus caused a different kind of national impact when veterans responded to the program by redeeming and cashing their adjusted service certificates in overwhelming numbers. Local posts of the veteran organizations, Veterans' Administration branches, and the Hearst newspapers' offices helped with the disbursement and collection of the necessary application forms. In Los Angeles, for example, Legion Post No. 8 mailed out 2,000 applications to all of its active and delinquent members. Across town, Lincoln Heights VFW Post No. 768 set up a Bonus headquarters for assistance that was open daily until 9:00 p.m. By May, all but 200,000 of the approximately 3.5 million veterans holding certificates had applied for immediate payment. On May 23, Postmaster-General (and DNC chair) Farley announced that the "great majority" of the bonds would be out on June 15 and that postal carriers "would go out of their way whenever necessary with a view toward effecting delivery." After receiving their bonds by mail, veterans were required to go to their post office to certify them for cashing. VFW and Legion national offices aided in the process by printing instructions on cashing the bonds in their monthly publications. Local posts again served as sources of information and assistance.[33]

Before the government issued the $1.9 billion in Bonus bonds, veterans received plenty of advice on how they should spend their money. John Thomas Taylor, the Legion lobbyist, urged Legionnaires in the *American Legion Monthly* to take advantage of new favorable lending policies for veterans adopted by the Federal Housing Administration to purchase new homes with their Bonuses. In the pages of the veteran organization's magazines, car companies began to advertise new vehicles and the advantages of "stretching your Bonus dollars" at Dodge used-car dealerships. A VFW editorial suggested that the grown men in their organization—and certainly their wives—needed no advice on how to spend their money. But the constantly underfunded VFW initiated a "War Chest Fund" to be used in future crises and requested that members contribute $10 of their Bonus money to the cause. Moreover, Commander Van Zandt also penned a column urging them to look into buying an FHA-financed house with their money. In Johnson City, Tennessee, a group of fifty-four veterans at the Soldiers' Home decided that they would launch a nationwide tour to persuade their buddies to spend their money freely. Using their own Bonus money to finance the caravan, the group planned out a 6,000-mile itinerary with stops at all of the nation's Soldiers' Homes from Roseburg, Oregon, to Biloxi, Mississippi. As the group's leader explained it, they wanted to "encourage the spending of Bonus money to help business." Great War veterans required no such prodding.[34]

As soon as it was clear that the Bonus would be paid, veterans knew quite well where their money would go. A Legion poll released in January showed that 54 percent of the 40,000 veterans who responded would use at least part of their Bonus money to settle old accounts and debts. From these figures, the Legion estimated that $623.6 million of the Bonus payout—31 percent of the total—would go toward paying outstanding bills. Bon Carr, a reporter for the *Los Angeles Times*, elaborated on this issue in an article titled "Bonus Dreams," wryly commenting, "You may have noted that every doctor walks a little more briskly now." More than 25 percent of the respondents to the survey indicated that they would buy new clothes for their wives and children. An equal percentage would outfit themselves with a new suit, overcoat, or shoes. New automobiles and trucks were the choice for 10 percent more. Another 10 percent would build or purchase a new home; 19 percent would repair their existing homes. Carr reported that a Los Angeles veteran named Frank would put his Bonus toward a new, sturdier house than his current home. Frank explained, "Boy, that's all going as first payment on a decent shack made out of solid brick instead of lemon meringue." Veterans' plans—from the grandiose to the wistful—were as varied as the 3.5 million men owed the Bonus. Pete, a partner in a service station, had a "Santa Claus list": a new set of teeth for his wife, an encyclopedia for his son, membership in a beach club for his family, and a set of "rare cactus plants" for himself. One veteran on a bus told Carr he would set up an auto camp motel in Gila Bend, Arizona. Another said he would spend the money to return to France in an attempt to regain his "freshness of soul." He hoped that when he got to France, he could return to the old sense of self he had had when he was "young and alive and glad of it." In all, only 10 percent planned to save the money.[35]

On June 15, Bonus "baby bonds" worth $1.9 billion swiftly spread throughout the nation. Exultant veterans wasted no time in cashing their bonds. The average payment, $581, equaled nearly 30 percent of the mean household income of men in the World War veterans' age bracket. To destitute veterans, it was nothing short of a new lease on life. Between June 15 and June 20 alone, the Post Office reported that $524 million worth

U.S. Postal Assistant George F. White (2nd from R) posing with American World War I veterans while delivering government bonus bonds on his rural route in Norwood Park, Illinois, June 15, 1936. Hulton Archive, courtesy of Getty Images.

of baby bonds had been redeemed. By June 30, some $800 million had flowed into the economy thanks to Bonus payment, nearly 1 percent of the Gross National Product for the entire year. Correspondingly, the federal deficit for June was the largest ever in peacetime. By November, 1936, only 138,131 out of the 3.5 million Bonus certificates remained uncollected. Between June 15 and October 31, $1.3 billion entered into circulation through the payment of the Bonus. And the national economic data for 1936 suggest that veterans spent their money as they had been planning since January.[36]

While Bonus payment clearly changed the lot of veterans, it also made the summer and fall of 1936 the most prosperous period since 1929. In 1936, the measure of economic recovery was 2.5 times greater than the previous two years. Unemployment fell from 20.1 to 16.9 percent; the GNP rose at a then-record rate of 14.1 percent. Consumption rose by $6.2 billion, with the Bonus payments equal to 16 percent of the total. Veterans' plans to purchase clothing for themselves and their families came to fruition. The Federal Reserve Board Index of Department Store Sales shot upward. When seventy-six corporations released their earnings reports in the week before the election, there was a 47 percent increase over the 1935 third-quarter reports. Bonus payment operated as the most efficient and direct of any federal fiscal stimuli. It more quickly moved into the economy than works programs, went directly to beneficiaries, and did so without a permanent expansion of the bureaucracy. Moreover, the Bonus payments were, in part, discretionary income since they came in a large lump sum, whereas WPA wages and direct relief payments were at barely subsistence levels. The vibrancy of the 1936 economic recovery, then, can be traced almost exclusively to the Bonus payment, not the public works projects of the WPA or any other relief and recovery effort. Bonus supporters who had long argued for "pump priming" and national recovery through immediate payment had been right after all.[37]

By the time the election season kicked off in the late summer of 1936, the "second" New Deal legislation and payment of the Bonus had reconfigured the political landscape for FDR's reelection campaign. With the "second" New Deal, FDR helped transform the relationship between the federal government and American citizens. In the process, Roosevelt adopted a more antagonistic attitude toward the business community and the "economic royalists" who opposed him. The WPA initiated approximately $5 billion in public work projects that employed millions of Americans. The Wagner Act served as an organizational boon to labor unions, giving working people across the nation hope for better wages and working conditions. The Social Security Act established a system of old-age pensions, unemployment insurance, and disability coverage. FDR's "soak-the-rich" tax bill of 1935, whether one considers it merely a symbolic reform or a real progressive tax measure, mimicked the Share the Wealth Society's concern with the concentration of wealth and sought to recalibrate the tax structure. And, finally, Bonus payment caused a wave of economic recovery with its distribution after June 15.[38]

The landscape of veteran politics was likewise transformed. Veterans and their organizations responded to the administration's "second" New Deal legislative efforts, sharper anticapitalist rhetoric, and Bonus payment to bring them back into the fold. The CCC and the WPA absorbed a sizeable contingent of unemployed veterans. During 1935, the VA sent thirty veterans a day from their offices to either a WPA project or a VA hospital. By July 1936, 250,000 veterans had found employment in the WPA.

Moreover, the tone of FDR's 1936 campaign began to match the vitupera-tive anticapitalist rhetoric employed by veterans since the late 1920s. Most important, however, expeditious Bonus payment washed away most vet-erans' resentments toward the administration. In 1934 and 1935, the Bonus provided the ideological touchstone for the New Deal Dissidents and the impetus behind their impressive mobilization. This visceral manifestation of the struggle between Wall Street and Main Street that drew so many Americans into conflict with the administration found resolution with payment of the Bonus. Veterans no longer acted as a foundational bloc in the New Deal Dissident coalition.[39]

On the verge of the summer campaign, Legion Commander Murphy and VFW Commander Van Zandt confirmed that veterans' groups would no longer serve as sites of dissident mobilization. They each released pointed statements about the possible intrusion of politics into their orga-nizations during the 1936 campaign. In April, Murphy wrote a column that was distributed to the officers of all Legion posts. Murphy expected that Legionnaires, as good Americans, would be active in the upcoming elec-tion, which promised to be "the most bitterly fought in recent times." But he cautioned his fellow veterans to keep their organization out of partisan politics. Murphy wrote, "There is every reason why we should take part as individuals in the elections to come—there is every reason why we should guard jealously our traditional and constitutional pledge against political activities as an organization." Louis Johnson, who had helped tap Murphy for the commander spot, sent the clippings to Steve Early, who then for-warded them on to DNC chair Farley. Early explained to Farley, "We can thank Louis Johnson and Harold Phillips [the Legion's national publicity director, a fellow Democrat appointed by Murphy] for this message by the National Commander of the Legion. It is very much worthwhile noting." Farley replied, "It is really worthwhile." In June, VFW Commander Van Zandt followed suit. As the party conventions approached, Van Zandt mailed a sharply worded directive against partisan politics to every VFW post. He explained that "if a man wants to be a Democrat or a Republican outside of his VFW activities, that's alright [*sic*], but we're not going to tolerate any electioneering in our midst." Van Zandt announced that "no politics will be allowed in our ranks" and threatened VFW members who persisted with such activity with expulsion. He wrote, "If we find any of our men trying to promote either political party thru the organization, we will kick them out, that's all." In each case, Democratic officials viewed this as a positive development for the party, eliminating potential vehicles for mobilizing veterans still put out by the Roosevelt administration's policies. For administration officials, neutrality by the veterans' organizations was all they sought.[40]

Once the 1936 campaign season heated up, however, Democratic Party officials made sure that these positive developments with veterans continued. Republicans had created a Republican National Service League in 1924 to cultivate the veteran vote. Democrats had responded in kind in 1928. But, in July, with so much at stake with regard to veterans, Farley, the DNC chair, dedicated the party's resources to setting up a new Veterans' Advisory Committee (VAC), with Louis Johnson as chairman. Paul V. McNutt, a former Legion commander and governor of Indiana, and Paul C. Wolman, a former commander of the VFW and a member of the VFW's Bonus Cash Payment Campaign Committee, joined Johnson on the fourteen-person committee. The VAC's primary mission was to mobilize the veteran vote at the grassroots level. The committee set up efforts in every state under the direction of veteran chairmen approved by the state party chairmen. The veteran chairmen then reported directly to Johnson and Farley. In a letter to Steve Early describing the incipient political organization, Johnson explained the merit of the state-by-state structure. He wrote that "the efforts of these men properly directed will be the most valuable and lasting contribution to lining the veterans up for President Roosevelt." The goal was clear. According to Johnson, "There is just one yardstick in this whole matter . . . and that is the reelection of Roosevelt."[41]

Once the committee had a chance to choose state chairmen and establish the network, the Veterans Advisory Committee coordinated the national messages that the grassroots structures were empowered to convey. It created and released a series of publications promoting the president's reelection. In the most powerful of these, entitled "Veterans: 1932 versus 1936," the VAC juxtaposed images of the suffering of the Depression, including multiple photographs of the Bonus March and its rout, with images of veterans at CCC and WPA worksites. The cover featured a down-and-out veteran in 1932 sitting sullenly in his service cap. The 1936 veteran stood tall and erect as he used surveyor's equipment, presumably at some CCC or WPA site. A more incendiary juxtaposition—literally—showed first a photograph of an Army soldier setting fire to the Bonus marchers' dwellings, followed by an image of a veteran wielding an acetylene welder's torch on a government worksite in Virginia. The pamphlet ended with the question "Now . . . what do *you* think?"[42]

Cover image of the Democratic National Committee's Veterans' Advisory Committee 1936 campaign pamphlet, "Veterans: 1932 versus 1936." Courtesy of the Democratic National Committee and the Franklin D. Roosevelt Library.

In June, the Republican Party nominated two World War I veterans for the 1936 presidential ticket: the moderate Kansas governor Alf Landon at the top and the more conservative Colonel Frank Knox as his running mate. While there were certainly more important political reasons for the choice, Republicans undoubtedly hoped that Landon and Knox would appeal to veterans angered by Roosevelt's treatment of them in the Economy Act and by the two Bonus vetoes. The Republicans veterans' efforts included disparaging Roosevelt's military record and touting Landon's veteran status. Moreover, Republican National Committee's veteran speakers blasted Roosevelt on the Bonus vetoes and what they described as his antiveteran attitude.[43]

The Democratic Veterans Advisory Committee counterpunched—and hard. The VAC issued multiple pamphlets outlining Roosevelt's record of service as Assistant Secretary of the Navy during the Great War. More to the point, the VAC undercut Landon's appeal to veterans by innocently spelling out Landon's service record: fifty days of training in Virginia at the war's end. The VAC also mailed to the state chairmen another pamphlet, this one titled "Veterans Have Full Recognition Under the New Deal," and a lengthy speech written by Johnson to refute the Republican charges. The pamphlet listed sixteen of the New Deal's accomplishments for the nation as a whole, including the litany of New Deal relief and recovery programs—and the repeal of prohibition. Then, under the subheading "Recall the Veterans' Plight in 1932? Here's What the Roosevelt Administration Has Done for *You*," twelve more accomplishments just for veterans were laid out, with "Bonus enacted and promptly paid" at the top of the list. Johnson wrote the speech for the state veteran chairmen to use on local radio stations. "You are at liberty to use it in whole or in part, and under your own or any name you choose," Johnson advised. He suggested to the state chairmen that they would find all of the material they would need in the speech and the pamphlet. Indeed, the speech was replete with choice lines. One read, "Driven by desperation, the desperation of a poor loser, the Republican high command has been foolish enough to think that the veteran vote can be regimented for the Republican candidate . . . by attempting to build up the idea that President Roosevelt has been the enemy of all of the veterans." The speech ended with a point-by-point refutation of this idea—nearly verbatim from the circular produced by Johnson in January. Although he had already shown himself to be an effective partisan fighter, Johnson demonstrated considerable savvy in the politics of the radio era. "We would suggest that the small stations which will give you free time be not ignored—all of them have their 'listeners-in,'" the national VAC chairman explained.[44]

The publications and Johnson's efforts on behalf of the president ap-peared to have some positive impact and were appreciated by the White House. On August 19, Johnson wrote to Steve Early that "our organization is really working and ought to help." Early responded that he valued the former Legion commander's efforts and noted that Johnson's presentations of the "contrasts between the president's policy respecting veterans and that of the preceding Administration" were "excellent and intelligent." On Sep-tember 16, Johnson wrote Early again, exulting in the "almost unbelievable" declaration by Van Zandt at the VFW convention that the organization would "stay out of party politics." He enthused, "Things are breaking our way so nicely on the Veteran set-up that I am almost afraid to breathe." A week later, Johnson updated Early after the Legion convention in Cleveland and reported that the Legionnaires were "more than two to one for Roose-velt." Johnson added that "many left the Convention Thursday as crusaders for the president's reelection. We are over the big hurdle." Early concurred. His response outlined the veterans' situation as the administration viewed it in late September: "Frankly there has not been the slightest stir in the field of veterans' affairs, in so far as White House correspondence and other re-ports reveal. I am inclined to agree with you that the situation on the whole is encouraging and most promising with regard to veterans."[45]

In the home stretch of the election, the VAC reported weekly to the White House on the ground activities of its veterans' network and in-cluded reports of each state's veteran political climate. In Illinois, A. A. Sprague, the veteran state chairman, detailed the mobilization there for the veteran vote. He told the VAC that "during the closing week of the campaign, the United Democratic Servicemen will hold 9 more meetings for veterans." Sprague added, "There was a splendid turnout of ex-service-men last night in a parade tendered to President Roosevelt . . .[with] up-wards of 3,500 ex-servicemen wearing distinctive white helmets, each of which bore the name 'Roosevelt' across the front." In Washington, chair-man Walter Pollitz wired in, "Our organization is producing results. The rank and file of the veterans are anxious to wear our lapel pins and are untouched by the Republican Bonus talk." Veteran state chairman Earle W. Reynolds reported from Michigan that, "the first time in the history of the Democratic Party, real active work has been started in staunch Re-publican strongholds . . . really believe we will win." From Pennsylvania, a state that voted for Hoover in 1932, chairman Ellwood Baumann described a very positive veteran outlook. Bauman predicted, "I can now say that the veteran vote in Pennsylvania will be from 60 to 75% Democratic." In part, he based this conclusion on signed pledges to vote for FDR from 38,000 of the 52,000 veterans in Allegheny County. In what surely must be a co-incidence, no veteran grassroots reports came out of Maine—one of the two states Roosevelt would lose to Alf Landon in November. Regardless, this movement of veterans into the New Deal's camp was welcome news to the Democratic Party and to the administration. The mended rift be-tween FDR and veterans not only gave the president an advantage over his Republican opponent but also severely hampered the viability of the third-party movement that had seemed so portentous in 1935.[46]

In the summer of 1936, Father Coughlin, Reverend Gerald L. K. Smith, and Dr. Francis Townshend, an advocate of old-age pensions, banded together to form the Union Party. Between May and December 1935, Coughlin wavered in his criticism of the president. In December, however, Coughlin deemed the New Deal incompatible with the National Union of Social Justice's goals. Months later, he declared that the NUSJ would endorse candidates of any party with principles consistent with his own. Finally in May, Coughlin signaled that he would be starting the Union Party to challenge the president. On June 19, Representative William Lemke (Nonpartisan, ND) became the incipient party's standard-bearer. Lemke had earned a minor political reputation by sponsoring farm mort-gage relief bills passed by Congress in 1934 and 1935. In 1936, he joined with Senator Lynn Frazier (Nonpartisan, ND) to sponsor the Frazier-Lemke bill for farm mortgage relief utilizing currency expansion. When the administration's allies in Congress killed the bill, the furious Lemke decided to join forces with Coughlin, a vocal supporter of the measure, and run on the third-party ticket against FDR. Townshend and Smith fol-lowed Lemke's announcement with a declaration that they had begun a "loose working agreement" with the Coughlin-Lemke forces. Coughlin hit the airwaves that night with his official endorsement of Lemke.[47]

Coughlin, Smith, and Townshend attempted to rally their supporters around Lemke, but with diminishing enthusiasm and disappointing re-sults. Despite a platform dubbed "a marvel of inclusive appeal to every crackpot and malcontent in the land," there was literally no center holding the three factions together. Of the Union Party, historian Alan Brinkley has written that it was "diverse and shapeless" and a victim of "basic in-ternal weakness." To make matters worse, the rumpled and dry Lemke left much to be desired as a candidate. Even with the dwindling enthusiasm,

Father Charles E. Coughlin rallies followers in Detroit, 1935 or 1936. New York World-Telegram & Sun Collection, courtesy of the Library of Congress.

however, some believed that the Union Party, with Lemke's name on thirty-four state ballots, might have an impact on what most predicted to be a very tight election. The week of the election, *Time* wrote, "In a few close states in the West Mr. Lemke may take enough votes away from Franklin Roosevelt to give Alf Landon a chance to carry them." Coughlin confidently predicted that Lemke would get nine million votes. If not, Coughlin vowed to end his radio broadcasts forever.[48]

• • •

On November 3, 1936, FDR blasted his way to the most lopsided electoral victory since the one-party era of the 1820s. Vermont and Maine alone cast their electoral votes for Landon. Roosevelt won a staggering 60 percent of the popular vote for the largest winning margin in U.S. history. Democrats increased their already significant majorities in both houses of Congress. In the Senate, Democrats now held an astounding seventy-six of the ninety-six seats. FDR's coattails also extended down into the governors' races with Democrats taking twenty-six of the thirty-three gubernatorial elections. All conceded that it was an historic election. Jim Farley called it "probably the greatest vote of confidence" ever given to a sitting president. Political commentator Arthur Krock went further, calling Roosevelt's victory "the most overwhelming testimonial of approval ever received by a national candidate in the history of the nation." Democratic worries over Landon's appeal—exacerbated by the usually reliable *Literary Digest* polls indicating a Landon lead all the way until election day— and over the Union Party's potential for cutting into Roosevelt's vote total were washed away in joyful celebrations held throughout the country.[49]

Despite the backing of a coalition that claimed millions, if not tens of millions, of members, Lemke received only 850,000 votes nationally, fewer than 2 percent of the votes cast. Even in states where Lemke polled better than 2 percent, such as North Dakota (13.41%), Minnesota (6.58%), Massachusetts (6.45%), Rhode Island (6.29%), Oregon (5.27%), and Wisconsin (4.79%), his votes did not come close to tilting the balloting to Alf Landon. The absence of Huey Long from the insurgency, Roosevelt's "turn to the left" in 1935 and 1936, the inadequacies of William Lemke as a candidate, and the poorly matched egomaniacs who served as the party's triumvirate all played a part in the Union Party's woeful electoral results. Many observers believed that the incompatible goals and personalities of the three principals undermined the party's ability to affect the election. But this would have been equally true in April or May of 1935. The key differences between the movement's vitality in 1935 and its lackluster campaign in 1936 was that there was neither a galvanizing issue like the Bonus nor a broad level of veteran participation in the dissident coalition. The efforts of the Roosevelt administration and the Democratic Party had denied the Union Party both the Bonus as a coalition-building issue and the backbone of veteran political activism that had made the New Deal Dissidents such a potent force in 1935. After the election, Coughlin declared that he would retire from political life. Though he would shortly change his mind, he never again reached the dizzying heights attained during the

Bonus battle of the spring of 1935. The New Deal Dissident movement rose and fell, its fortunes synchronized with the rhythms of veteran politics.[50]

If the Republican Party hoped to siphon off veterans disaffected by the New Deal by featuring two World War I veterans on the ticket, the gambit failed. By nominating the moderate Landon—who made increasingly conservative speeches as the election wore on—and the true conservative Knox, Republicans showed that they misunderstood the ideological positions that had sparked veteran political activism against the New Deal. For example, in May 1936, the *National Tribune*, the veteran newspaper with long ties to the party of Lincoln, publicly endorsed Senator Fred Steiwer of Oregon, a Bonus leader and a progressive, for the Republican presidential nomination. When the Landon-Knox ticket emerged from the party's convention in June, the editorial board of the *National Tribune* declined to support any candidate, claiming neutrality, as did many other Republican progressive outlets. The silence was very much appreciated by Democratic stalwarts. Louis Johnson, the successful chairman of the DNC's Veterans' Advisory Committee, telegrammed the *Tribune*'s editor after the 1936 electoral landslide, thanking him for the paper's "fair and impartial attitude." The Republican Party could not translate years of veteran political activism and two FDR Bonus vetoes into broad support for an all-veteran presidential ticket because veterans' critique of the New Deal's policies had been from the left, not the right.[51]

The election of 1936 resulted in the resounding political triumph of the New Deal. On many fronts and in many different ways, FDR forged a new political coalition during the election that would dominate national politics for decades to come. But the victory was a triumph in the arena of veteran politics as much as in any other. With the resolution of the Bonus, no other single issue existed that could so effectively mobilize and galvanize the remaining New Deal Dissidents into a focused and meaningful political coalition. Moreover, with the implementation of the "second" New Deal and the changed tone of the Roosevelt presidency, veterans' perceptions of FDR as an adversary and a tool of Wall Street lost hold. Even so, the Roosevelt administration's political initiatives left nothing to chance by actively courting disaffected veterans. The administration's political countermobilization of the veteran organizations utilized artful behind-the-scenes maneuvering to help turn them into political neutrals rather than potent opponents. If veterans could not be turned into ardent New Deal supporters, at the very least their voices, so powerful in American political culture, would no longer be raised in opposition to the president.[52]

The Bonus, so fiercely fought by FDR from 1932 to 1935, became the source of the strongest period of economic recovery for veterans and nonveterans alike just in time for the 1936 election. Indeed, the Bonus-driven economic boom may very well have been the election's deciding factor.[53] The veteran organizations and the New Deal Dissidents had been right after all. The immediate and widespread fiscal stimulus of the Bonus succeeded where the early New Deal recovery efforts had failed. Unfortunately for Roosevelt, this was a lesson ignored until the sharp contraction of the "Roosevelt Recession" during 1937 and 1938. Only then would FDR turn unflinchingly to deficit spending as a method for economic stimulation. And only then would the nation move permanently toward full recovery. Still, veteran politics had cast a long shadow over the New Deal era. And that shadow would be remembered when the nation became engulfed in a second world war and sought to define postwar policies for sixteen million new veterans.[54]

Conclusion
GI Bill Legacies

The long hard fight of the veterans of World War I for decent
treatment has formed the foundation of this piece of veterans'
legislation.
—Representative Chet Holifield (D, CA) on the GI Bill, May 16, 1944

On June 22, 1944, World War II servicemen and servicewomen
learned that their military duty would translate into social and economic
benefits of unparalleled proportions. Thanks to the Servicemen's Readjustment Act, then more popularly known as the GI Bill of Rights, approximately sixteen million veterans gained access to federally funded vocational training and education benefits; generous unemployment stipends;
and low-interest home, farm, and business loans. The origins of the GI
Bill have been traced to the concerns over the social and economic reintegration of veterans and the political consequences if that reintegration
failed. To be sure, the fear of rampant postwar unemployment and the
potential for attendant political unrest, a fear grounded in the historical
experience of the Bonus March, played a major role in the origins of the
legislation. But, as the preceding chapters demonstrate, the Bonus March
was just one expression of veterans' political activism during the 1930s.
Indeed, by 1944, previous debates over veterans' issues, the interorganiza-
tional dynamics between the American Legion and the VFW that gave life
to those debates, and elected officials' concerns over the "soldiers' vote" all
continued to shape the political terrain as they had during the New Deal
era. Unlike the post–World War I period, however, veteran lobbyists now
found Congress and the Roosevelt administration equally committed to
liberal veterans' welfare legislation. With the GI Bill's passage, the federal

government created the most expansive system of social provisioning in the history of the country. By extension, then, the explosive veteran politics of the New Deal period also played a hand in shaping the social, economic, and political contours of the post–World War II era.[1]

As early as 1942, the Roosevelt administration explored the issue of veteran benefits for the World War II cohort. A number of overlapping federal agencies and special commissions investigated methods of offering veteran benefits as one component of larger postwar planning efforts. Early discussions for postwar preparations originated in the National Resources Planning Board (NRPB). The NRPB urged that men and women who had participated in both the military and the economic mobilization be granted educational and vocational training as part of a coordinated effort aimed at expanding social welfare provisioning for the entire citizenry. Another planning committee working under the auspices of the NRPB, the Conference on Postwar Readjustments of Civilian and Military Personnel (also known as the Postwar Manpower Conference, or PMC) investigated historical precedents for veterans' educational benefits at the state and national levels. After studying Wisconsin's Educational Bonus Law of 1919 and Canadian veterans' benefits, the Conference set its sights beyond mere monetary compensation and instead focused on educational and vocational training for veterans. In a July 28, 1943, fireside chat, President Franklin D. Roosevelt outlined a skeletal plan for veterans based on the PMC recommendations. The president prodded Congress to prepare the necessary legislation on several key veterans' issues: mustering-out pay; medical care; and education, unemployment, and pension benefits. FDR used tropes reminiscent of the conversation around the Bonus March in pleading that soldiers "must not be demobilized into an environment of inflation and unemployment, to a place on a bread line, or on a corner selling apples."[2]

In late 1943, the scuttling of the progressive-minded NRPB at the hands of a conservative Congress undermined the political viability of the PMC and NRPB reports. However, another special committee operating under the auspices of the Navy and War Departments, the Armed Forces Committee on Postwar Educational Opportunities for Service Personnel, had taken also up the issue. Named the Osborn Committee after its chairman, Brigadier General Frederick H. Osborn, the committee advanced legislative proposals that featured a provision for one year of educational or vocational training for veterans who had served more than six months in the armed forces, with only a limited number of exceptionally talented ex-service personnel qualifying for extended education benefits. These Osborn Committee recommendations became the groundwork for the administration's legislative submissions to Congress.[3]

On October 27, 1943, President Roosevelt lauded the Osborn Committee's recommendations and announced the administration's legislative proposals for returning veterans. He urged Congress to act promptly on the educational benefits bill, as well as the other veteran-related proposals on a "mustering-out" pay and unemployment benefits. The president's request found willing congressional participants. In fact, when the administration offered its proposals, twenty-six other veterans' bills were already circulating in various congressional committees. Such legislation was clearly popular among the electorate, as polling showed 90 percent of Americans in favor of government-financed educational benefits for returning veterans and 70 percent willing to pay higher taxes to pay for veterans' benefits. By the end of 1943, as an election year approached, 243 veterans' bills clogged the congressional docket. Despite the broad support, however, the success or failure of specific veterans' bills once again hinged on the positions and actions of the major veteran organizations. And, as during the period from 1929 to 1936, the organizational competition between the VFW and the Legion played a significant part in the final shape and outcome of World War II veterans' legislation.[4]

World War II sent a shock wave through the veterans' lobby. Just days before the attack on Pearl Harbor that drew the United States into the war, the Senate heard from the American Legion, the VFW, and DAV on two bills pending before the Finance Committee. One would grant pensions to the widows and children of all World War I veterans regardless of the causes of the former doughboy's death. The other granted $40-a-month pensions to all but the wealthiest veterans over the age of sixty-five. Once again tying veterans to the New Deal Dissidents, the *New York Times* scornfully described the proposed legislation as "a universal Townshend plan for veterans and their relatives." The bills' initial outlays, if passed, were estimated at $7 million annually, but the pension plans together might total $20 billion and would range out to the 2000 fiscal year. After U.S. entry into World War II, however, veterans' organizations' efforts on behalf of the Great War cohort became eclipsed by the enormous war mobilization and the waging of another battle: that over World War II soldiers' membership.[5]

In 1942, the American Legion took up the question of membership for World War II veterans. The Legion encountered two major problems when it came to the recruitment of new members. First, the organization's charter clearly stated that it was a Great War veterans' organization only. Second, it opened its doors only to honorably discharged veterans. Even if the Legion changed its charter to welcome World War II veterans, the uncertain length of the war for current soldiers would effectively delay recruiting until the war's end. At first, Legionnaires expressed ambivalence over the issue. While many posts clamored to admit new veterans, others opposed being taken over by a younger generation after all of the hard work that had been done already by the former doughboys. Different ages, needs, and bureaucratic struggles would lead to strife among members, opponents argued. And, besides, they added, the new generation would want its own organization, just as Legionnaires had in 1919. (As late as February 1944, an officer's poll in the South Pacific found seven hundred enlisted men nearly evenly split, 53–47, on the question "Do you approve of the American Legion's absorbing the veterans of this war?") A New Englander on the National Executive Committee was unmoved by the calls for new members, remaining "definitely opposed to absorbing the men engaged in the present war." In May, the Legion decided to submit the matter to the membership for consideration at the next convention. At the convention in September, delegates opted to amend the Legion's constitution and charter to accept World War II veterans, but only after an honorable discharge. Legion champions in Congress quickly pushed through the necessary legislation. On October 29, 1942, FDR signed Public Law 767 amending the Legion charter's wording to include the new group of honorably discharged veterans.[6]

In 1943, the Legion moved to usher new veterans into the organization. In May, Legion leaders kicked off a recruitment drive, announcing that they hoped for eight or nine million new members. The National Executive Committee laid out a plan for "actively and immediately identifying ourselves with the veterans of this war." In more crass terms, the World War II liaison committee urged that Great War veterans "sell the Legion" to the new cohort of World War II veterans. They hoped that Legion activities developed during the 1920s and 1930s such as junior baseball, boys' state encampments, and scholarship contests had given the younger men a sense of Legionnaires' traditions, patriotism, and service. The plan included the mobilization of the entire Legion to give speeches, radio broadcasts, entertainments, and "send-off parties" for the new generation of soldiers. Leaders urged the doughboy generation to treat the new men "not as youngsters but as comrades in arms." By the summer of 1943, the Legion set a new record of 1,136,290 members. Yet, especially in view of the number of World War II veterans, this number was not dramatically higher than the 1931 total of 1,053, 909.[7]

At the 1943 convention, in Omaha, the Legion's push for new members and, not coincidentally, for veterans' legislation to attract the new cohort took on greater urgency. Only 42,000 World War II veterans had been added to the rolls since the last convention. To address this shortcoming, Legionnaires elected Warren H. Atherton to the commandership on the basis of his record of enthusiastic recruiting in California. This went hand in hand with other efforts, including a $250,000 appropriation for "an intelligent, aggressive campaign to inform eligible veterans of the advantages offered by the American Legion" and an authorization for the National Executive Committee to establish a special committee to develop new veterans' welfare legislation. A reporter for *Time* explained the goal: "to go hot and heavy after the veterans of World War II." But he also located the impetus for the membership drive in the competition between veteran organizations, adding that the Legion "is acutely worried by the gains in membership which have been made by its hated rival, the Veterans of Foreign Wars."[8]

As described by *Time*, the VFW had made impressive strides in organizing new recruits during the war. Unhampered by any charter restrictions on potential members and not having to wait until soldiers were discharged, the VFW saw its rosters grow dramatically, often in newly created overseas posts. One hundred fifty thousand soldiers who were serving (or who had served) overseas had joined the VFW, resulting in a 75 percent increase in enrollment from 1941's 200,000 members. Once again *Time* captured the stakes of the membership competition between the Legion and the VFW, declaring it the "a battle for more political power than any organization has wielded in U.S. history." With the millions of veterans from World War II, the author contended that "[the organizations] might dominate U.S. politics for decades." The VFW, he concluded, was "sitting pretty."[9]

At the 1943 VFW encampment, in New York City, the topics of new members and new veterans' legislation also dominated the proceedings. VFW leaders proudly touted the organization's impressive membership gains. To help pad their numbers, the delegates created an extension department to systematize the sending of invitations and blank membership cards to men overseas. The delegates also took up the issues of postwar veteran welfare policies, dedicating an entire session to the matter highlighted by an address by VA Director Frank T. Hines. Commander Robert T. Merrill introduced the VFW's program by telling the 2,500 delegates that FDR's plans as laid out in his summer fireside chat were not sufficiently comprehensive. In fact, an encampment resolution declared that the federal government was "guilty of gross negligence in its failure to increase the compensation and pension awards of disabled veterans and their dependents in relation to the greatly increased costs of living since Dec. 7, 1941." The VFW's program, in contrast, included six months' pay continuance after discharge; educational aid to those whose schooling had been interrupted; pension and adjusted compensation; extended veterans preference; widow and orphan pensions; and open hospitalization. Commander Merrill also argued that employment was a key issue, claiming that there was "too much talk and not enough action on the idea of making sure our men in service will have jobs waiting for them after the war." Merrill charged government, business, and organized labor with devising "a job security program which will definitely assure those in the armed forces that they won't have to stand in line for handouts in another depression." The VFW leadership presented the program to Roosevelt and then watched as the president's messages to Congress in October and November failed to equal their expectations.[10]

On December 21, 1943, the VFW changed tactics and pitched to the House Military Affairs Committee a $15 billion Bonus as an alternative to a $300 mustering-out payment for discharged soldiers under deliberation in Congress at Roosevelt's behest. The VFW's proposal touted by its legislative chairman, Omar Ketchum, nearly replicated the original Bonus: $1 a day for stateside veterans (maximum $800) and $1.50 a day for overseas veterans (maximum $1,200). *New York Times* reporter John D. Morris not so subtly criticized the proposal: "The beginnings of another bonus movement, whose first World War counterpart did not get under way until two years after the armistice of 1918, was thus laid even before peace was in sight." On January 12, 1944, Ketchum testified before the Committee that linking demobilization pay to adjusted compensation would "save double administrative costs" since a Bonus was sure to be brought up again at war's end. The VFW found congressional support from William Lemke (R, ND), the former Union Party presidential candidate, who led an ad hoc caucus on "Immediate and Adequate Mustering Out Pay." The DAV supported the VFW plan, but Legion leaders quickly refused to support the Bonus proposal and urged Congress to pass the mustering plan as suggested by the Roosevelt administration. The Legion had very good reasons to oppose the linking of a Bonus with the mustering-out payment. Legion leaders wanted a small muster-out sum so that they could continue to put together an expansive benefits package. A Bonus would be potentially fatal to what a special Legion committee in Washington was planning.[11]

While the VFW pushed its Bonus plan, the Legion set out to pass its own comprehensive veterans' benefits package. Between December 15, 1943, and January 6, 1944, a special Legion committee chaired by John Stelle, the former governor of Illinois, and dominated by Harry Colmery, former Legion national commander, drafted its own legislation. The 1943 national convention had authorized the committee; a November National Executive Committee meeting had chosen the personnel and set it in motion. The Legion bill relied on the foundations of proposals circulated throughout 1942–1943, but the Legion's proposal packaged all of the administration's veterans' provisions into one omnibus bill. It also broadened the provisioning on the length of educational benefits for all, regardless of "worthiness," and shortened the required length of service for access to benefits from six months to ninety days. Moreover, the Legion proposal made it clear that the benefits would be administered through the Veterans' Administration rather than by multiple federal agencies, clearing up a source of ambiguity in (and veterans' hostility to) the administration's proposals. At the start of the 1944 congressional session, J. Bennett "Champ" Clark, the Democratic senator from Missouri and a Legion founding member, introduced the bill in the Senate. In the House, the powerful chairman of the World War Veterans' Legislation Committee, John E. Rankin (D, MS), shepherded legislation based on the Legion's proposals.[12]

Public relations efforts sponsored by the American Legion quickly generated wide support for the measure. A Legion publicity officer felicitously dubbed the legislation the "GI Bill of Rights," a label that stuck nearly instantaneously. The Hearst newspaper chain threw its considerable weight behind the bill and even loaned out the talents of two writers to assist the drive. The Legion lobbied Congress intensively for the measure, now combining official and back-channel lobbying with the types of public opinion appeals employed by the VFW during the Bonus struggle. As in the past, the Legion trotted out officials before the Senate Finance Committee to propound the bill's merits. Commander Warren Atherton declared, "I am elated that more preparation is being made today for World War II veterans than was made in 1917–18 for World War I veterans." The

tried-and-true Legion method of direct constituent contact with legislators—"the barrage"—was again an important lobbying tactic. The national
organization's network of grassroots political activists, however, employed
a wider range of tactics aimed at gaining public approval for the GI Bill,
including appearances by post-level officials on local radio shows and a
massive petition-gathering drive. On February 12, for example, the Legion
sent out a letter accompanied by an audio recording of a one-minute announcement on the GI Bill that post commanders were to take to their
local radio stations for airing. Legion leaders also sent movie trailers touting the bill to lower-level officials for use by local theaters, bypassing the
Hollywood distribution chain. Through these tactics, the Legion raised
public awareness of the bill and kept the pressure on Congress.[13]

In February 1944, despite the Legion's publicity blitz, deep and potentially fatal cracks over the GI Bill appeared in the U.S. veterans' lobby.
On February 3, the VFW's Bonus proposal lost out to the administration's mustering-out bill, thanks in no small part to the Legion's behind-
the-scenes lobbying. As a result, on February 16, leaders from the VFW,
DAV, and two other minor organizations drafted a letter to Champ Clark,
chairman of the Veterans' subcommittee of the Senate Finance Committee, expressing concerns that the GI Bill was being hastily and danger-
ously pushed through Congress. The real fear, as these leaders saw it,
was that the costly benefits, especially the education provisions, might
be so expensive that they would "jeopardize the entire structure of veteran benefits and provoke another Economy Act." The next day, one of
the letter's signatories, Omar Ketchum, the VFW's legislative chairman,
wired all national and departmental officers an acerbic message on the
GI Bill. Ketchum opened the message, "A new high in a 'grab' for prestige was recently reached by a large veteran organization when it came up
with the so-called 'GI Bill of Rights' and is now attempting to stampede
the Congress into its immediate enactment." He objected to the omnibus
strategy and the speed with which the wide-ranging bill was being moved
through Congress. Ketchum blamed this on the Legion's enormous desire
to get credit for the measure with World War II veterans. The VFW lobbyist complained that "'this GI Bill of Rights' was accompanied by a blare
of trumpets; rolling of drums; and steam roller pressure to grab the spotlight and sweep aside all competition. . . . Unless they [Legion leaders]
hurry, other points may become law or policy before they can take credit."
Ketchum ended by urging VFW members to restrain from supporting the
measure.[14]

Warren Atherton, national commander of the American Legion, gives petitions
in favor of the GI Bill to congressional supporters on the Capitol steps, 1944.
Courtesy of the American Legion.

In March, the same dissenting veteran organizations proposed another
even larger Bonus alternative for World War II veterans in place of the
omnibus GI Bill. This Bonus would distribute $4 a day to overseas soldiers
and $3 to those in home theater operations and would range up to $4500
per soldier in total. Payment of the proposed "Veterans' Adjusted Service
Pay Act of 1944" would be in the form of nonnegotiable tax-free bonds.

According to the joint statement, the new Bonus was a replica of the old one: "The purpose of the bill is to adjust, in a measure, the differences in pay of those serving in the armed forces and civilians employed in war industry." Nine members of Congress jointly introduced a bill on this basis. A writer for *Time* was staggered by the audacity of the proposal, writing that, when alerted to the proposal's features and costs, "sober citizens blinked as if they had been slugged." Legion lobbyists and Senator Clark worried, too. A divided veterans' lobby might jeopardize the GI Bill just as it had during the Bonus battle. Legionnaire Stelle sent back a mixed message to the Legion legislative committee. On the one hand, he wrote, "This letter can't beat the GI Bill." But he cautioned, "Senator Clark asked me to get those other organizations off his neck, if we can. They offer a wonderful excuse for some members of Congress to oppose the bill."[15]

On February 22, a special meeting of Legion and VFW officials at the Statler Hotel in Washington, DC, one reminiscent of the November, 1935, summit over Bonus legislation, persuaded the VFW leaders to join the Legion in support of the GI Bill. Representative Ernest McFarland (D, AZ), a long-term Legionnaire, and Paul Wolman, past VFW commander, proved instrumental to the settlement. David Camelon, a Hearst reporter who was aiding the Legion's publicity efforts, used his position as a quasi neutral (he belonged to neither organization) to arrange the meeting between the leaders. Camelon argued to Legionnaires that "I was sure that the VFW leaders really wanted to share the credit. . . . In his internal memo, VFW legislative director Ketchum had dwelt upon 'prestige,' 'credit,' and 'the spotlight.'" To assuage the VFW conferees, the Legion delegation offered to amend the GI Bill to include some specific VFW proposals on funding for hospitalizations. More than likely, this very negligible face saving accommodation worked because VFW leaders saw the legislative writing on the wall. Much as in the last phases of the Bonus struggle, they now felt compelled to join with the Legion for fear that they would get no credit for passing a very popular measure if the Legion's bill carried the day. Worse still, in the event of the bill's demise, they would get blamed for its derailment.[16]

The National Publicity Division of the Legion issued a press statement extolling the repaired rupture between the two organizations as removing the last hurdle to legislative approval of the GI Bill. Legion legislative director Francis M. Sullivan proclaimed that the "joining of forces by the American Legion and the VFW representing as they do the two major veterans' organizations, behind the omnibus bill increases the prospects of the early passage of this measure." The VFW's Wolman declared, "I think we made history here. The combined efforts of the two organizations make it certain that ample and adequate care shall be available for our boys when they come home." The first draft of the news release included language on how the VFW's inclusions had led to some revisions of the bill. But all wording that suggested that the bill was a collaborative effort, rather than a Legion bill that the VFW had just signed onto, was struck from the final version of the statement. So, too, were comments by Legionnaire Stelle, chair of the GI Bill drafting committee, expressing these generous sentiments: "There is ample credit for all of us if we are seeking credit. We welcome the participation of the VFW."[17]

While the Legion tried to hoard the credit, only the VFW of all the dissenting veterans' groups was brought into the partnership. Ketchum testified in both the House and the Senate that the VFW endorsed the amended GI Bill. The Disabled American Veterans national organization, however, opposed the measure up through its passage. Millard Rice, the DAV legislative chairman, continued to argue that the bureaucratic strain of such an ambitious program for the able-bodied would lead to the suffering of disabled veterans and that the financial strain would lead to another Economy Act. In a letter to a Senate Finance Chair Walter F. George (D, GA), Rice called the measure an "ominous" bill. With the Legion and the VFW in agreement, however, Congress had all the evidence it needed that the two largest veteran organizations—the foundations of the veterans' lobby—now supported the legislation.[18]

On March 24, 1944, the Senate voted unanimously in favor of the Legion's bill, a bill sponsored by eighty-one members of the Senate. In the House, however, Rankin's committee bogged down, in no small measure because of the chairman himself. Rankin viewed the educational features with skepticism, believing that only a small percentage of already privileged veterans would take advantage of them. Moreover, he treated the unemployment features with outright disdain. An ardent white supremacist, Rankin feared the impact of the unemployment provisions on the work habits of the African Americans in his state and region. African Americans would not quickly rejoin the work force, he argued, if they were being paid generous unemployment benefits. Rankin complained further that it would "spoil" them. Once a bill modified to meet many of Rankin's objections to the unemployment and education features emerged from the committee, the resulting House version of the Bill passed unanimously, too.[19]

Although early deliberations over veterans' welfare were folded into the workings of New Deal planning agencies, liberal ideas about social provisioning did not generate the momentum for the GI Bill. More traditional notions of patriotism and of citizenship based on military service gave the legislation its cultural and political resonance. In the congressional and public debates, however, the historically grounded fears over veterans' unemployment and the militancy of veteran politics were constants in the rhetoric supporting the bill. Both the Bonus March and the dangerous association of veterans with the radical New Deal Dissidents that had threatened dictatorship in 1935 seasoned the discussion. Representative Ernest W. McFarland commented, "It is our belief that we should take care of our veterans when they come home, not ten years after the war. The stark tragedy of Anacostia Flats must not be relived—we must face this problem today." Representative Samuel A. Weiss (D, PA) bellowed in congressional debate, "Lest we forget, our heroes and starving veterans of World War . . . . were run out of the national Capital at the point of bayonets and with tear gas when they came to fight for their rights—simple rights—to work and earn a livelihood in a democracy." Legion commander Atherton warned in a radio address that veterans "will be a potent force for good or evil in the years to come. . . . They can restore our democracy or scrap it." None other than Eleanor Roosevelt, who had expressed strong concerns over the veterans' lobby in 1935, cautioned that veterans might be "a dangerous pressure group in our midst" and that the federal government should "adjust our economic system so that opportunity is open to them, or we may reap the whirlwind." Representative Maury Maverick (D, TX), a friend to veterans and one himself, cautioned that if World War II veterans returned to conditions as Great War veterans had, the United States would this time certainly face "a dictatorship."[20]

As pervasive in the public debates was the sentiment that the federal policies for Great War veterans had simply been wrong, requiring years of veteran activism to overturn them. To those who expressed this, the GI Bill would be an offering of atonement. Representative Thomas J. Lane (D, MA) explained, "We have the opportunity to make up for past mistakes." Pat Kearney, a past VFW commander and now a congressman from New York, added that the GI Bill "provides assurances that the ghastly mistakes in the treatment of veterans that marked the last war will not be repeated." Representative Thomas D'Alesandro, Jr., commented that "the bill will prevent a repetition of the tragic mistakes under which World War I veterans suffered and will guarantee just treatment to our veterans."

Representative Weiss made it simple: "Mr. Speaker, my pledge to GI Joe is: History shall not repeat itself."[21]

Even though veterans' legislation enjoyed near-universal approval, large discrepancies existed between the House and Senate versions of the GI Bill. In the House-Senate Conference, the unemployment and education benefits came under renewed attack by Rankin. The conference stood deadlocked, and it appeared that the Senate version was doomed. Only a dramatic last-minute intervention by a previously absent conferee, Representative John S. Gibson (D, GA), broke the deadlock and allowed the GI Bill to emerge in a form very close to the Senate version. Once agreed upon, the conference version easily passed both houses on June 13 and became law on June 22, 1944, in a celebratory White House signing. Flanked by members of Congress, senators, and leaders of both the Legion and the VFW, Roosevelt proclaimed that the bill gave "emphatic notice to the men and women in our armed forces that the American people do not intend to let them down." At the recommendation of his adviser, Samuel Rosenman, he attempted to wrest some of the political credit for what was increasingly seen as a Legion initiative. FDR noted in his first sentence that the bill "substantially carries out most of the recommendations made by me in a speech on July 28, 1943, and more specifically in messages to Congress dated October 27, 1943, and November 23, 1943."[22]

Regardless of who claimed the credit, the GI Bill was landmark legislation. In its final form, the law offered exceptionally generous benefits to all veterans other than those dishonorably discharged. Veterans were eligible for low-interest home, farm, and business loans. They could receive unemployment pay of $20 a week for up to fifty-two weeks. For education and vocational training, military personnel who had begun their service before the age of twenty-five and who had served for at least ninety days would receive one year of benefits. For each year of service, the government would pay for an additional year of education, up to four years total. Moreover, veterans pursuing education and training would receive cash stipends of $50 a month for single veterans, $75 for those who were married. The bill's administration coupled federal enrollment, certification, and funding with a decentralized local management that channeled veterans to approved programs and distributed loan money. To those who had witnessed the convergence of veterans with the New Deal Dissident movement in 1935, there would be one final but unspoken irony in these GI Bill's provisions: the material benefits conferred by the GI Bill for farm

Franklin D. Roosevelt signs the Servicemen's Readjustment Act, popularly known as the GI Bill, in front of congressional and veteran organization sponsors, June 22, 1944. Courtesy of the Franklin D. Roosevelt Library.

and home ownership and education matched nearly exactly those found in Huey Long's Share Our Wealth program.[23]

The bill had a powerful impact on the lives of veterans and on the postwar United States. Overall, 51 percent of veterans used the educational and vocational benefits. Veterans poured into the nation's colleges and universities. By 1947, veterans accounted for 49 percent of college enrollments. Vocational training was an equally important form of social provision. Indeed, some 5.6 million veterans used vocational training, while only 2.2 million veterans attended colleges and universities. Fourteen percent of veterans received unemployment benefits. Some 29 percent of veterans took out low-interest home, farm, and business loans. In 1947 alone, for example, the Veterans' Administration approved 640,298 loans.[24]

This staggering level of federal funding in housing and education provided the foundations for the social and economic transformations of the postwar United States. VA home mortgages lay at the heart of the housing expansion and the suburbanization processes of those years. Higher education and vocational training for those who would not have had previous access to such socioeconomic tools provided the basis for an expanding middle class and for postwar economic prosperity. Moreover, the success and popularity of the federal program for veterans helped maintain the postwar political consensus on the benefits of an activist federal government. A recent study suggests that once again a federal veterans' policy—the GI Bill—helped create the activist citizens of the post–World War II period. Critics correctly argue, however, that the GI Bill merely perpetuated—or, worse, extended—existing class, race, and gender cleavages in U.S. society. Those who have investigated the impact of the bill's reliance on local administration consistently have found that women, African Americans, and homosexual veterans suffered discrimination and unequal access to GI Bill benefits. Local administration of VA home loans also accelerated and consolidated strict residential segregation across the country. And yet, despite these significant—arguably tragic—shortcomings, the GI Bill remains one of the most successful and popular federal programs in the nation's history.[25]

If the GI Bill helped maintain the New Deal political consensus into the post–World War II period, it also paid short-term political dividends for Roosevelt. At the bill's signing, Roosevelt's uncertain fourth term election bid loomed. In May 1944, George Gallup, the director of the American Institute of Public Opinion, penned an article calling the potential presidential matchup between FDR and Thomas E. Dewey, the Republican governor of New York, "evenly matched." While the "fourth-term issue" and population shifts complicated the conventional political wisdom concerning Roosevelt's wartime reelection campaign, Gallup paid particular attention to the potential importance of the soldier vote in deciding the outcome. Even on the eve of the 1944 election, Arthur Krock of the *New York Times* considered the soldier vote critical to determining the winner. In sixteen battleground states, the estimated number of ballots to be cast by soldiers exceeded the very tight victory margin of FDR over the Republican nominee, Wendell L. Willkie, in the 1940 election. These sixteen states had a whopping 235 out of 531 electoral votes. The soldier vote could turn the election.[26]

Both the Republican and the Democratic tickets tried to sway the soldier vote using the GI Bill and FDR's past record on veterans' issues. At the VFW annual convention, in Chicago, Senator Harry Truman (D, MO), the Democratic vice presidential candidate, hailed the GI Bill as a "rather complete statement of what the country thinks the veteran is entitled to." Truman, a VFW member since the Great War, then told the delegates that "the veteran, who is going to be the most potent political factor in the country, must assume responsibility toward the Government as the Government has assumed responsibility toward him." On September 18, both vice presidential candidates, Governor John Bricker, a Republican from Ohio, and Truman, delivered addresses to the Legion national convention. Bricker ripped Roosevelt for his 1933 Legion speech denying veterans a special status of citizenship. He did, however, give his support to the GI Bill as a "good beginning." Truman concurred, devoting two-thirds of his address to trumpeting the virtues of the GI Bill and the president's support of the measure. On October 10, Bricker once again assailed the administration over its veterans' policies, proclaiming that FDR exhibited "a violent antagonism towards veterans' legislation." Bricker began with the Economy Act and moved through the New Deal Bonus vetoes, complaining about "the paradox" of Roosevelt's tight-fisted attitude toward veterans when he was "the most prolific spender in the world." Bricker conceded that there were a few "minor" exceptions, but "the overall picture of his great treatment of the men who fought our battles is not one of which this nation can be proud." This attack, however, was a dubious one, even by the loose standards of American presidential campaigns. If Republicans failed to nail down Roosevelt as an enemy of the veteran when he *had* vetoed veterans' legislation, this tactic would clearly be a tough sell in 1944, when Roosevelt initiated, supported, and signed the expansive veterans' benefit package.[27]

In the closest vote of his four campaigns, Roosevelt carried the 1944 election over Thomas Dewey. The evidence on the soldiers' vote, possible to glean only thanks to special wartime federal soldiers' ballots, suggests that it aided in Roosevelt's victory. On the day after the election, the *New York Times* reported that "the support of the men and women in the armed forces would be a strong factor in building up the [president's] final majority." In New York City's separate tabulation, GI ballots came in at 72 percent for FDR, 12 percent higher than the civilian vote. (New York state received 420,000 soldiers' ballots.) In Philadelphia, GIs' ballots supported Roosevelt by a two-to-one margin. In Oklahoma, FDR received 65.6 percent of the soldier vote but only 59 percent of the total vote. In December, the *New York Times* investigated the soldier vote from more than thirty states. More than 4.4 million soldiers voted in the election, a much higher figure than anticipated. In the seven states where separate tallies where kept for the soldier vote (Arkansas, Colorado, Maryland, New Jersey, Oklahoma, Pennsylvania, and Rhode Island), they "confirmed indications immediately after the election that President Roosevelt was a stronger favorite of the military than the civilian voters." The margin for FDR was 51.5 percent in the civilian population and 59.3 percent among soldiers. This difference actually led Dewey to lose the state of New Jersey and its electoral votes.[28]

While the GI Bill helped FDR in 1944, it entrenched the VFW and the Legion as the twin pillars of the American veterans' lobby for decades to come. Both emerged from the war more powerful than at any other time in their history by absorbing the new cohort of World War II veterans. As early as May 1944, the *New York Times* cited congressional sources who predicted that "the American Legion will become the greatest political force in the country, even greater than labor, as its membership expands with veterans of this war." By December 1945, the Legion membership stood at 1,666,802 (650,000 new), while the VFW's had reached 1,250,000, including more than a million new members. As more soldiers were discharged in 1946, the Legion's membership rolls surged to 3.3 million. In October 1946, a *Collier's* article touted that the Legion was gaining 70,000 recruits a week! According to the author, the sales pitch was easy: "Better join our club, boys. We're the biggest, the richest [assets around $250,000,000]; we can do the most for you." In response to the Legion's 1945–1946 surge, the VFW began referring to the GI Bill as the Good Intentions Bill and yet again endorsed (to little enthusiasm) its large Bonus plan to aid veterans who were not benefiting from the GI Bill. The two organizations continually battled throughout the rest of the twentieth century over members and over credit for the GI Bill. But they remain the two largest veterans' organizations to this day.[29]

While their roles in the *creation* of the GI Bill proved a boon to the Legion and the VFW, the legislation's *implementation* conferred even more power on the organizations over upstart rivals. As predicted, World War II veterans created organizations of their own; the American Veterans of World War II (AMVETS) and the liberal American Veterans' Committee were the best and largest examples. A *Time* article published immediately following the GI Bill signing fretted over World War II veterans' domination of American politics over the next forty years, predicting, "Potentially, they are a pressure group which can make the GAR [Grand Army of the Republic] and American Legion look like Youth Day at City hall." But none of the World War II veterans' organizations superseded the Legion or the VFW as the main pillars of the veterans' lobby. World War II veterans simply joined the old guard by the millions. After all, the new organizations lacked money, whereas the Legion maintained a $15 million treasury and the VFW held $2 million. The new groups also lacked the institutional resources of the VFW and the Legion, whether measured in legislative lobbyists or in institutional veteran services available to returning GIs. The GI Bill's multiple provisions had made the VFW and the Legion even more necessary to World War II veterans as they sought to navigate a larger range of entitlements and of bureaucratic obstacles. As Charles Hurd of the *New York Times* described it, the new veterans were learning that conditions "have entrenched the Legion and Veterans of Foreign Wars so strongly that the young veteran of today, particularly if he has a personal problem, must turn to the older agencies for assistance and, in turn, he finds himself morally bound to support them." *Time*'s veteran correspondent predicted—wrongly—that the fledgling World War II veteran organizations "would probably evaporate." Regardless, throughout the twentieth century, the Legion and VFW continued to dominate the veterans' welfare system as mediators for individual veterans and as lobbyists on veterans' behalf.[30]

In the period from 1919 to 1944, World War I veterans battled with the federal government over pensions and adequate compensation for wartime military service. At the onset of the war, progressive federal veterans' policies were developed to prevent the corruption found in the Civil War pension system. During the 1920s, however, those policies produced a sustained backlash by veterans and their organizations, who worked tirelessly to liberalize the federal government's treatment of former soldiers. The newly formed American Legion superseded all of the other veteran groups as its members and leaders played a central role in the creation and maintenance of a new federal veterans' bureaucracy and welfare system. But the Legion leadership also suppressed grassroots demands for policies with which the leadership disagreed, most notably nonservice-connected pensions and the payment of the Bonus. Even before the Great Depression provoked a large outcry by veterans who argued that as former defenders of the country they were wards of the state and worthy of relief, a rival for Great War veterans arose in the formerly moribund Veterans of Foreign Wars. In 1929, prior to the Crash, the VFW began to mobilize veterans for immediate Bonus payment and general pensions. This new rivalry and the expansion of veterans' aims that it set in motion created the foundation upon which veteran politics would be based throughout the Depression era.

The Bonus March is remembered as the apotheosis of veteran political activism. In some ways—the magnitude of the demonstrations, the public consternation over both the march and its dispersal—this was true. The Bonus March needs to be reconsidered, however, as part of a much longer political mobilization, one in which the veteran organization rivalry played a formative role. In 1931–1932, by challenging a reluctant Legion leadership over prepayment and by politicizing veterans seeking the Bonus, the VFW produced the environment of veteran political activism from which the Bonus March emerged. The impact of the march and of the marchers' removal on the nation's politics was undeniable. But just because no demonstration materialized after 1932 on the order of the Bonus March does not mean that veterans grew complacent or were coopted by FDR's New Deal benevolence. On the contrary, oppositional veteran politics became a central feature of the New Deal era.

From 1933 to 1936, veterans' political mobilizations against the Economy Act's deep reductions in veterans' benefits and for early payment of the Bonus pitted them against the Roosevelt administration. This critical response to early New Deal policy made veterans the vanguard of the "New Deal Dissidents," the social protest movement associated with Senator Huey P. Long and Father Charles E. Coughlin. In 1934–1935, the Bonus provided the glue that held together an otherwise incompatible coalition of Long, Coughlin, and veterans. Indeed, by the late spring of 1935, the battle over its passage brought the politically threatening dissident movement to a climax. Payment of the Bonus in 1936, even though it was accomplished despite Roosevelt's veto, deprived the dissidents of their one common rallying cry, helping to undermine the strength of their third party electoral challenge. Moreover, FDR and the Democratic Party worked very hard in 1935 and 1936 to neutralize the veteran organizations as vehicles for veterans' opposition. Not coincidentally, the massive cash infusion of the Bonus money into the economy in the summer prior to the election made the autumn of 1936 the most prosperous quarter since the Crash and aided substantially in Roosevelt's reelection. Thus, veteran politics was a central causal factor in both the political origins of the "Second" New Deal and Roosevelt's electoral triumph of 1936.

As this concluding chapter explains, the dynamics of veteran politics since 1929—the organizational rivalries, fear of the soldier vote, and the ferocity of the battles—all provided the context for the GI Bill. But, by 1944, the federal governments' new obligations to veterans were of a piece with the larger transformation that had occurred in American political life during the New Deal era; the federal government had assumed un-paralleled responsibilities for the social and economic security of *all* citizens. The size and scope of the GI Bill projected this new understanding of citizenship, unequally and problematically to be sure, across the second half of the twentieth century. While this tectonic political shift is typically associated with New Deal labor, social welfare, and relief programs, veterans' policy must also be considered a vital factor in the creation of both the New Deal state and the New Deal political consensus. Modern conservatism, when it arose as a political force late in the twentieth century, capitalized on deep fissures that had formed in the New Deal consensus and targeted the New Deal state. Yet, the modern veterans' lobby, built from 1919 to 1944 and entrenched thanks to the GI Bill, remained one of the most powerful interest groups in U.S. politics. This legacy of the New Deal era—neither ironic nor tragic—lays bare the connections linking civic organizations, social policy, and electoral politics for generation after generation of Americans. It serves simultaneously as a guide—and as a warning.

Postscript

A GI Bill for the Twenty-first Century?

In 1945, the editors at *The New Republic* assessed the relationship between veterans and earlier manifestations of twentieth-century liberalism. The progressive standard-bearers recognized that liberals of the post–World War I period had joined with fiscal conservatives on veterans' issues and "had a good many cutting things to say about bonus and pension 'grabs' and were much more interested in combating the American Legion in politics than in improving [veterans'] social services." The editors hoped this time that liberals would embrace veterans' welfare for ideological as well as practical political reasons. They wrote, "The progressives may ignore, if they so choose, the question of whether men who have served their country in uniform are entitled to special economic consideration in the name of patriotism. They cannot afford to ignore the fact that the fate of a generation is at stake and that the setting-up of a wide and socially constructive system of benefits is of the deepest significance to the future of the democratic philosophy."[1]

The New Republic advised postwar liberals to amplify the GI Bill's provisions with a liberal expansion of the welfare state. They explained, "The benefits for veterans . . . are in embryo the kind of benefits that a rational state might well consider for all of its citizens." Postwar liberals' decision to forgo this route for all citizens is a topic others have explored. In short, macroeconomic Keynesian fiscal policy became the cornerstone of postwar liberalism, not the expansion of the welfare state beyond veterans—even though the scale and sweep of the GI Bill's largesse essentially obscured the distinction for years. When Great Society programs of the 1960s attempted to expand socioeconomic opportunity to all citizens regardless of veteran status, these efforts caused a spirited backlash that was a major factor in the ascendency of modern conservatism.[2]

It is especially noteworthy, then, that in 2008, as Americans faced an economic calamity that—while still unfolding—evokes images of the Great Depression, Congress overwhelmingly passed, and the conservative president George W. Bush signed, a new version of the GI Bill for the veterans of the all-volunteer forces serving in the Iraq and Afghanistan wars. (After the preceding chapters, the passage of the GI Bill during an election year requires no comment.) The legislation replaced the much-maligned Montgomery GI Bill, offering educational benefits that pay the highest in-state public tuition rate and providing books, fees, and a living stipend to recipients. It extended the "use-or-lose" benefit requirement from ten to fifteen years and allowed reenlisting service members to transfer their educational benefit to their spouse and/or children. An early, ardent supporter of the 2008 GI Bill was the junior member of the Senate Committee on Veterans Affairs and eventual Democratic presidential candidate, Barack Obama (D, IL).[3]

During his campaign for the presidency, Obama addressed the 2007 Veterans of Foreign Wars encampment, held in Kansas City, Missouri. The 2007 encampment received generous media coverage because, over three successive days, the veteran delegates were treated to speeches by four major candidates in the 2008 presidential campaign and by President Bush. The storylines that emerged focused first on the differences in Iraq policy articulated by Senators Hillary Rodham Clinton, Barack Obama, and John McCain and former Senator Fred Thompson, and then on President Bush's spirited defense of his administration's policy in Iraq. Lost in the media coverage was the fact that all of the presidential hopefuls dedicated substantially more time in their addresses to the issues of veterans' benefits than to the Iraq War. Most notably, Senator Obama told the veterans, "I'll keep faith with America's veterans by helping them achieve their dreams. We need a GI Bill for the twenty-first century. An Obama administration will expand access to education for our veterans and increase benefits to keep pace with rising costs." Obama closed by saying, "And I will be clear that whatever disagreements we have on [national security] policy, there will be no daylight between us when it comes to honoring these men and women who serve and keeping faith with our veterans. This is not a partisan issue. This is a moral obligation." In the campaign, Obama frequently mentioned that his maternal grandfather had benefited from the 1944 GI Bill after his service in "Patton's Army" and that the new veterans deserved the same level of federal assistance.[4]

On January 20, 2009, Barack Obama was sworn in as the first African American president of the United States at a moment of profound economic crisis. With the GI Bill old news, the country awaited the announcement of a new stimulus package from the Democratic Congress and the new president. Between 1929 and 1936, Bonus advocates had argued that its payment would offer a sure path to economic recovery. In 2008, however, a bipartisan fiscal stimuli plan, the Economic Stimulus Act, passed with little commentary on whether putting $152 billion into the hands of consumers *could* affect economic growth. The only question was how much money *should* be doled out by the tax rebates enacted by the legislation.[5] After the harrowing securities and financial collapse of late 2008, however, economists bandied about numbers ranging from $700 billion to $1 trillion as the appropriate level of necessary new federal spending commitments to avert an economic calamity similar to the Great Depression. (For a sense of scale, the $2 billion Bonus payout would be equal to just $30 billion in 2009 dollars.) While it is too early to tell if the return of the GI Bill, the resurrection of Keynesian economics, and the election of a Democratic president (albeit a self-described "pragmatic" one) are harbingers of a period of a new and ascendant twenty-first century liberalism, many speak of a return to "New Deal" priorities and programs under an Obama administration. Unlike the New Deal, though, veteran politics will probably have very little impact on the contours of the Obama agenda. Between the bipartisan embrace of liberal veteran benefits and public support for government deficit spending during an economic recession, veterans and veteran organizations will no longer be called upon to make the arguments both for veterans' welfare and the country's economic welfare as they were from 1929 to 1936. With the United States involved in two wars, in Iraq and in Afghanistan, that will usher in a new cohort of more than 1.5 million more veterans, this should be a relief to liberals and nonliberals, veterans and nonveterans alike.

Notes

INTRODUCTION

1. Oliver McKee, Jr., "The Political March of the Veterans," *The Commonweal* (November 12, 1930): 40–42.

2. For studies of the Bonus March, see Roger Daniels, *The Bonus March: An Episode of the Great Depression* (Westport, CT: Greenwood Press, 1971); Donald J. Lisio, *The President and Protest: Hoover, Conspiracy, and the Bonus Riot* (Columbia: University of Missouri Press, 1974), reprinted as *The President and Protest: Hoover, MacArthur, and the Bonus Riot* (New York: Fordham University Press, 1994); and Paul Dickson and Thomas B. Allen, *The Bonus Army: An American Epic* (New York: Walker, 2005). For accounts that consider the Bonus March more broadly, see Jennifer D. Keene, *Doughboys, the Great War, and the Remaking of America* (Baltimore: Johns Hopkins University Press, 2001), and Lucy G. Barber, *Marching on Washington: The Forging of an American Political Tradition* (Berkeley: University of California Press, 2002).

3. For a selective list of New Deal narratives that employ the March in this way, see Arthur M. Schlesinger, Jr., *The Age of Roosevelt: The Crisis of the Old Order* (Boston: Houghton Mifflin, 1957); Schlesinger, *The Age of Roosevelt: The Coming of the New Deal Order* (Boston: Houghton Mifflin, 1958); William E. Leuchtenburg, *Franklin D. Roosevelt and the New Deal, 1932–1940* (New York: Harper and Row, 1963); and David M. Kennedy, *Freedom From Fear: The American People in Depression and War, 1929–1945* (New York: Oxford University Press, 1999). For the FDR statement, see Lisio, *President and Protest*, 103. Few New Deal studies continue sustained discussions of veterans' issues after 1933. The notable exceptions are Frank Freidel, *Franklin D. Roosevelt: Launching the New Deal* (Boston: Little, Brown, 1973); James E. Sargent, *Roosevelt and the Hundred Days: Struggles for the Early New Deal* (New York: Garland, 1981); and Julian E. Zelizer, "The Forgotten Legacy of the New Deal: Fiscal Conservatism and the Roosevelt Administration, 1933–1938," *Presidential Studies Quarterly* 30.2 (2000): 331–358.

4. On the GI Bill, see Davis R. B. Ross, *Preparing for Ulysses: Politics and Veterans During World War II* (New York: Columbia University Press, 1969); Keith W. Olson, *The GI Bill, the Veterans, and the Colleges* (Lexington: The University Press of Kentucky, 1974); Michael J. Bennett, *When Dreams Came True: The GI Bill and the Making of Modern America* (Washington, DC: Brassey's, 1996); Keene, *Doughboys*, 205–214; Edwin Amenta and Theda Skocpol, "Redefining the New Deal: World War II and the Development of Social Provision in the United States," in Margaret Weir, Ann Shola Orloff, and Theda Skocpol, eds., *The Politics of Social Policy in the United States* (Princeton: Princeton University Press, 1988); and Kathleen Jill Frydl, "The GI Bill," Ph.D. diss., University of Chicago, 2000; Suzanne

Mettler, "The Creation of the GI Bill of Rights of 1944: Melding Social and Participatory Citizenship Ideals," *Journal of Policy History* 17.4 (2005): 345–374, and *Soldiers to Citizens: The G.I. Bill and the Making of the Greatest Generation* (New York: Oxford University Press, 2005). For the limitations of the GI Bill, see David H. Onkst, "'First a Negro . . . Incidentally a Veteran': Black World War Two Veterans and the G.I. Bill in the Deep South, 1944–1948," *Journal of Social History* 31 (Spring 1998): 517–544; Margot Canaday, "Building a Straight State: Sexuality and Social Citizenship Under the 1944 G.I. Bill," *Journal of American History* 90 (December 2003): 935–957; Lizabeth Cohen, *A Consumer's Republic: The Politics of Mass Consumption in Postwar America* (New York: Knopf, 2003); and Ira Katznelson, *When Affirmative Action Was White: An Untold Story of Racial Inequality in the Twentieth Century United States* (New York: Norton, 2005), 113–142.

5. See especially, Schlesinger, *The Age of Roosevelt*, vols. 1–3 (Boston: Houghton Mifflin, 1957–1960); Leuchtenburg, *Franklin D. Roosevelt and the New Deal, 1932–1940*; Kenneth S. Davis, *FDR: The New Deal Years, 1933–1937* (New York: Random House, 1979); and Kennedy, *Freedom From Fear*. For Bonus March studies that do this, see Daniels, *The Bonus March*; Keene, *Doughboys*; and Dickson and Allen, *The Bonus Army*.

6. For postrevolutionary veterans, see John P. Resch, *Suffering Soldiers: Revolutionary War Veterans, Moral Sentiment, and Political Culture in the Early Republic* (Amherst: University of Massachusetts Press, 1999); Laura Jensen, *Patriots, Settlers, and the Origins of American Social Policy* (New York: Cambridge University Press, 2003); and Leonard L. Richards, *Shays's Rebellion: The American Revolution's Final Battle* (Philadelphia: University of Pennsylvania Press, 2002).

7. On Civil War pensions and politics, see Stuart McConnell, *Glorious Contentment: The Grand Army of the Republic, 1865–1900* (Chapel Hill: University of North Carolina Press, 1992); Richard Franklin Bensel, *The Political Economy of American Industrialization, 1877–1900* (New York: Cambridge University Press, 2000); and Mark W. Summers, *Party Games: Getting, Keeping, and Using Power in Gilded Age Politics* (Chapel Hill: University of North Carolina Press, 2004).

8. On Civil War veteran welfare and state-building during the Gilded Age and the Progressive era, see Patrick J. Kelly, *Creating a National Home: Building the Veterans' Welfare State, 1860–1900* (Cambridge, MA: Harvard University Press, 1997); Theda Skocpol, *Protecting Soldiers and Mothers: The Political Origins of Social Policy* (Cambridge, MA: Belknap Press, 1992); Ann Shola Orloff, *The Politics of Pensions: A Comparative Analysis of Britain, Canada, and the United States, 1880–1940* (Madison: University of Wisconsin Press, 1993); K. Walter Hickel, "War, Region, and Social Welfare: Federal Aid to Servicemen's Dependents in the South, 1917–1921," *Journal of American History* 87: 4 (March 2001): 1362–1391; and Hickel, "Entitling Citizens: World War I, Progressivism, and the Origins of the American Welfare State, 1917–1928," Ph.D. diss., Columbia University, 1999.

9. For more general discussions of the relationship between military veterans and the state, see Eliot A. Cohen, *Citizens and Soldiers: The Dilemmas of Military Service* (Ithaca: Cornell University Press, 1985); and Samuel P. Huntington, *The Soldier and the State: The Theory and Politics of Civil-Military Relations* (Cambridge, MA: Harvard University Press, 1957).

10. In a recent assessment of the "new directions" in political history, Meg Jacobs and Julian E. Zelizer call for a reexamination of the links between citizens and their government. They describe the need for studies of "the political and voluntary institutions through which Americans gained their political standing, and mediating institutions that connected citizens to elected officials." Meg Jacobs and Julian E. Zelizer, "The Democratic

Experiment: New Directions in American Political History" in Meg Jacobs, William J. Novak, and Julian E. Zelizer, eds., *The Democratic Experiment: New Directions in American Political History* (Princeton: Princeton University Press, 2003), 2. For the importance of the relationships among war, voluntary associations, and democracy, see Theda Skocpol et al., "How Americans Became Civic," in Theda Skocpol and Morris P. Fiorina, eds., *Civic Engagements in American Democracy* (Washington, DC: Brookings Institution Press, 1999); and Skocpol et al., "Patriotic Partnerships: Why Great Wars Nourished American Civic Voluntarism," in Ira Katznelson and Martin Shefter, eds., *Shaped by War and Trade: International Influences on American Political Development* (Princeton: Princeton University Press, 2002), 134–180. For more on the importance of existing organizational structures to social protest movements, see Aldon D. Morris, *The Origins of the Civil Rights Movement: Black Communities Organizing for Change* (New York: Free Press, 1984); and Charles M. Payne, *I've Got the Light of Freedom: The Organizing Tradition and the Mississippi Freedom Struggle* (Berkeley: University of California Press, 1995).

 11. As Julian E. Zelizer suggests in a state-of-the-field essay, "the tension between scholars who study elite politics and grassroots politics quickly dissipates when policy is made the center of inquiry." Julian E. Zelizer, "Introduction: New Directions in Policy History," *Journal of Policy History* 17.1 (2005): 1–11; quotation, 4. For more on the symbiotic relationship between voluntary associations and the federal government, see Skocpol et al., "How Americans Became Civic"; and Skocpol et al., "Patriotic Partnerships."

 12. Important works on how federal policies affect political participation include Andrea Louise Campbell, *How Policies Make Citizens: Senior Political Activism and the American Welfare State* (Princeton: Princeton University Press, 2003); Paul Pierson, "When Effect Becomes Cause: Policy Feedback and Political Change," *World Politics* 45 (1993): 595–628; and Joe Soss, "Lessons of Welfare: Policy Design, Political Learning, and Political Action," *American Political Science Review* 93 (1999): 363–380. For the importance of "policy feedback," or the manner in which federal policy helps produce political participation in veterans and their dependents, see Suzanne Mettler, "Bringing the State Back in to Civic Engagement: Policy Feedback Effects of the G.I. Bill for World War II Veterans," *American Political Science Review* 96 (June 2002): 351–365; Mettler, *Soldiers to Citizens*; Hickel, "War, Region, and Social Welfare"; and Hickel, "Entitling Citizens." For an excellent comparative study of European veterans that explores these issues, see Deborah Cohen, *The War Come Home: Disabled Veterans in Britain and Germany, 1914–1939* (Berkeley: University of California Press, 2000).

 13. On the ideological implications of conscription, see Keene, *Doughboys*, 4–5. For labor relations, see Jeffrey Haydu, *Making American Industry Safe for Democracy: Comparative Perspectives on the State and Employee Representation in the Era of World War I* (Urbana: University of Illinois Press, 1997); and Joseph A. McCartin, *Labor's Great War: The Struggle for Industrial Democracy and the Origins of Modern American Labor Relations, 1917–1921* (Chapel Hill: University of North Carolina Press, 1997). For race relations, see William G. Jordan, *Black Newspapers and America's War for Democracy, 1914–1920* (Chapel Hill: University of North Carolina Press, 2001); David Levering Lewis, *W. E. B. Du Bois: Biography of Race, 1868–1919* (New York: Holt, 1993); and Chad L. Williams, "Vanguards of the New Negro: African American Veterans and Post–World War I Racial Militancy" *Journal of African American Studies* 92.3 (2007): 347–370.

 14. The group of historians, political scientists, and sociologists working under the rubric of "American Political Development" have already demonstrated the importance of veteran pensions in their studies of state formation. For excellent summaries on the

contributions of the American Political Development school, see Julian E. Zelizer, "Stephen Skowronek's *Building a New American State* and the Origins of American Political Development," *Social Science History* 27.3 (2003): 425–441; and Jacobs and Zelizer, "The Democratic Experiment: New Directions in American Political History," 1–19.

15. The best overview of U.S. veterans' policy in the interwar period is William Pyrle Dillingham, *Federal Aid to Veterans, 1917–1941* (Gainesville: University of Florida Press, 1952).

16. For Roosevelt's speech, see "FDR speech to American Legion Convention, October 2, 1933," in President's Personal File (hereafter PPF): Speeches, Box 15, Franklin D. Roosevelt Library (hereafter FDRL).

17. For the best discussion of New Deal liberalism and its transformation, see Alan Brinkley, *The End of Reform: New Deal Liberalism in Recession and War* (New York: Knopf, 1995).

18. To date, historians have concentrated on the American Legion because it was the largest of the interwar veteran organizations with a cadre of prominent national leaders. But the Legion is also more extensively studied because it maintains a library and extensive official archive at its national headquarters in Indianapolis. The VFW national headquarters in Kansas City, Missouri, on the other hand, holds very little archival material save for the complete set of its monthly publication, *Foreign Service*. On the American Legion, see William Pencak, *For God and Country: The American Legion, 1919–1941* (Boston: Northeastern University Press, 1989); Raymond Moley, Jr., *The American Legion Story* (New York: Duell, Sloan, and Pearce, 1966); Alec Duncan Campbell, "The Invisible Welfare State: Class Struggles, the American Legion, and The Development of Veterans' Benefits in the Twentieth–Century United States," Ph.D. diss., UCLA, 1997; and Thomas A. Rumer, *The American Legion: An Official History, 1919–1989* (New York: M. Evans, 1990). For the sparse literature on the VFW, see Mary Katherine Goldsmith, "The Veterans of Foreign Wars of the United States : The History of a Veterans' Organization, Its Function in Assisting Veterans, Influencing National Legislation, and Interpreting and Promoting Americanism, 1899–1948," M.A. thesis, University of Kansas City, 1963; the most recent official history of the organization, Herbert Molloy Mason, Jr., *VFW: Our First Century, 1899–1999* (Lenexa, KS: Addax, 1999); Stephen R. Ortiz, "Rethinking the Bonus March: Federal Bonus Policy, the Veterans of Foreign Wars, and the Origins of a Protest Movement" *Journal of Policy History* 18.3 (2006): 275–303; Ortiz, "The 'New Deal' for Veterans: The Economy Act, the Veterans of Foreign Wars, and the Origins of New Deal Dissent" *Journal of Military History* 70.2 (2006): 415–438; and Ortiz, "'Soldier-Citizens': The Veterans of Foreign Wars and Veteran Political Activism From the Bonus March to the GI Bill," Ph.D. diss., University of Florida, 2004.

19. Two studies delineate a more antagonistic relationship between veterans and FDR, usually using the 1935 Labor Day hurricane and the deaths of veteran CCC workers in the Florida Keys as an entry point. See Gary Dean Best, *FDR and the Bonus Marchers, 1933–1935* (Westport, CT: Praeger, 1992), and, echoing Best's argument, Dickson and Allen, *The Bonus Army,* 224–259.

20. Many have argued for a periodization of the New Deal that finds relatively distinct phases of the Roosevelt presidency, typically referred to as the "first" and "second" New Deals. In this interpretive schema, the "first" New Deal concentrated on structural economic reform from 1933 to 1935 with only minimal emphasis on social reform. The "second" New Deal, 1935–1937, refers to the period of wide-ranging social reform legislation and Roosevelt's accompanying "turn to the left." For the best discussions, see Schlesinger,

The Age of Roosevelt: The Politics of Upheaval (Boston: Houghton Mifflin, 1960);Brinkley, *The End of Reform*; Mark Leff, *The Limits of Symbolic Reform: The New Deal and Taxation, 1933-1939* (Cambridge: Cambridge University Press, 1984); and Edwin Amenta, Kathleen Dunleavy, and Mary Bernstein, "Stolen Thunder: Huey Long's 'Share Our Wealth,' Political Mediation, and the Second New Deal," *American Sociological Review* 59.5 (October 1994): 678–702.

21. Alan Brinkley's seminal study of Long and Coughlin offers anecdotal evidence that suggests that veterans actively participated in Long's and Coughlin's organizations because of each man's support for the immediate cash payment of the Bonus. Yet, Brinkley accepts the Bonus as simply a matter of interest group politics, not the ideologically divisive issue it was to become. As a result, Brinkley overlooks the importance of the Bonus, veteran organizations, and veteran political activism to the Long and Coughlin movements. See Alan Brinkley, *Voices of Protest: Huey Long, Father Coughlin, and the Great Depression* (New York: Knopf, 1982), especially 182, 194–198. The newest study of the Bonus March, Dickson and Allen's *The Bonus Army*, very briefly alludes to this coalition and the importance of the Bonus to it.

CHAPTER 1

1. For the self-conscious styling of the Legion on the model of the Grand Army of the Republic, see Pencak, *For God and Country*, 27–34.

2. For two recent works emphasizing the role of Progressivism in World War I, see Robert H. Zieger, *America's Great War: World War I and the American Experience* (Lanham, MD: Rowan & Littlefield, 2000), and Alan Dawley, *Changing the World: American Progressives in War and Revolution* (Princeton: Princeton University Press, 2005). For Progressives' dealings with soldiers, see Nancy K. Bristow, *Making Men Moral: Social Engineering During the Great War* (New York: New York University Press, 1996).

3. For discussion of the War Risk Insurance Act and the political milieu from which it emerged, see William H. Glasson, *Federal Military Pensions in the United States* (New York: Oxford University Press, 1918); Gustavus A. Weber, *The Bureau of Pensions: Its History, Activities, and Organization* (Baltimore, MD: Johns Hopkins University Press, 1923); Gustavus A. Weber and Laurence F. Scheckebier, *The Veterans' Administration: Its History, Activities, and Organization* (Washington, DC: The Brookings Institute, 1934), 89–201; Hickel, "War, Region, and Social Welfare," 1368–1372; and Dillingham, *Federal Aid to Veterans*, 4–13. Rayburn quotation found in Pencak, *For God and Country*, 177. Roosevelt quotation, "Roosevelt Backs Soldier Insurance," *New York Times* (hereafter *NYT*), August 27, 1917, 3.

4. For the most thorough discussion of the insurance and family allotment provisions, see Hickel, "War, Region, and Social Welfare" and "Entitling Citizens: World War I, Progressivism, and the Origins of the American Welfare State, 1917–1928"; see also Dillingham, *Federal Aid to Veterans*, 21–38. For disability coverage, see Dillingham, *Federal Aid to Veterans*, 39–42; Weber and Scheckebier, *The Veterans' Administration*, 117–128; and Pencak, *For God and Country*, 177–178.

5. For more on hospitalization and vocational rehabilitation policies, see Dillingham, *Federal Aid to Veterans*, 58–72 and 131–144, respectively; Weber and Scheckebier, *The Veterans' Administration*, 153–169 and 104–117, respectively; and Scott Gelder, "'A Hard-Boiled Order': The Reeducation of Disabled WWI Veterans in New York City," *Journal of Social History* 39.1 (Fall 2005): 161–180.

6. Pencak, *For God and Country*, 49, 63–65; Rumer, *The American Legion*, 8–78.

7. Pencak, *For God and Country*, 48–77; Rumer, *The American Legion*, 104–109; Campbell, "The Invisible Welfare State," 262–328.

8. Pencak, *For God and Country*, 50–51; Williams, "Vanguards of the New Negro," 357–360; Daniels, *The Bonus March*, 67–70. For a history of the Disabled American Veterans organization, see "Wars and Scars: The History of Disabled American Veterans," on the DAV Web site, http://www.dav.org/about/history.html (accessed February 28, 2008).

9. On the VFW's origins, see Mason, *VFW*, 28–49; and George T. Trial, "The American Veterans of Foreign Service and the Veterans of Foreign Wars," *The Ohio State Archeological and Historical Quarterly* 57.1 (1948): 79–93. Membership requirement from the mission statement of *Foreign Service*, the VFW's monthly publication. Rabing statement, "Foreign War Veterans," *NYT*, August 26, 1917, 9.

10. Mason, *VFW*, 49–68. Estimated membership totals in Goldsmith, "The Veterans of Foreign Wars of the United States," 194–195.

11. On VFW leadership, see Mason, *VFW*, 54–95, and Goldsmith, "The Veterans of Foreign Wars of the United States," 1–92. On Woodside, see Mason, *VFW*, 51, and 1930 Census for Allegheny County, Pennsylvania.

12. On race and the American Legion, see Pencak, *For God and Country*, 68–69. For the VFW, see references to race and African American posts in *Foreign Service*, 1919–1941, especially August 1934 encampment edition with invitation to a party held by a "colored" Louisville post.

13. Results of 1935 Legion survey in William Gellermann, *The American Legion as Educator* (New York: Bureau of Publications, Teachers College, Columbia University, 1938), 24–25, 270. The 1938 survey is found in Pencak, *For God and Country*, 80–83. For the sake of analysis, the occupation of salesmen is categorized as clerical work. In the 1935 Legion survey, 6 percent of respondents were salesmen.

14. This statistical summary is based on two sources in the author's possession: a VFW roster and scrapbook dated 1935–1941 from Kankakee, Illinois, and the Fiftieth Anniversary program commemorating the 1932 mustering of Gaspar J. Salaz Post No. 2350, Elko, Nevada. In each document, the roster of veterans from 1935 and 1932, respectively, can be found. The rosters were cross-referenced with 1930 U.S. Census population schedules to find profiles on the locatable members. This was made possible, in part, because in 1930 census takers asked questions to identify veterans and the wars in which they fought. For Kankakee, some 111 of the posts' 167 members (66 percent) were located this way; for Elko, 17 of the 34 members were located (50 percent). Median home values can be found on the "Historical Census Browser" Web page maintained by the University of Virginia Library at http://fisher.lib.virginia.edu/collections/stats/histcensus/index.html (accessed March 7, 2008). Since it is likely that only the most stable and prosperous remained in these locations from 1930 to 1932 and 1935 (the worst years of the Depression), the social characteristics revealed here are, if anything, probably skewed upward.

15. On the American Legion, see Pencak, *For God and Country*, and Rumer, *The American Legion*, 110–186. On the VFW, see Mason, *VFW*, 54–95, and Goldsmith, "The Veterans of Foreign Wars of the United States." On the role as claims agents, see Dillingham, *Federal Aid to Veterans*, 6.

16. Ibid.

17. For a detailed overview of the literature on the role of "iron triangles" or "subgovernments" in policy formation, see Jeffrey M. Berry, "Subgovernments, Issue Networks, and Political Conflict," in Richard A. Harris and Sidney M. Milkis, eds., *Remaking American Politics* (Boulder, CO: Westview Press, 1989), 239–260.

18. Rumer, *The American Legion*, 110–120; Pencak, *For God and Country*, 75; Weber and Scheckebier, *The Veterans' Administration*, 212–218. For more on veteran discontent with vocational training, see Gelder, "'A Hard-Boiled Order.'"

19. Pencak, *For God and Country*, 159, 178–185, 207; Dillingham, *Federal Aid to Veterans*, 13–15, 43; Weber and Scheckebier, *The Veterans' Administration*, 217–225.

20. Pencak, *For God and Country*, 112, 115–117, 119; Mason, *VFW*, 57, 60.

21. Pencak, *For God and Country*, 72, 197–199; Dillingham, *Federal Aid to Veterans*, 145–150.

22. Daniels, *The Bonus March*, 23–28; Pencak, *For God and Country*, 75–77, 197–200; Dillingham, *Federal Aid to Veterans*, 145–150; Weber and Scheckebier, *The Veterans' Administration*, 229–231; *Foreign Service* (June 1919): 8 and (November 1920): 1; "Thousands March in Bonus Parade," *NYT*, October 16–17, 1920, 1.

23. Daniels, *The Bonus March*, 32–33; Dillingham, *Federal Aid to Veterans*, 153–156.

24. Daniels, *The Bonus March*, 28–37; Pencak, *For God and Country*, 67, 200; Weber and Scheckebier, *The Veterans' Administration*, 231; Keene, *Doughboys*, 173–174. Johnson, "Marshalling Votes," *Time*, May 19, 1923, 8. Smoot quotation, "Tinkering," *Time*, May 12, 1923, 7.

25. Pencak, *For God and Country*, 197–200; Daniels, *The Bonus March*, 28–37; and Dillingham, *Federal Aid to Veterans*, 153–155. Mellon in "Mr. Mellon Proposes," *Time*, November 19, 1923, 8.

26. Daniels, *The Bonus March*, 37–40; Pencak, *For God and Country*, 197–200; Weber and Scheckebier, *The Veterans' Administration*, 231–234.

27. Daniels, *The Bonus March*, 39.

28. Pencak, *For God and Country*, 171, 185; Weber and Scheckebier, *The Veterans' Administration*, 152–153; Dillingham, *Federal Aid to Veterans*, 15–16, 45–46, 69.

29. Weber and Scheckebier, *The Veterans' Administration*, 468.

30. Resolution No. 141, *Proceedings of the 27th Annual Encampment of the Veterans of Foreign Wars of the United States*, 1926 (Washington, DC: U.S. Government Printing Office, 1927), 264. Legion membership totals in *National Tribune*, February 7, 1935, and VFW's in Goldsmith, "The Veterans of Foreign Wars of the United States," 194. Letter from Royal C. Johnson to Herbert Hoover, dated April 1, 1929, in "World War Veterans—Correspondence, 1929," Box 371, Subject Files Herbert Hoover Presidential Library (hereafter SFHH).

31. Dillingham, *Federal Aid to Veterans*, 50–51; Pencak, *For God and Country*, 189–190; Mason, *VFW*, 79–80. Carver quotation in "Urges Army Pension to All Disabled," *NYT*, April 7, 1929, 18.

32. *Foreign Service* (September 1929): 4. Resolutions, *Proceedings of the 30th Annual Encampment of the Veterans of Foreign Wars of the United States, 1929* (Washington, DC: U.S. Government Printing Office, 1930), 267. Daniels, *Bonus March*, 42. Interestingly, no mention of Wright Patman, the future congressional Bonus leader and at the time a freshman congressman from Texas, can be found in the VFW encampment minutes. This is despite the fact that Patman proposed a Bonus bill in the House just days after Brookhart's proposal. For more on Patman, see Nancy Beck Young, *Wright Patman: Populism, Liberalism, and the American Dream* (Dallas: Southern Methodist University Press, 2000).

CHAPTER 2

1. Veteran unemployment data found in Keene, *Doughboys*, 180–181; "Veterans Ask Hoover to Call Work Parley," *NYT*, May 15, 1931, 1. Veterans' bonus applications in *Foreign Service* (February 1930): 4. O'Neil in Pencak, *For God and Country*, 84.

2. O'Neil quotation on Pencak, *For God and Country*, 84, 188. "Tells of Legion Employment Plan," *NYT*, November, 12, 1930, 5.

3. Copy of November 22, 1929, Duff telegram in *Foreign Service* (December 1929): 27 and February, 1930: 4. Letter from Hezekiah N. Duff to Herbert Hoover, dated January 29, 1930, in "VFW, 1930," Box 359, SFHH.

4. Rumer, *The American Legion*, 186–188; Lisio, *The President and Protest*, 26–30.

5. Cited in letter from Frank T. Hines to Herbert Hoover, dated September 10, 1930, in "VFW, 1930," Box 359, SFHH. For VFW encampment information, see *Proceedings of the 31st Annual Encampment of the Veterans of Foreign Wars of the United States, 1930* (Washington, DC: U.S. Government Printing Office, 1931) and *NYT* and *Washington Post*, September 1–6, 1930.

6. Daniels, *The Bonus March*, 42–43; Lisio, *The President and Protest*, 30–32; Pencak, *For God and Country*, 200–201. On Taylor's assistance in Hoover speech, Pencak, *For God and Country*, 201.

7. Young, *Wright Patman*, 36. "'Mellon Gag' Help Applied to Legion," *Washington Post*, December 29, 1930, 2.

8. "News and Notes from Capital Veterans' Activities," *Washington Post*, December 21, 1930, R6; "News of Veterans' Activities," *Washington Post*, December 28, 1930, R3.

9. "47 Bills to Help Veterans Listed," *Washington Post*, January 3, 1931, 2.

10. Petitions in Daniels, *The Bonus March*, 43, 71; *Washington Post*, "Mellon Condemns Veterans' Cash Bill," January 22, 1931, 12; "3 Representatives Make Addresses to Men at House Wing," January 22, 1931, 1. Petition squabble in "Patman Justifies Veterans Petition," *Washington Post*, December 28, 1930, M1. Alfieri and VFW marchers in *Washington Post*, "200 Veterans Start on Hike to Washington to Push Aid," January 27, 1931, M22; "Bonus Plea Voiced By 'Army' Remnant," January 28, 1931, 3.

11. Rumer, *The American Legion*, 190–191; "The Veterans' 'Gold Rush,'" *Literary Digest* (February 14, 1931): 5; and *Washington Post*, "Compromise Plan On Bonus Studied," January 25, 1931, M22; "Executive Board Acts on Veterans' Increasing Demands," January 26, 1931, 1. MacNider and Chadwick quotations in Pencak, *For God and Country*, 202.

12. Wolman testimony in House Committee on Ways and Means, *Payment of Soldiers' Adjusted-Compensation Certificates: Hearings Before the House Committee on Ways and Means*, 71st Congress, 3rd Session, 1931, 129–135; "The Veterans' Bonus—Calamity or Blessing?" *Literary Digest* (February 14, 1931): 5–6; "Cash for Veterans' Certificates Urged," *Washington Post*, January 28, 1931, 3.

13. Lisio, *The President and Protest*, 36–39; Daniels, *The Bonus March*, 43–45; "The Veterans' Bonus—Calamity or Blessing?" *Literary Digest* (February 14, 1931): 5–6.

14. Lisio, *The President and Protest*, 38–42; Herbert Hoover Veto Message, February 26, 1931, in "Veterans' Bureau Correspondence, 1931, January-February," Box 356, SFHH; "Needy Served First," *Time*, March 19, 1931, 11.

15. "The Veteran's 'Gold Rush,'" *Literary Digest* (March 14, 1931): 5–6; Letter from Frank T. Hines to Herbert Hoover, August 12, 1932 in "World War Veterans—Bonus Correspondence, 1931, March–December," Box 372, SFHH; *Foreign Service* (January 1932): 17; Letter from Arthur H. Vandenberg to Herbert Hoover, August 10, 1931, in "Trips—1931, September 21, Detroit, American Legion Convention," Box 37, SFHH.

16. *Foreign Service* (March 1931): 5 and (April 1931): 4.

17. VFW membership growth in Goldsmith, "The Veterans of Foreign Wars of the United States," 194; post growth obtained from *Foreign Service*, January 1929 to December 1931. Report in *Proceedings of the 32nd Annual Encampment of the Veterans of Foreign*

Wars of the United States, 1931 (Washington, DC: U.S. Government Printing Office, 1932), 244–246.

18. Internal Memorandum to Walter H. Newton, August 8, 1931, in "VFW, 1931–1933," Box 359, SFHH.

19. Hines's speech and Wolman retort in *Proceedings of the 32nd Annual Encampment of the Veterans of Foreign Wars*, 38–46.

20. Letter from Royal C. Johnson to J. Edgar Hoover, dated August 28, 1931, in " Trips—1931, September 21, Detroit, American Legion Convention," Box 37, SFHH. Address of President Hoover to the Thirteenth Convention of the American Legion, September 21, 1931, in "Congratulatory Correspondence American Legion Address Detroit Sept. 21, 1931, A-D," Box 47, President Personal File, Herbert Hoover Presidential Library (hereafter PP-FHH). Daniels, *The Bonus March*, 51. Letter from Gilbert Bettman to Walter [*sic*] Richey, dated September 25, 1931, in "Congratulatory Correspondence American Legion Address Detroit Sept. 21, 1931, A-D," Box 47, PPFHH. In his zeal, Bettman confused the names of Hoover's two secretaries, Walter Newton and Larry Richey.

21. H. L. Mencken, "The Case for the Heroes," *The American Mercury* 24 (December, 1931): 409–410.

22. Report of the Director of Publicity, *Proceedings of the 34th Annual Encampment of the Veterans of Foreign Wars of the United States* (Washington, DC: U.S. Government Printing Office, 1933), 197–199. *Foreign Service* (January 1932): 17.

23. Alfieri in Dickson and Allen, *The Bonus Army*, 46, and "Fifty Veterans on Hike to Urge Bonus," *NYT*, December 15, 1931, 56. *Foreign Service* (January 1932): 19–21. Emphasis added.

24. Daniels, *The Bonus March*, 55. *Foreign Service*, December 1931 to March 1932.

25. *Foreign Service* (February 1932): 10–12, 24.

26. Daniels, *The Bonus March*, 52, 61–64; Young, *Wright Patman*, 45–46; *Foreign Service* (May 1932): 6–8; *NYT*, April 2–11, 1932.

27. *NYT*, "Veterans' Views Stated" and "Stevens Tells Legion Views," April 6, 1932, 1–2; Pencak, *God and Country*, 202.

28. *NYT*, "Veterans' Views Stated," April 6, 1932, 1; "Seek Legion Meeting Over Bonus" and "VFW Chief Challenges Stevens," April 7, 1932, 16; "Post Demands Stevens Retract," April 8, 1932, 2; "Defense of Stevens Causes Near Riot," April 1, 1932, 12. Copy of Luther letter dated April 5, 1932, found in "World War Veterans, Bonus Correspondence, 1932, January–June," Box 373, SFHH.

29. Of the Bonus March accounts that mention this episode, most downplay its importance as a key precursor. For the most recent example, see Dickson and Allen, *The Bonus Army*, 59. For the best coverage of this march, see "Paraders Present Appeals for Bonus," *Washington Post*, April 9, 1932, 4, and "Parade to Capitol in Plea for Bonus," *NYT*, April 9, 1932, 3; and *Foreign Service* (May 1932): 6–7.

30. For DeCoe, Ray, and Wolman testimony, see House Committee on Ways and Means, *Payment of Adjusted-Compensation Certificates: Hearings Before the House Committee on Ways and Means*, 72nd Congress, 1st Session, 1932, 81–83, 188–191, 207–210; *NYT* and *Washington Post*, April 2, 6, 8, 11, 14, and 16, 1932; Daniels, *The Bonus March*, 52, 61–64; "Pro Bono Politico," *Time*, April 11, 1932, 19; Memorandum from Raymond Benjamin to Larry Richey, dated April 13, 1932, in "World War Veterans, Bonus Correspondence, 1932, January–June," Box 373, SFHH.

31. Letter from John A. Weeks to Walter H. Newton, dated January 9, 1932, in "World War Veterans, Bonus Correspondence, 1932, January–June," Box 373, SFHH. Legion totals

in Pencak, *For God and Country*, 83–86. See also *National Tribune*, February 7, 1935. VFW post total from *Foreign Service* (April–July 1932).

32. *Foreign Service* (May 1932): 15; "The Soldier Racket," *The Christian Century* 49 (May 11, 1932): 598–599; Letter from Tunis Benjamin to Theodore Joslin, dated April 8, 1932, in "World War Veterans, Bonus Correspondence, 1932, January–June," Box 373, SFHH.

33. For the most thorough description, see Daniels, *The Bonus March*, 65–122, Lisio, *The President and Protest*, 51–165 and Dickson and Allen, *The Bonus Army*, 56–183. Keene, *Doughboys*, 179–198, and Barber, *Marching on Washington*, 75–97, provide excellent short descriptions. The *Washington Post* coverage from late May until July, 1932 is excellent. For more on Waters, see W. W. Waters, *B.E.F.: The Whole Story of the Bonus Army* (New York: John Day, 1933) and Dickson and Allen, *The Bonus Army*, 56–60.

34. Ibid.

35. Letter from Royal C. Johnson to The President, dated June 10, 1932, in "World War Veterans, Bonus Correspondence, 1932, January–June," Box 373, SFHH. *NYT*, "Two Veterans Groups Deny Part in 'March,'" June 9, 1932, 19; "Stevens Corrects French Idea That Legion Backs 'B.E.F.,'" June 24, 1932, 3; "Offers to Spank Bonus March," June 10, 1932, 12; 'Reds Urge Mutiny in the Bonus Army," June 19, 1932, 1. See also Dickson and Allen, *The Bonus Army*, 61, 70, 100, 103–104, 140.

36. *NYT*, "Reds Inspired Bonus Marchers," June 10, 1932, 12; "Brooklyn March Planned," June 5, 1932, 3. See also Dickson and Allen, *The Bonus Army*, 61, 70, 100, 103–104, 140.

37. Daniels, *The Bonus March*, 80; *NYT*, "Two Veterans' Groups Deny Part in 'March,'" June 9, 1932, 3; "135 Veterans Leave Hartford," June 12, 1932, 2; see also "Veterans in Heated Annapolis Session," *Washington Post*, June 19, 1932, 20. Ironically, Dickson and Allen's work includes a photograph of the Chattanooga truck without mentioning the clearly legible "VFW" painted on its side panels. See Dickson and Allen, *The Bonus Army*, 59.

38. "7,000 in Bonus Army Parade in Capital," *NYT*, June 8, 1932, 1. VA records in Frank T. Hines to Herbert Hoover, dated August 2, 1932, in "World War Veterans-Bonus Reports, Descriptions, and Statements, 1932, August," Box 376, SFHH.

39. " Glassford's 'Ads' of Free Food For Veterans Curbed," *Washington Post*, June 4, 1932, 1; "135 Veterans Leave Hartford," *NYT*, June 12, 1932, 2. Frontline Post activities in VA Report, Hines to Theodore G. Joslin, dated July 27, 1932, in "World War Veterans—Bonus Reports, Descriptions, and Statements, 1932, July 26–31," Box 376, SFHH.

40. On Glassford, see Lisio, *President and Protest*, 51–55, and *BEF News*, August 13, 1932: 6. On Heffernan, see obituary in *Youngstown Vindicator*, April 21, 1977. On Rice Means, see *National Tribune*, April-August 1932, and Mason, *VFW: Our First Century*. On Butler, see Hans Schmidt, *Maverick Marine: Smedley D. Butler and the Contradictions of American Military History* (Lexington: University Press of Kentucky, 1987).

41. *NYT*, June 3, 7–9, 1932. *Washington Post*, May 25 and June 3–12, 1932.

42. *Washington Post*, "Veterans in Heated Annapolis Session," June 19, 1932, 20; "Quenstedt Is Again VFW Commander," June 20, 1932, 5. Ranken's specific message to the Maryland encampment is unknown, but the passing of the resolution had been hotly contested on June 18, only to be withdrawn after his address.

43. Letter from Francis Ralston Welsh to J. Edgar Hoover and Lawrence Richey, dated June 13, 1932, in "World War Veterans, Bonus Correspondence, 1932, January–June," Box 373, SFHH.

44. Letter from Royal C. Johnson to The President, dated June 10, 1932, in "World War Veterans, Bonus Correspondence, 1932, January–June," Box 373, SFHH. Johnson floor

speech in *Congressional Record*, 72nd Congress, 1st session, 12716–12717, and *Washington Post*, "First U.S. Step Is Taken to Aid Veterans Here," June 12, 1932, 1.

45. "The Legion's Chickens Come Home to Roost," *The Christian Century* 49 (June 22, 1932): 78.

46. The single best treatment of the Bonus Army removal remains Lisio, *President and Protest*, 139–225. The most recent treatment is Dickson and Allen, *The Bonus Army*, 152–206.

47. Keene, *Doughboys*, 197–198 and Daniels, *The Bonus March*, 41–64. No good study exists for the National Economy League, but George Wolfskill, *The Revolt of the Conservatives: A History of the American Liberty League, 1934–1940* (Boston: Houghton Mifflin, 1962), and "Cut In Veterans' Aid of $450,000,000 Asked to Abolish 'Racket,'" *NYT*, May 5, 1932, 1, are good starting points.

48. Lawrence G. Pugh to Herbert Hoover, dated August 6, 1932, in "World War Veterans—Bonus, Public Comment on Presidential Action, Protesting, 1932, Aug 6–10," Box 375, SFHH; Frank J. Murray to Herbert Hoover, dated August 1, 1932, in in "World War Veterans—Bonus, Public Comment on Presidential Action, Protesting, 1932, Aug 1," Box 375, SFHH; and John Henry Bartlett, *The Bonus March and the New Deal* (Chicago: M. A. Donohue, 1937), 128.

49. Elmer quotation in Lisio, *President and Protest*, 112. For the best breakdown of the House vote, see Daniels, *The Bonus March*, 116–117. For more on the Bonus in the 1932 campaign, see Lisio, *President and Protest*, 279–285.

50. For more on the "forgotten man" speech and the Long-Roosevelt conversation, see Samuel I. Rosenman, *Working With Roosevelt* (New York: Harper and Brothers, 1952), 61–62 and 69–70. For the best description of the 1932 Democratic Convention, see Schlesinger, *The Crisis of the Old Order*, 297–311. For the most recent, see Donald A. Ritchie, *Electing FDR: The New Deal Campaign of 1932* (Lawrence: University of Kansas Press, 2007).

51. For Tugwell's assessment, see R. G. Tugwell, *The Brains Trust* (New York: Viking Press, 1968), 357–359; Lisio, *President and Protest*, 285; and Daniels, *The Bonus March*, 218. See notes 2 and 3 to introduction for complete Bonus March and New Deal historiography.

52. Lawrence G. Pugh to Herbert Hoover, dated August 6, 1932 in "World War Veterans—Bonus, Public Comment on Presidential Action, Protesting, 1932, Aug 6–10," Box 375, SFHH; George E. Parker to Theodore Joslin, dated July 29, 1932, in "World War Veterans Bonus, Public Comment on Presidential Action, opposed, 1932, July 29," Box 375, SFHH; and A. Cuehler (?) to Herbert Hoover, undated, in "World War Veterans—Bonus, Public Comment on Presidential Action, Protesting, 1932, Aug 2," Box 375, SFHH, (emphasis in the original).

53. *Foreign Service* (September 1932): 4–5. Argonne Post No. 107 to Herbert Hoover, dated August 6, 1932; Pvt. Martin Glendon Post No. 298 to Herbert Hoover, dated August 8, 1932; Pvt. Martin Glendon Post No. 298 to Herbert Hoover, dated August 8, 1932; and Herbert Dunlavy Post No. 581 to Herbert Hoover, undated; in "World War Veterans—Bonus, Public Comment on Presidential Action, Protesting, 1932, Aug 6–10," Box 375, SFHH.

54. Lisio, *The President and Protest*, 244–245; *NYT*, "Legion Post Backs Hoover," July 29, 1932, 6; "Vermont Veterans Condemn March," July 31, 1932, 3.

55. South End Post No. 105 to Herbert Hoover, dated August 4, 1932, in "World War Veterans—Bonus, Public Comment on Presidential Action, Protesting, 1932, Aug 4," Box 375, SFHH. Vincent B. Costello Post No. 15 to Herbert Hoover, dated August 3, 1932, in "World War Veterans—Bonus, Public Comment on Presidential Action, Protesting, 1932,

Aug 3," Box 375, SFHH. *NYT*, "Keystone Legion Denounces Hoover," August 21, 1932, 2; "Ohio Legion Asks for Bonus," August, 17, 1932, 2; "31 State Legions Listed for Bonus," August 29, 1932, 2.

56. VFW membership data in Goldsmith, "The Veterans of Foreign Wars of the United States," 194, and "Again Bonuseers," *Time*, September 12, 1932, 9–11; post data obtained from *Foreign Service*, January 1929 to December 1932.

57. *Proceedings of the 33rd Annual Encampment of the Veterans of Foreign Wars of the United States*, 1932 (Washington, DC: U.S. Government Printing Office, 1933), 260, 267–268.

58. "Hoover Won't Try to Bar Bonus Vote," *NYT*, August 30, 1932, 19; *Time*, "Again Bonuseers," "Riot Report," September 19, 1932, 9; "Portland Thorn," September 26, 1932, 8–9. George E. Leach to Walter Newton, dated September 11, 1932, in "World War Veterans—Bonus Correspondence, 1932, September," Box 373, SFHH. See also Lisio, *The President and Protest*, 244–257.

59. *Time*, "That's a Secret," October 10, 1932, 9; "Yes or No," October 17, 1932, 13; "Coolidge Contributes," October 24, 1932, 14. *NYT*, "The Text of Governor Roosevelt's Speech to 30,000 in Pittsburgh Baseball Park," October 20, 1932, 18; "Hoover Aides Map Bonus Attack," October 21, 1932, 10. "Where Roosevelt Stands on the Bonus," *Literary Digest* (October 29, 1932): 5–6.

CHAPTER 3

1. The list of New Deal political narratives is virtually endless. A necessarily incomplete list includes Schlesinger, *The Age of Roosevelt, Vols. 1–3*; Kenneth S. Davis, *FDR: The New Deal Years, 1933–1937* (New York: Random House, 1979); Leuchtenburg, *Franklin D. Roosevelt and the New Deal, 1932–1940*; Leuchtenburg, *The FDR Years: On Roosevelt and His Legacy* (New York: Columbia University Press, 1995); Anthony J. Badger, *The New Deal: The Depression Years, 1933–1940* (New York: Farrar, Strauss, & Giroux, 1989); Kennedy, *Freedom From Fear*; and George T. McJimsey, *The Presidency of Franklin Delano Roosevelt* (Lawrence: University Press of Kansas, 2000).

2. The Economy Act remains one of the most underexamined pieces of New Deal legislation. For the best discussion of the centrality of fiscal conservatism to FDR and the first stages of the New Deal, see Freidel, *Franklin D. Roosevelt*, 237–254, 448–453; Sargent, *Roosevelt and the Hundred Days*; Kelly McMichael Stott, "FDR, Lewis Douglas, and the Raw Deal," *Historian* 63.1 (2000): 105–120; and Julian Zelizer, "The Forgotten Legacy of the New Deal: Fiscal Conservatism and the Roosevelt Administration, 1933–1938," *Presidential Studies Quarterly* 30.2 (2000): 331–358.

3. I employ the term "New Deal Dissidents" by borrowing from Alan Brinkley's discussion of "dissident ideology" in *Voices of Protest: Huey Long, Father Coughlin, and the Great Depression* (New York: Knopf, 1982), especially 143–168. Other terms such as progressives, insurgents, native radicals, and populists lack the specificity, both historical and historiographical, of New Deal Dissidents. For more on New Deal Dissidents, see also Schlesinger, *The Age of Roosevelt, Vol. 3*; David H. Bennett, *Demagogues in the Depression: American Radicals and the Union Party, 1932–1936* (New Brunswick, NJ: Rutgers University Press, 1969); and David Horowitz, *Beyond Left and Right: Insurgency and the Establishment* (Urbana: University of Illinois Press, 1997).

4. Mason, *VFW*, 79–80; "Urges Army Pension to All Disabled," *NYT*, April 7, 1929, 18; and letter from Royal C. Johnson to Herbert Hoover, dated April 1, 1929, in "World War Veterans—Correspondence, 1929," Box 371, SFHH.

5. Lisio, *President and Protest*, 8–26; Pencak, *For God and Country*, 188–191; Dillingham, *Federal Aid to Veterans*, 50–54; *Time*, "Pension Beginnings," July 7, 1930, 16–17, and "Pensions Win," July 14, 1930, 17; "President Warns Senate of Veto," *NYT*, June 23, 1930, 1.

6. Lisio, *President and Protest*, 8–26; *Time*, "Pension Beginnings," July 7, 1930, 16–17; "Pensions Win," July 14, 1930, 17; *NYT*, "Congress Adjourns With Hoover Victory," July 4, 1930, 1; "President Warns Senate of Veto of Veterans' Bill," June 23, 1930; 1, "Hoover Excoriates the Veterans' Bill; House to Back Veto," June 25, 1930; 1; and "House Upholds Veto," June 27, 1930; 1; Walter H. Newton to Ernest Jahncke, memorandum dated August 24, 1932 in "World War Veterans—Disabled Soldiers Hospitalized, 1929–1932 and undated," Box 371, SFHH.

7. *Time*, "Pension Beginnings," July 7, 1930, 16–17; "Pensions Win," July 14, 1930, 17.

8. Pencak, *For God and Country*, 190. Newton and Watson in *Foreign Service* (August 1930): 5, 7.

9. Rumer, *The American Legion*, 200; Pencak, *For God and Country*, 190. Murphy in "Report of National Legislative Committee," *Digest of Minutes, National Executive Committee Meeting, May 4 and 5, 1933*, American Legion National Headquarters Library (hereafter ALNHL).

10. Pencak, *For God and Country*, 171; Lisio, *President and Protest*, 22; and Frank T. Hines to Walter H. Newton, dated August 4, 1932, in "Veterans' Bureau—Correspondence, 1932, August," Box 357, SFHH. Representative critical publications are Roger Burlingame, *Peace Veterans: The Story of a Racket and a Plea for Economy* (New York: Minton, Balch, 1932); National Industrial Conference Board, *The World War Veterans and the Federal Treasury* (New York: National Industrial Conference Board, 1932); Robert Cruse McManus, "Billions for Veterans," *Current History* 36 (August 1932): 557–562; Lawrence Sullivan, "The Veteran Racket," *Atlantic Monthly* 151 (1933): 393–402; Sullivan, "The Soldier Racket," *The Christian Century* 49 (May 11, 1932): 598–599.

11. On the NEL, see Wolfskill, *The Revolt of the Conservatives*; "Cut in Veterans' Aid of $450,000,000 to Abolish "Racket,'" *NYT*, May 5, 1932, 1; Grenville Clark to Herbert Hoover, dated July 19, 1932, and National Economy League Declaration of Purposes and Plan of Organization in "National Economy League, 1932," President's Personal File 178, Herbert Hoover Library (hereafter PPFHH)

12. On the AVA, see *NYT*, "Anti-Bonus Men Organize," September 29, 1932, 3; "Ex-Soldiers Advise $450,000,000 Savings," December 12, 1932, 9. For implied connection among AVA and the Chamber of Commerce and the National Economy League, see *American Legion Monthly* (March 1933): 22–23.

13. *Joint Committee on Veterans' Affairs: Hearings on Veterans' Affairs, December 9, 1932*, 72nd Congress, 2nd Session, 1932; "Cabinet Is Consulted," *NYT*, November 20, 1932, 1; Freidel, *Launching the New Deal*, 51; Pencak, *For God and Country*, 170–175; and Rumer, *The American Legion*, 196–201. For reporting on the Joint Committee, see *Washington Post*, December 7, 9, 21–22, 1932, and January 4, 5, 10, 12, 1933; *Foreign Service* (February 1933): 4–5, 10–11, 25 and (March 1933): 10; Bullitt in "Veterans' Cut Plans Stir Ire at Hearing," *NYT*, December 21, 1932, 6.

14. *NYT*, "Denounce Critics of Aid to Veterans," December 14, 1932, 12; "Legion Chief Voices Reawakened Spirit," December 25, 1932, 9; *American Legion Monthly* (January 1933): 42, (February 1933): 55, and (March 1933): 22–23, 55–58; Rumer, *The American Legion*, 197; Pencak, *For God and Country*, 174; and *Washington Post*, January 4–12, 1933.

15. *Foreign Service* (January 1933): 4, (February 1933): 4, and (March 1933): 31. Veterans of Foreign Wars, Department of New York, *An Expose of the National Economy League*, in "Military Pensions," Vertical File, Franklin D. Roosevelt Library (hereafter FDRL).

16. Rumer, *The American Legion*, 197; Pencak, *For God and Country*, 174; *Foreign Service* (February 1933): 4; and *American Legion Monthly* (April 1933): 15, 56–60.

17. VFW Post 2235, Neponset, Mass., to FDR, March 3, 1933; Raymond G. Price, Corp. Matthews-Purnell Post 518, Camden, NJ, to FDR, March 10, 1933; and Comrade W. E. Dowling of Corp. John McGotty Post 1941, Irvington, NJ, to FDR, February 18, 1933, in "Veterans of Foreign Wars, 1933–1936," President's Personal File (hereafter, PPF) 87, FDRL. Clifford Ellig to FDR, telegram dated March 4, 1933, in "American Legion, January–June 1933," Box 1, OF 64, FDRL. Albert B. Marquis to FDR, letter dated March 6, 1933, in "Public Reaction, March 4, 1933," Box 7 D–M, folder M, PPF 200B, FDRL.

18. On the fundamental fiscal conservatism of FDR, Douglas's instructions to work on cuts in veteran benefits, and the importance of balancing the budget to the early New Deal, see Freidel, *Launching the New Deal*, 237–254; Stott, "FDR, Douglas, and the Raw Deal, passim; and Sargent, *Roosevelt and the Hundred Days*, 68–74. FDR message found in Franklin D. Roosevelt, "A Request to the Congress for Authority to Effect Drastic Economics in Government," in Samuel Rosenman, ed., *The Public Papers of Franklin D. Roosevelt, Vol. 2* (New York: Random House, 1938), 49–54.

19. Sargent, *Roosevelt and the Hundred Days*, 242; Franklin D. Roosevelt, "A Message to Veterans to Share the Spirit of Sacrifice," April 1, 1933, in Rosenman, ed., *The Public Papers of Franklin D. Roosevelt, Vol. 2*, 99–100; and Dillingham, *Federal Aid to Veterans*, 73–78.

20. Sargent, *Roosevelt and the Hundred Days*, 242; Dillingham, *Federal Aid to Veterans*, 73–78; and *National Tribune*, June 22, 1933. In the summer of 1933, the *National Tribune* ran weekly stories listing veterans' suicides compiled from the news wires.

21. FDR Address in American Legion National Broadcast, March 5, 1933, in "American Legion, Jan.–June, 1933," OF 64, Box 1, FDRL, and "Legion's Plans Stressed by National Commander," *Washington Post*, March 6, 1933, 4.

22. Johnson was a Democratic Party loyalist from West Virginia. He was later appointed Assistant Secretary of War by FDR, who carried on a voluminous secret correspondence within the administration on veteran issues. On Louis Johnson's ties to the FDR administration and for the Legion's response to the Economy Act, see Pencak, *For God and Country*, 192–197. Louis Johnson to FDR, March 28, 1933, in "American Legion, January–June, 1933," OF 64, Box 1, FDRL. "Battle Orders" quotation in Pencak, *For God and Country*, 191–192; *American Legion Monthly* (May 1933): 14–15, 45; and "Legion's Head Promises Full Faith in President," *Washington Post*, March 16, 1933, 5.

23. *Digest of Minutes, National Executive Committee Meeting, May 4 and 5, 1933,* AL-NHL and *National Tribune*, May 11, 1933.

24. See Pencak, *For God and Country*, 110, 170–175, 192–197; Rumer, *The American Legion*, 196–201. *Legion News* in *American Legion Monthly* (June 1933): 39. Early and Taylor in Pencak, *For God and Country*, 193. Murphy in *American Legion Monthly* (May 1933): 16–17, 56–59.

25. *Foreign Service* (April 1933): 4.

26. Ibid.

27. Ibid., 5–6.

28. *Foreign Service* (May 1933): 5–7 and (February 1934): 4.

29. *Foreign Service* (May 1933): 30.

30. *Foreign Service* (May 1933): 4–7 and (July 1933): 5.

31. L.M. Tate Post 39 to FDR in "Economy Program, 1933, T," PPF 200f, Box 159, FDRL; Harry S. Roberts, Huntington Park Post 952, to Colonel Howe, July 7, 1933, in "Veterans of Foreign Wars, 1933–1934," Official File (OF) 84, FDRL; Kenneth A. Bixler and W. R.

Ambrose to FDR, March 10, 1933, in "Economy Program, 1933, U–V," PPF 200f, Box 159, FDRL; and Harry C. Hoffman, City of Detroit Post 334, to Secretary Howe, undated, in "World War Veterans, June 5–June 13, 1933," OF 95, FDRL.

32. Copy of letter from Joe Heffernan to James Farley, July 1, 1933, in "Veterans of Foreign Wars, 1933–1934," OF 84, FDRL.

33. Chart of American Legion Membership totals from 1920–1934 in *National Tribune*, February 7, 1935. VFW post growth information found in *Foreign Service* (January–December 1933) and "Report of the Adjutant General's Department" and "Report of the Chief of Staff," *34th National Encampment of the VFW, 1933* (Washington, DC: U.S. Government Printing Office, 1934), 152–163, 182–185. July 1, 1933 announcement by VFW National Headquarters, quoted in *National Tribune*, July 27, 1933.

34. E. Burns telegram to FDR, March 12, 1933, in "Economy Program, 1933," PPF 200F, Box 156, FDRL; L. Cole telegram to FDR, April 25, 1933, in "Veterans Administration, Federal Hospital Board, April–July, 1933," OF 86, Box 4, FDRL; and M. E. Depew telegram to FDR, March 11, 1933, in "Economy Program, 1933," PPF 200F, Box 156, FDRL.

35. Disabled Veteran to FDR, September 8, 1933, in "Veterans Administration, August–Sept., 1933," OF 8, Box 1, FDRL; Floyd O. Jellison telegram to FDR, March 14, 1933, in "Economy Program, 1933," PPF 200F, Box 157, FDRL; Carrell S. Huston to FDR, June 11, 1933, in "World War Veterans, June 5–June 13, 1933," OF 95, Box 1, FDRL; and *National Tribune*, June 22, 1933.

36. Letter from Lorry A. Jacobs to Marvin H. MacIntire, May 5, 1933, in "World War Veterans, Jan.–May, 1933," OF 95, Box 1, FDRL, and letter from Roy Roberts to Steve Early, May 9, 1933, in "World War Veterans, Jan.–May, 1933," OF 95, Box 1, FDRL.

37. On the ideological formation of World War I soldiers see Keene, *Doughboys*; Mark Meigs, *Optimism at Armageddon: Voices of American Participants in the First World War* (New York: New York University Press, 1997); Nancy K. Bristow, *Making Men Moral: Social Engineering During the Great War* (New York: New York University Press, 1996). For the historical revisionism of the Great War during the 1920s and 1930s, see Warren I. Cohen, *The American Revisionists: The Lessons of Intervention in World War I* (Chicago: University of Chicago Press, 1967).

38. Pencak, *For God and Country*, 193; Dillingham, *Federal Aid to Veterans*, 76–77; Freidel, *Franklin D. Roosevelt: Launching the New Deal*, 449; and Sargent, *Roosevelt and the Hundred Days*, 242–260. "Whittling Down Roosevelt Economy," *Literary Digest* (June 17, 1933): 3–4. Lewis Douglas to James S. Douglas, June 8, 1933, quoted in Sargent, *Roosevelt and the Hundred Days*, 247.

39. Johnson in *American Legion Monthly* (September 1933): 14–15; *Foreign Service* (September 1933): 4.

40. For Steiwer's membership in VFW Post 81, Portland, Oregon, see *Foreign Service* (July 1933). Frederick Steiwer to Cicero Hogan, June 20, 1933, quoted in Sargent, *Roosevelt and the Hundred Days*, 260. Patman in *American Legion Monthly* (October 1933): 21–25, 42.

41. Address of Representative Everett M. Dirksen, August 29, 1933, in *34th National Encampment of the VFW, 1933* (Washington, DC: U.S. Government Printing Office, 1934), 41.

42. On VFW ties, see James J. Lorence, *Gerald J. Boileau and the Progressive-Farm-Labor Alliance*, (Columbia: University of Missouri Press, 1994): 22–45, 75; Everett M. Dirksen, *The Education of a Senator* (Urbana: University of Illinois Press, 1998), 91, 131–132; and, for Robinson, *Foreign Service* (February 1933): 10. On Dirksen membership and Boileau committee position see *34th National Encampment of the VFW, 1933*, 40, 136. *National Tribune*, August 3, 1933. For an example of the floor debate contributions of Steiwer, Long,

and Robinson, see *Congressional Record*, vol. 77, part 5, 73rd Congress, 1st Session (May 26–June 7, 1933): 4614–4321.

43. Attendance estimates in *Chicago Daily Tribune*, August 28, 1933. Address of Senator Arthur Robinson, August 30, 1933, *in 34th National Encampment of the VFW, 1933* (Washington, DC: U.S. Government Printing Office, 1934), 53, 54. Address of Rice W. Means, August 30, 1933, in *34th National Encampment of the VFW, 1933*, 51. Butler Address reprinted in *Foreign Service* (December 1933): 30.

44. Address of Senator Elmer Thomas, August 28, 1933, in *34th National Encampment of the VFW, 1933*, 15–21.

45. Long's appearance at the VFW encampment came within a day of a much-publicized altercation at a Long Island country club in which Long received a probably well-deserved black eye. Dogged by reporters over the incident, Long addressed the encampment in what Brinkley calls "one of the surliest and most vituperative speeches he had ever made." See Brinkley, *Voices of Protest*, 65–66, for story and quote.

46. Address of Senator Huey Long, August 29, 1933, in *34th National Encampment of the VFW, 1933*, 31–39. The "sapling bill" was Long's dismissive term for the Reforestation Act that created the Civilian Conservation Corps.

47. *Foreign Service* (October 1933): 10, 39; Dirksen, *The Education of A Senator*,132–133; "Long Amid Bedlam Denounces Foes," *NYT*, August 30, 1933, 21; "Battle-Scarred 'Kingfish' Fans V.F.W. Frenzy," *Washington Post*, August 30, 1933, 1. The VFW leadership sent formal apologies to the Milwaukee newspapers for Long's "violent abuse" of the assembled newspapermen. See "Veterans Offer Apologies for Speech by Long," *Chicago Daily Tribune*, August 30, 1933, 3.

48. *34th National Encampment of the VFW, 1933*, 253–269.

49. Ibid., 255.

50. Ibid., 117, 255, and *Foreign Service* (October 1933): 9. For list of resolutions, see *34th National Encampment of the VFW, 1933*, 236–269. Quotation in *Foreign Service* (October 1933): 8.

51. Commander James E. Van Zandt to the President, September 22, 1933, in "VFW, 1933–1936," PPF 87, FDRL, and *Foreign Service* (November 1933): 12.

52. "Roosevelt Trip to Give Legion Address Likely," *Washington Post*, October 1, 1933, 1; John C. Fischer to Stephen F. Early, September 15, 1933, in "American Legion, July–Dec., 1933," OF 64, Box 1, FDRL. Johnson quoted in Pencak, *For God and Country*, 194.

53. FDR speech to American Legion Convention, Oct. 2, 1933, in PPF: Speeches, Box 15, FDRL. See also, *Washington Post*, "Legion Looks to President for Guidance" and "Roosevelt to Address Legion Meeting in Chicago Today," October, 2, 1933, 1–2; "Cuban Crisis Is Watched by Roosevelt Aboard Train," October 3, 1933, 1.

54. Dillingham, *Federal Aid to Veterans*, 78; Louis A. Johnson to FDR, October 9, 1933, in "American Legion, 1933," PPF 350, FDRL; and *NYT*, "Legion Declares for Sound Dollar," October 6, 1933, 1; "Roosevelt Holds Firm on Economy in Talk to Legion," October 3, 1933, 1.

55. Commander Frank O. Gangwisch to FDR, in "Soldier's Bonus, 1933," OF 95c, Box 2, FDRL. Van Zandt and Lake image in *Foreign Service* (November 1933): 12 and (December 1933): 4–5.

56. *National Tribune*, October 26, 1933; *NYT*, "Today, on the Radio," September 28, 1933, 19; "Radio Programs Scheduled," October 29, 1933, XX10; and *Foreign Service*, October 1933 to March 1934. See *Foreign Service*, October 1933 to April 1934, for Van Zandt's breakneck tour of VFW posts across the nation.

57. *National Tribune*, December, 14, 1933; "Butler for Bonus out of Wall Street," *NYT*, December 10, 1933, N8; "Break for Vets Asked by Butler,"*Atlanta Constitution*, December 11, 1933, 1. For more on the mercurial Butler, see Hans Schmidt, *Maverick Marine: General Smedley D. Butler and the Contradictions of American Military History* (Lexington: University Press of Kentucky, 1987).

58. Dillingham, *Federal Aid to Veterans*, 74–78; Pencak, *For God and Country*, 196; Rumer, *The American Legion*, 213–215.

59. *Foreign Service* (January 1934): 12, 25; (March 1934): 27; (February 1934): 30, 32.

60. *Foreign Service* (January 1934): 5.

61. Rumer, *The American Legion*, 213–215; Dillingham, *Federal Aid to Veterans*, 78; Pencak, *For God and Country*, 196; and *Foreign Service* (May 1934): 5. Harold L. Ickes, March 31, 1934, diary entry in *The Secret Diary of Harold L. Ickes: The First Thousand Days, 1933–1936* (New York: Simon and Schuster, 1953), 158.

62. Ickes, March 31, 1934, diary entry in *The Secret Diary of Harold L. Ickes*, 158; Krock in "In Washington: Progressives' Defection on Veto a Striking Move," *NYT*, March 30, 1934, 20; "Veterans Again in the Saddle," *Boston Herald*, March 29, 1934, 8; James F. Byrnes, *All in One Lifetime* (New York: Harper, 1958), 75–76; and Stott, "FDR, Lewis Douglas, and the Raw Deal," 117–119.

63. "Veterans Hail Congress," *NYT*, March 30, 1934, 2; *National Tribune*, May 11, 1934; *Foreign Service* (May 1934): 5, 9; and Pencak, *For God and Country*, 196. Kelly and Taylor Reports in *Digest of Minutes, National Executive Committee Meeting, May 3 and 4, 1934*, ALNHL.

64. Long's "Every Man A King" address, reprinted in Henry M. Christman, ed., *Kingfish to America: Share Our Wealth* (New York: Schocken, 1985), 44 (emphasis added). On Coughlin support of FDR policy, see Reverend Charles E. Coughlin, *Driving Out the Money Changers* (Detroit, MI: Radio League of the Little Flower, 1933): 83–91. On 1934 speech, "Bonus Payment Now Urged by Coughlin," *NYT*, February 26, 1934, 3.

CHAPTER 4

1. To date, little dialogue exists between scholars who study the political history of the New Deal and the handful of scholars who have investigated veteran political activism for the Bonus. While quick to discuss the Bonus March of 1932 and to contrast it with FDR's humane treatment of subsequent Bonus Marchers, historians of New Deal politics dismiss the fight for the Bonus from 1934 to 1936 as a minor episode, insignificant to the larger New Deal political narrative. Arthur M. Schlesinger's classic narrative of the period, for example, devotes two perfunctory paragraphs separated by nearly five hundred pages of text to the Bonus fight and its ultimate passage. See Schlesinger, *The Politics of Upheaval*, 10, 504. Meanwhile, scholars such as Roger Daniels, William Pencak, and Jennifer Keene who have studied veteran activism for the Bonus either do so through the lens of the Bonus March or do not systematically link the 1934–1936 battle to the larger political milieu.

2. Schlesinger, *The Coming of the New Deal*, 15; Lisio, *President and Protest*, 291–294; Dickson and Allen, *The Bonus Army*, 207–216; and Daniels, *The Bonus March*, 219–226.

3. See Ernest Lundeen, "Big Business vs. the Veteran," in *Foreign Service* (December 1933): 10, 29. For more on Ludeen, see Richard M. Valelly, *Radicalism in the States: The Minnesota Farm-Labor Party and the American Political Economy* (Chicago: University of Chicago Press, 1989), and *Foreign Service* (March 1934): 9, 27. *NYT*, February 19–21, 1934.

4. Ironically, Lundeen had been kicked out of the VFW in 1917 for his House vote against the U.S. declaration of war. See Mason, *The VFW*, 46–47; Lundeen, "Big Business vs. the Veteran"; *Foreign Service* (January 1934): 5 and (February 1934): 5. *NYT*, February 19–21, 1934.

5. *NYT*, "In Washington: Presidential Veto Appears Possible on Veterans' Bill," February 28, 1934, 18; "Challenging the President," March 10, 1934, 12; and "63 to 27 the Final Vote," March 29, 1934, 1.

6. *Foreign Service* (March 1934): 9, 27. For Rainey quotation, "Bonus Vote Order Forced on House Over Veto Threat," *NYT*, February 21, 1934, 1. For extensive coverage of the Lundeen discharge, see *NYT* and *WSJ*, February 19–22, 1934; and Daniels, *The Bonus March*, 228–229.

7. *Foreign Service* (March 1934): 22, 27.

8. James E. Van Zandt to the President, telegram dated February 28, 1934, in "Soldier's Bonus, 1934," OF 95c, Box 3, FDRL. Report of the Director of Publicity, *35th National Encampment of the VFW, 1934* (Washington, DC: U.S. Government Printing Office, 1935), 237.

9. *Foreign Service* (April 1934): 22, 27.

10. Post totals in *Foreign Service*, December 1933 to April 1934. Handy quote in *National Tribune*, May 17, 1934. Van Zandt quote in "Why Patman Bill Is Urged," *NYT*, April 7, 1934, 14; *NYT*, "Bowie Challenged on Legion Charge," April 7, 1934, 9; and *National Tribune*, April 19, 1934.

11. National Economy League statement "Warn of 'Disaster' in Bonus Payment," in *NYT*, March 5, 1934, 34; Van Zandt in "Why Patman Bill is Urged," *NYT*, April 7, 1934, 14.

12. Long's "Every Man a King" address, reprinted in Henry M. Christman, ed., *Kingfish to America: Share Our Wealth* (New York: Schocken, 1985), 44. See VFW resolution No. 64, *34th National Encampment of the VFW, 1933*, 255. *NYT*, "$139,000,000 Voted by Senate Revives Veteran Benefits," February 28, 1934, 1; "Long's War Record Attacked," April 6, 1934, 4. For Legion commentary on Long and VFW, see Kelly Report in *Digest of Minutes, National Executive Committee Meeting, May 3 and 4, 1934*, ALNHL.

13. For the changed tone in the relationship between Coughlin and FDR beginning in 1934, see Brinkley, *Voices of Protest*, 124–126. Brinkley does not mention Coughlin's turnaround on the Bonus. For Coughlin address, see "United States Incorporated," February 25, 1934, in Charles E. Coughlin, *Eight Lectures on Labor, Capital, and Justice* (Royal Oak, MI: Radio League of the Little Flower, 1934), 83–99. For quotation, 95.

14. Coughlin, *Eight Lectures on Labor, Capital, and Justice*, 95–98, and "Bonus Payment Now Urged by Coughlin," *NYT*, February 26, 1934, 3.

15. For Patman and Coughlin relationship, see Young, *Wright Patman*, 38, 55, 64–65. For Thomas and Coughlin, see Brinkley, *Voices of Protest*, 121, 138.

16. *National Tribune*, March 8, 1934.

17. *NYT*, "House Votes Bonus, 295–125, After Disorderly Debate," March 13, 1934, 1; "In Washington: House Revolt on Bonus Makes Target of Leaders," March 13, 1934, 20; "A Rebellious Congress," March 15, 1934: 22. "Honeymoon's End," *Time*, March 26, 1934, 9–10.

18. *Foreign Service* (April 1934): 4–5, 27.

19. *National Tribune*, May 17, 1934; Dickson and Allen, *The Bonus Army*, 220–221; and Daniels, *The Bonus March*, 228–232.

20. *NYT*, "Bonus Rises Again to Beset Senate," June 6, 1934, 1; "Important Bills Failed of Passage," June 20, 1934, 2; *Los Angeles Times*, "Senators Foes to Bonus Bill," June 7, 1934, 3; "March 27, 1934 Veto Message on Patman Bonus Bill [not used]," FDR Speech File, 673–696, Container 17, "January 3, 1934–May 3, 1934, FDRL; *Foreign Service* (July 1934): 12, 29;

and Report of G. K. Brobeck, Legislative Representative, in *35th National Encampment of the VFW, 1934*, 242–247. The VFW published a list of ten senators who had perfect voting records on veteran affairs. Cutting and Robinson, both VFW members, made the list. So did Huey Long.

21. "Roosevelt Asks Aid of Veterans," *NYT*, October 2, 1934, 2; *Foreign Service* (November 1934): 16–17.

22. "VFW Plans Crusade Against Communists," *NYT*, September 30, 1934, 24; *35th National Encampment of the VFW, 1934*, 113–117.

23. Ibid.

24. *35th National Encampment of the VFW, 1934*, 115–121; "VFW Rejects Plan to Join in Politics," *NYT*, October 5, 1934, 8.

25. Ibid., 119, 121.

26. *35th National Encampment of the VFW, 1934*, 120; *Foreign Service* (November 1934): 4.

27. Louis Johnson to Stephen B. Early, telegram dated October 16, 1934, and Confidential Memorandum to Mr. Early relating Louis Johnson phone conversation dated August 29, 1934, in "American Legion, 1934," OF 64, box 1, FDRL; "Address of the President at the Dedication of the Veterans Hospital, Roanoke, Virginia, October 19, 1934," FDR Speech Files, 741–762, October 19, 1934–January 17, 1935, FDRL; and "The Roosevelt Week," *Time*, October 29, 1934, 9.

28. *NYT*, "Predicts Bonus Victory," October 21, 1934, 29; "VFW Bonus Plea Put to Roosevelt," October 23, 1934, 22; "Asks Legion's Bonus Aid," October 24, 1934, 17.

29. *NYT*, "Roosevelt to the Veterans," October 20, 1934, 14; "Roosevelt's View Stirs Legion Head," October 20, 1934, 8.

30. "Miami Meet," *Time*, November 5, 1934, 9–10; *NYT*, "Legion Floor Fight Looms Over Bonus," October 22, 1934, 16; "Warns Legion Not to 'Rock Boat,'" October 23, 1934, 1; "'Bonus Now' Urged in Legion Report," October 25, 1934, 1.

31. *NYT*, October 24–26, 1934; Pencak, *For God and Country*, 204; "Miami Meet," *Time*, November 5, 1934, 9–10; Morris A. Beale to Louis W. Howe, November 9, 1934, in "Veterans' Administration, 1934–35 (misc.)," OF 8, Box 3, FDRL; and Flier attached to letter dated November 3, 1934, from J. L. Fox to Louis M. Howe, OF 95c, Box 3, "Soldier's Bonus, 1934," FDRL.

32. *NYT*, "Legion Committee to Consider Bonus," October 30, 1934, 12; "Hines Sees Chance to Drop Bonus Demand," November 2, 1934, 2; "To Push Bonus Fight Says New Legion Head," November 10, 1934, 1; "Legion Head, at Brilliant Banquet, Pledges Work for 'Bonus' Payment," *Atlanta Constitution*, November 1, 1934, 1; John Thomas Taylor, "Memorandum of Address to the National Executive Committee," November 19–24, 1934, ALNHL; and Press Statement of Frank N. Belgrano, Jr., November 28, 1934, in "Veteran Welfare-Adjusted Compensation-Federal-1935," ALNHL.

33. For the view of the Democratic gains in the 1934 election as a great FDR victory, see *NYT*, "Democratic Sweep Dazes Opponents" and "Democrats Gain Ten Senate Seats," November 7, 1934, 5, 11; Schlesinger, *The Age of Roosevelt, Vol. 2*, 489–511. Statistical summary of 74th Congress in Michael J. Dubin, *United States Congressional Elections, 1788–1997: The Official Results* (Jefferson, NC: McFarland, 1998), 500–510. House Roll Call on the Bonus in *NYT*, March 13, 1934, 2; "Line-up for 1935," *Time*, November 19, 1934, 12–15. VFW opinion in *Foreign Service* (December 1934): 4, 14.

34. Charles E. Coughlin, "The National Union for Social Justice, Nov. 11, 1934," in Coughlin, *A Series of Lectures on Social Justice* (Royal Oak, MI: Radio League of the Little Flower, 1935), 8, 17. Brinkley, *Voices of Protest*, 133–134.

35. For radio programming on Armistice Day, 1934, see "On the Radio Today," in *NYT*, November 11, 1934, X14. Coughlin, "The National Union for Social Justice, November 11, 1934," in *A Series of Lectures on Social Justice*, 7, 11. While the launch of Coughlin's National Union drew widespread commentary from contemporary chroniclers and subsequent generations of historians, no account of Coughlin or the National Union for Social Justice investigates this matter of timing.

36. Coughlin, "The National Union for Social Justice, November 11, 1934," in *A Series of Lectures on Social Justice*, 11, 18–19.

37. Louis Johnson to Marvin McIntyre, letter dated December 10, 1934, in "American Legion, 1934," OF 64, box 1, FDRL, and Garland R. Farmer, Henderson, Texas, October 31, 1934, letter to FDR, in "Soldiers' Bonus, 1934," OF 95c, Box 3, FDRL.

38. Copy of FDR letter to Garland R. Farmer, dated December 27, 1934, in "Soldiers' Bonus, 1934," OF 95c, Box 3, FDRL, and "Roosevelt Takes Stand Against Bonus Payment," *NYT*, January 1, 1935, 1.

39. Stephen Early to Garland R. Farmer, telegram dated December 27, 1934, in "Soldiers' Bonus, 1934," OF 95c, Box 3, FDRL. For national coverage, see *NYT, Washington Post, and WSJ*, January 1,1935. *Washington Post*, January 1–2, 1935. Garland R. Farmer to Steve Early, letter dated January 18, 1935, and Major L. R. Elkins to Garland R. Farmer, letter dated January 1, 1935, in "Soldiers' Bonus, 1934," OF 95c, Box 3, FDRL.

40. For Van Zandt prediction that FDR would sign a Bonus Bill in the coming session, see *National Tribune*, January 3, 1935. The rest of the paragraph is from *National Tribune*, January 10, 1935.

41. Emphasis added, *National Tribune*, January 10, 1935. Later, the VFW claimed that an investigation of Farmer's service record showed only thirteen days in actual service. See *Foreign Service* (February 1935): 17. Van Zandt comments in *National Tribune*, January 10, 1935, and "Bonus Fight Compromise Is Weighed," *Washington Post*, January 2, 1935, 1.

42. "Legion Chief Hits Warning on Bonus," *NYT*, January 2, 1935, 8.

CHAPTER 5

1. Alan Brinkley's seminal study of Long and Coughlin offers anecdotal evidence that suggests that veterans actively participated in Long and Coughlin's organizations because of each man's support for the immediate cash payment of the Bonus. Yet Brinkley accepts the Bonus as simply a matter of interest-group politics, not the ideologically divisive issue it was to become. As a result, Brinkley overlooks the importance of the Bonus, veteran organizations, and veteran political activism to the Long and Coughlin movements. See Brinkley, *Voices of Protest*, esp. 182, 194–198.

2. FDR's State of the Union Address—the first one referred to by that phrase—can be found in Franklin D. Roosevelt, "Annual Message to Congress, January 4, 1935," in Samuel Rosenman, ed., *The Public Papers of Franklin D. Roosevelt, Vol. 4* (New York: Random House, 1938), 15–25. The 1935 Congressional session ultimately produced the signature legislation of the New Deal: the Social Security Act, the Wagner Act, and the Works Progress Administration. Byrns in "Early Bonus Vote Pledged In House On Congress Eve," *NYT*, January 3, 1935: 1; "Roosevelt and the Bonus," *Los Angeles Times*, January 3, 1935, A4. Veteran Bonus Marcher in Dickson and Allen, *The Bonus Army*, 222–223 and "Shouts at President, Veteran Arrested," *NYT*, January 5, 1935, 4.

3. John Russell to Frank Belgrano, January 12, 1935 in "Veteran Welfare-Adjusted Compensation-Federal-1935," ALNHL; Daniels, *The Bonus March*, 235; *National Tribune*, February 7, 1935; and Vinson quote in Young, *Wright Patman*, 57.

4. *Foreign Service* (February 1935): 4, 17. Patman quote and Patman-Belgrano feud in Young, *Wright Patman*, 59, and Pencak, *For God and Country*, 204–205.

5. *Foreign Service* (March 1935): 7, 12–13; "VFW Supports Patman on Bonus," *NYT*, February 9, 1935, 4; *National Tribune*, February 14, 1935.

6. For good summaries of the House Committee and Floor battles, see Daniels, *The Bonus March*, 234–235; Rumer, *The American Legion*, 219–220; Pencak, *For God and Country*, 204; and Young, *Wright Patman*, 57–60. See also, *NYT*, March 7–14, 1935, *Washington Post*, March 7–14, 1935, and *National Tribune*, March 14, 1935.

7. *NYT*, "Assails Roosevelt in Debate on Bonus," March 21, 1935, 17; "Inflationary Bill Chosen by House on Bonus, 202-191," March 22, 1935, 1; *Washington Post*, "In Congress," March 21, 1935, 2; "Bonus Bill Test Won by Patman; Final Vote Today" and "How Members of House Voted on the Patman Bonus Measure," March 22, 1935, 1, 6. Vinson quoted in Daniels, *The Bonus March*, 235. *NYT*, "Inflation Bonus Adopted in House by Vote of 318–90," "Vote on Bonus Bill," and "The Bonus Bill," March 23, 1935, 1, 2, 14; "House Votes Greenback Bonus, 318 to 90, Defying Roosevelt," *Washington Post*, March 23, 1935, 1.

8. "Between You and Me," *Washington Post*, March 22, 1935, 2; *NYT*, "35 Members in House Drop Party Lines to Join in Drive for Liberal Legislation," March 10, 1935, 1; "House 'Mavericks' Threaten a Fight," April 14, 1935, E10. Information on the Liberal Bloc and Progressive Group in James L. Lawrence, *Gerald J. Boileau and the Progressive-Farmer-Labor Alliance: Politics of the New Deal* (Columbia: University of Missouri Press, 1994), 114–116.

9. *Washington Post*, May 3–12, 1935; Henry Morgenthau, Jr., to FDR, letter dated June 6, 1934, in Henry Morgenthau, Jr. Papers, Box 517, "The President, May, 1934–July, 1934," FDRL; and McAdoo and Clark in *Congressional Record*, vol. 79, part 7, 74th Congress, 1st Session, Senate, May 6–May 23: 7058–7068, and "The Senate and the Bonus," *Los Angeles Times*, May 8, 1935, A4.

10. *Washington Post*, May 3–12, 1935, quotation in "Patman Bonus Passed by Senate, 55–33" and "Veto Seen to Doom Pay Now," May 8, 1935, 1; "Joyride," *Time*, May 20, 1935, 14; "Payment of Bonus With New Money Voted by Senate," *Los Angeles Times*, May 8, 1935, 1; and "Senate Passes Patman Bonus Bill With Two Billion, But It Might Uphold Veto," *NYT*, May 8, 1935, 1.

11. *Washington Post*, May 9–15, 1935, and *NYT*, May 9–5, 1935.

12. *NYT*, "Compromise Bonus Pushed for Senate," April 23, 1935, 10; "Bonus Forces Split on Their Next Move," June 9, 1935, E10; *Literary Digest*, "Topics of the Day" (May 4, 1935): 4-5; and "Joyride," *Time*, May 20, 1935, 14.

13. For a sample of Van Zandt's exhausting schedule, see *Foreign Service* (February–June 1935). *NYT*, "Compromise Bonus Pushed for Senate," April 23, 1935, 10; "Senate Kills Cash Bonus," May 24, 1935, 1. *Literary Digest*, "Topics of the Day" (May 4, 1935): 4–5 and "Topics of the Day" (May 18, 1935): 6–7.

14. Frank N. Belgrano, Jr., "Let's Have the Truth!," in *American Legion Monthly* (March 1935): 24–25, 54; Memorandum for Steve Early from Colonel Monroe Johnson and Louis Johnson, April 4, 1935, in OF 95c, box 3, "Soldiers bonus, January–April, 1935," FDRL; and "Joyride," *Time*, May 20, 1935, 14.

15. VFW post formation totals and "Hello America" proceedings in *Foreign Service* (February–July 1935). *National Tribune*, May 9, 1935.

16. Charles E. Coughlin, "The Future of the National Union, February 3, 1935," in Coughlin, *A Series of Lectures on Social Justice*, 137–152. NUSJ estimate in Brinkley, *Voices of Protest*, 179.

17. Brinkley, *Voices of Protest*, 175–177; Charles Tully, *Father Coughlin and the New Deal* (Syracuse, NY: Syracuse University Press, 1965), 93–97; *Literary Digest* (May 4, 1935): 4–5 and (May 18, 1935): 6–7; and "Radio Priest Raps Regime," *Los Angeles Times*, May 9, 1935, 3.

18. Charles E. Coughlin, "Solidarity and Social Justice, May 5, 1935," in Coughlin, *A Series of Lectures, May 5th to June 9th, Incl.* (Royal Oak, Michigan: Radio League of the Little Flower, 1935), 9–14.

19. Ibid.; "Between You and Me," *Washington Post*, May 8, 1935, 2.

20. Coughlin, "Social Justice and the Distribution of Wealth, May 12, 1935," in Coughlin, *A Series of Lectures, May 5th to June 9th, Incl.*, 13–24.

21. "Senators Split as Bonus Fight Goes on Floor," *Washington Post*, May 3, 1935, 1; T. Harry Williams, *Huey Long* (New York: Alfred A. Knopf, 1969), 828–829; and "Tydings and Long Clash Over Bonus," *Los Angeles Times*, May 11, 1935, 1.

22. Speech in Henry M. Christman, ed., *Kingfish to America: Share Our Wealth, Selected Senatorial Papers of Huey P. Long* (New York: Schocken, 1985), 112–118, and Ernest G. Bormann, *A Rhetorical Analysis of the National Radio Broadcasts of Senator Huey P. Long* (Iowa City: University of Iowa Press, 1953), 71, 318–319.

23. Christman, ed., *Kingfish to America*, 112–118.

24. Ibid.

25. Brinkley, *Voices of Protest*, 169–170, 182, 195–196. Quotation, 196. Estimates in Williams, *Huey Long*, 700–701. "Hurja Starts Quiz of Long in D.C. Home," *Washington Post*, July 27, 1935, 13.

26. Frank R. Kent, *Los Angeles Times*, "The Great Game of Politics," May 15, 1935, 4; *Literary Digest*, "Topics of the Day"(April 27, 1935): 6 and "Topics of the Day" (May 4, 1935): 4–5; Brinkley, *Voices of Protest*, 210–215; *Foreign Service* (April 1935): 9; and "Patman Bill Veto Ready and Strong, The Capital Hears," *NYT*, May 14, 1935, 1.

27. Johnson quoted in Brinkley, *Voices of Protest*, 6; "Dr. Peale Attacks Father Coughlin," *NYT*, May 13, 1935, 16; and Raymond Gram Swing, *The Forerunners of American Fascism* (New York: Julian Messner, 1935).

28. Sinclair Lewis, *It Can't Happen Here* (New York: Doubleday, 1935). For the breaking Butler story, see "General Butler Bares 'Fascist Plot,'" *NYT*, November 21, 1934, 1. For the best accounts of the Butler Plot, see Schmidt, *Maverick Marine*, 223–231 and Jules Archer, *The Plot to Seize the White House: The Shocking True Story of the Conspiracy to Overthrow FDR* (New York: Skyhorse), 2007.

29. FDR to Colonel House, February 16, 1935, in "House, Colonel Edward," PPF 222, FDRL. For the Farley quote and the most thorough discussion of the Hurja Poll, see Edwin Amenta, Kathleen Dunleavy, and Mary Bernstein, "Stolen Thunder: Huey Long's 'Share Our Wealth,' Political Mediation, and the Second New Deal," *American Sociological Review* 59.5 (October 1994): 687–689. Farley to cabinet in Ickes diary, May 10, 1935, entry, *The Secret Diary of Harold L. Ickes*, 360.

30. According to senior archivist Robert Clark of the Franklin D. Roosevelt Library and Museum, the public-reaction mail regarding the Bonus bill veto is "one of the largest single issue reactions that the White House received. PPF 200 L: Public Reaction: Bonus Bill Veto (Containers 164–210) totals 47 boxes, approximately 37,600 pages. By comparison, the reaction mail to the Court Packing Plan (located in Official File 41: Judiciary Reorganization Act of 1937) totals 47 boxes. Reaction mail to the Third Term issue (OF 2526:

Third Term) totals 50 boxes." This tally does not include the substantial reaction mail in OF 95c: "In Favor of the Bonus." Quotation from e-mail message, Robert Clark to author, July 29, 2002, in author's possession. "Joyride," *Time*, May 20, 1935, 14.

31. Richard Demmary to FDR, April 30, 1935, in "In Favor of the Bonus: D–G, 1935," OF95c, Box 4, FDRL; Frank Anderson to FDR, undated, in "Soldiers' Bonus—Approval of, A," OF 95c, Box 3, FDRL; Edwin A. Lake, Brooklyn, NY, to FDR, May 12, 1935, in "Bonus Bill Veto, 1935, Against," PPF 200L, Cont. 169, FDRL; and Joseph Eugene Dash, Chicago, IL, letter to FDR, May 16, 1935, in "Bonus Bill Veto, Against," PPF 200L, Cont. 174, folder 3, FDRL.

32. Joseph P. Nash, Cleveland, OH, to FDR, May 11, 1935 in "Bonus Bill Veto, Against," PPF 200L, Cont. 184, folder 5, FDRL; Winfield Phelps, Minneapolis, MN, to FDR, May 10, 1935, in "Bonus Bill Veto, Against," PPF 200L, Cont. 182, folder 4, FDRL; Robert L. Turner to H. B. Caultonborn (copy to FDR), May 20, 1935, in "Bonus Bill Veto, Against," PPF 200L, Cont. 169, FDRL; and John O'Connell, Long Island City, NY, to FDR, July 16, 1935, in "Soldiers' Bonus—In Favor of, H–K," OF 95c, box 4, FDRL.

33. James O. Sabin to Patman, copy to White House, April 17, 1935, in "In Favor of Bonus, Q–S, May, 1935," OF 95c, box 4, FDRL; R. S. Appleton, Attleboro, MA, to FDR, May 10, 1935, in "Bonus Bill Veto, Against," PPF 200L, Cont. 182, folder 2, FDRL; Benjamin C. Tunis, Watervliet, MI, to FDR, May, 1935, in "Bonus Bill Veto, Against," PPF 200L, Cont. 182, folder 4, FDRL.

34. E. J. Hawes, Drexell Hill, PA, telegram to FDR, May 10, 1935, in "Bonus Bill Veto, Against," PPF 200L, Cont. 192, FDRL; John Allen, Jersey City, NJ, to FDR, May 11, 1935, in "Bonus Bill Veto, Against," PPF 200L, Cont. 169, FDRL; and Frederick E. Rieger, Englewood, NJ, letter to FDR, May 10, 1935, in "Bonus Bill Veto, Pro," PPF 200L, Cont. 194, FDRL.

35. Harry R. Bowen, Troup, TX, letter to FDR, May 17, 1935, in "Bonus Bill Veto, Against," PPF 200L, Cont. 174, folder 3, FDRL, emphasis in original; E. L. Westbrook, Meridian, MS, letter to FDR, March 27, 1935, in "In Favor of Bonus, V–Z, Feb.–July, 1935," OF 95c, box 5, FDRL; E. Harry Schiome, New York, NY, letter to FDR, May 13, 1935, in "Bonus Bill Veto, Against," PPF 200L, Cont. 171, folder 1, FDRL; and E. F. Hackett, New York, NY, telegram to Marvin H. McIntyre, May 11, 1935, in "In Favor of Bonus, H–K, May, 1935," OF 95c, box 4, FDRL.

36. Memo sent FDR by ER, copy in Henry Morenthau, Jr., Papers, Box 517, "The President, Jan. 1935–March, 1935," FDRL. Schlesinger, *Politics of Upheal*, 10–11; Davis, *FDR: The New Deal Years*, 513; and on FDR, Morgenthau, Germany, and fiscal conservatism, Zelizer, "The Forgotten Legacy of the New Deal."

37. Ickes diary entry for May 3, 1935, Ickes, *The Secret Diary of Harold Ickes*, 356, and James A. Farley, *Jim Farley's Story: The Roosevelt Years* (New York: McGraw-Hill, 1948), 53–54.

38. Farley, *Jim Farley's Story*, 53–54; for Garner and Farley rumors, see "Senate Sends Bonus Today to Roosevelt," *Washington Post*, May 14, 1935, 1; "Roosevelt Forces Firm on Bonus Bill," *NYT*, May 15, 1935, 1; "Roosevelt to Deliver Bonus Veto in Person," *Los Angeles Times*, May 18, 1935, 1; Press Conference #205, May 17, 1935, in *Press Conferences of Franklin D. Roosevelt, 1933–1945*, FDRL; Henry Morgenthau, Jr. Diaries, May 20, 1935, Roll 2, Book 5:115, FDRL; Davis, *FDR: The New Deal Years*, 513; Rosenman, *Working With Roosevelt*, 94; Schlesinger, *Politics of Upheaval*, 10–11; and "Senators Break Long Filibuster, Hear Veto Today," *Washington Post*, May 22, 1935, 1.

39. "Praise and Blame Greet Bonus Veto," *NYT*, May 23, 1935, 1; *Literary Digest*, "Topics of the Day" (June 1, 1935): 5–7, and, for multiple thorough descriptions of the spectacle and reaction, *Washington Post* and *NYT*, May 23, 1935.

40. Text of veto message printed in Franklin D. Roosevelt, "The President Vetoes the Bonus Bill, May 22, 1935," in Rosenman, ed., *The Public Papers of Franklin D. Roosevelt, Vol. 4*, 182–193, and "Text of Roosevelt's Address Vetoing Patman Bonus Bill," *Washington Post*, May 23, 1935, 6.

41. Roosevelt, "The President Vetoes the Bonus Bill, May 22, 1935," in Rosenman, ed., *The Public Papers of Franklin D. Roosevelt, Vol. 4*, 185–186, and American Liberty League quoted in "Topics of the Day," *Literary Digest* (June 1, 1935): 6. On the issue of Roosevelt's rediscovery of fiscal restraint, William Leuchtenbrg's classic New Deal narrative accuses Roosevelt's veto message of sounding "for all the world like Grover Cleveland venting his indignation at the Silver Purchase Act." Leuchtenburg, *Franklin D. Roosevelt and the New Deal*, 147.

42. Roosevelt, "The President Vetoes the Bonus Bill, May 22, 1935," in Rosenman, ed., *The Public Papers of Franklin D. Roosevelt, Vol. 4*, 187–190, and *Washington Post*, May 23, 1935, 6.

43. Conspicuously, Long absented himself from the proceedings. After Long and Steiwer held up the vote allowing FDR to address the joint session with a failed filibuster, both of these Bonus champions in the Senate boycotted the session. Roosevelt, "The President Vetoes the Bonus Bill, May 22, 1935," in Rosenman, ed., *The Public Papers of Franklin D. Roosevelt, Vol. 4*, 187–190; "The President's Veto," *Los Angeles Times*, May 23, 1935, A4; *Washington Post*, "Between You and Me," "The Veto Message," Check to the Demagogues," and "Along the Potomac," May 23, 1935, 2, 8, 9; "Topics of the Day," *Literary Digest* (May 18, 1935): 6; and "Winter's End," *Time* May 27, 1935, 13. Schlesinger begins his account of the second New Deal with FDR's resurgence in the Bonus bill veto; Schlesinger, *The Politics of Upheaval*, 10–11, 290. Davis pinpoints Roosevelt's new initiative to a few days earlier, to a secret May 14 meeting with congressional Progressives—all of whom voted for the Patman Bonus bill—on the very day the Bonus bill was delivered to the White House. However, Davis also views the veto message as the first public manifestation of this change in attitude. Davis, *FDR: The New Deal Years*, 493, 510–511.

44. "Topics of the Day," *Literary Digest* (June 1, 1935): 4; *Washington Post*, "White House Rejection Beaten 45 Minutes After Message" and "The Veto Message," May 23, 1935, 1, 8; and *NYT*, "Bonus Movement Swift" and "Praise and Blame Greet Bonus Veto," May 23, 1935, 1.

45. For quotation, see Brinkley, *Voices of Protest*, 176. On comparison to Bryan see Brinkley, 176–177, "Young Crowd Halls New 'Emancipator,'" *Wall Street Journal*, May 23, 1935; 1, and "23,000 Cheer Coughlin Attack on the President," *NYT*, May 23, 1935; 1. Money-changers quotation in "Topics of the Day," *Literary Digest* (June 1, 1935): 6.

46. "23,000 Cheer Coughlin Attack on the President," *NYT*, May 23, 1935, 1.

47. "Roosevelt Wins 8-Vote Margin as Senate Kills Patman Bonus," *Washington Post*, May 24, 1935, 1 and "Senate Kills Cash Bonus," *NYT*, May 24, 1935, 1. Long and Steiwer and debate in *Congressional Record*, vol. 79, part 7, 74th Congress, 1st Session, Senate, May 6-May 23: 8034–8067 and Christman, ed., *Kingfish to America*, 112–130. Frank R. Kent, *Los Angeles Times*, "The Great Game of Politics," *Los Angeles Times*, May 17, 1935: 4. For similar analysis, see "In Washington: Some Kind of Bonus Held Sure Before Campaign," *NYT*, May 23, 1935, 22.

48. "Roosevelt Wins 8-Vote Margin As Senate Kills Patman Bonus," *Washington Post*, May 24, 1935, 1.

49. *Foreign Service* (June 1935): 4–5.

50. Ibid.

51. Legion leader's comment in "Bonus Forces Split on Their Next Move," *NYT*, June 9, 1935, E10. "Legion Head Defends Demands," *Los Angeles Times*, May 23, 1935, 3; "Belgrano Opposes Demonstration," *NYT*, May 25, 1935, 2; "Two Records: Hoover Vs. Roosevelt" in "American Legion, 1936," OF 64, Box 2, FDRL.

52. Alice Veterans McCoy letter to FDR, May 25, 1935, in "Bonus Bill Veto," PPF 200L, Cont. 167, folder M, FDRL; Howard H. Banker letter to FDR, May 22, 1935, in "Bonus Bill Veto," PPF 200L, Cont. 164, folder B, FDRL; R. H. Baker letter to FDR, May 24, 1935, in "Bonus Bill Veto," PPF 200L, Cont. 164, folder B, FDRL; Dr. Rodney D. Book letter to FDR, May 24, 1935, and copy of letter to Mel G. Underwood, May 24, 1935, in "Bonus Bill Veto," PPF 200L, Cont. 164, folder B, FDRL; P. A. Rishberger letter to FDR, May 22, 1935, in "Bonus Bill Veto," PPF 200L, Cont. 167, folder R, FDRL;

53. John W. Marshall letter to FDR, May 22, 1935, in "Bonus Bill Veto," PPF 200L, Cont. 167, folder M, FDRL; Michigan World War Veterans letter to FDR, May 23, 1935, in "Bonus Bill Veto," PPF 200L, Cont. 167, folder M, FDRL; Lawrence B. Parker, undated letter to FDR, in "Bonus Bill Veto," PPF 200L, Cont. 167, folder P, FDRL; and George C. Post telegram to FDR, May 22, 1935, in "Bonus Bill Veto," PPF 200L, Cont. 167, folder P, FDRL.

CHAPTER 6

1. For literature on the "second" New Deal, see note 20 in Introduction. Raymond Moley, *After Seven Years* (Lincoln: University of Nebraska Press, 1971), 305, 308–312. For a new appraisal of the WPA, see Jason Scott Smith, *Building New Deal Liberalism: The Political Economy of Public Works, 1933–1956* (New York: Cambridge University Press, 2005).

2. For an example of the Bonus's negative effect on other legislation, see *NYT*, "Bonus Vote Assurances Given," March 11, 1935, 2; "Hopes Are Fading for Security Bill," March 20, 1935, 4; "Congress Delays on New Deal Legislation," May 5, 1935, E4; and "Bonus Forces Split on Next Move," June 9, 1935, E10. For riders, see "New Bonus Push Opens," *Los Angeles Times*, July 25, 1935, 3. For the lengthy spat involving the VFW, Patman, and Belgrano, see *Los Angeles Times*, "Bonus Loss Blame Fixed," July 5, 1935, 2; "Lost Bonus Blame Laid by Veteran," August 30, 1935, 4; and "Head of Legion Defends Fight for Cash Bonus," September 3, 1935, 1. For the administration deal on the Bonus and new Bonus petition, see "Administration 'Deal' Shelves Bonus Issue for this Session," *Washington Post*, August 7, 1935, 1; "Price of Passage," *Time*, August 26, 1935, 17; and "Patman Bill Action Sure," *Los Angeles Times*, August 23, 1935, 0.

3. Henry Morgenthau, Jr., to FDR, dated September 4, 1935, in Henry Morgenthau, Jr., Papers, Box 517, "The President, September, 1935–December, 1935," FDRL.

4. *Foreign Service* (October 1935): 8–9, 28, 30.

5. "New Bonus Drive Pledged by VFW," *NYT*, September 18, 1935, 16. Eulogy delivered by Reverend Gerald Smith in *36th National Encampment of the VFW, 1935* (Washington, DC: U.S. Government Printing Office, 1936), 40–41.

6. Butler and Talmadge addresses in *36th National Encampment of the VFW, 1935*, 33–37 and 355–360.

7. Patman address in *36th National Encampment of the VFW, 1935*, 339–344. List of resolutions in *Foreign Service* (October 1935): 18–19. For more on the 1935 Labor Day Hurricane and the veteran work camps, see Gary Dean Best's anti-Roosevelt polemic *FDR and the Bonus Marchers, 1933–1935* (Westport, CT: Praeger, 1992), and Dickson and Allen, *The Bonus Army*, 224–251. List of resolutions in *Foreign Service* (October 1935): 18–19.

8. Bonus resolution in *Foreign Service* (October 1935): 18–19. Unsuccessful Lundeen resolution in "VFW Asks Congress for Gale Toll Inquiry," *Washington Post*, September 20, 1935, 1. It is unknown if Lundeen was related to the Farm-Labor congressman Ernst Lundeen.

9. Frank M. Kirwin, Department Adjutant, to Stephen Early, telegram dated September 10, 1935; memo on copy of Kirwin telegram sent to Anning Prall, dated September 11, 1935; and memorandum from Edna M. Savord, Secretary to Anning S. Prall to White House, September 14, 1935, in "Veterans of Foreign Wars, 1935–1937," OF 84, FDRL.

10. Confidential letter from Joe Heffernan to Steve Early, September 18, 1935, in "Veterans of Foreign Wars, 1935–1937," OF 84, FDRL. Heffernan is a fascinating character. A self-proclaimed "broken-down vet" who worked with Early on *Stars and Stripes*, Heffernan rose to prominence in Ohio Democratic circles during the 1920s, ultimately becoming mayor of Youngstown. Yet, in the summer of 1932, Heffernan led a group of one hundred Youngstown veterans to Washington, DC, to join in the Bonus March. In fact, Heffernan edited and printed the official news organ of the Bonus March, *The BEF News*. By 1935, Heffernan had been appointed to his FCC attorney post. For Heffernan's life, see obituary in *Youngstown Vindicator*, April 21, 1977. For roster of *Stars and Stripes* employees, see the Library of Congress American Memory Web site dedicated to *The Stars and Stripes*, especially the special section "A Closer Look at *The Stars and Stripes*," at http://memory.loc.gov/ammem/sgphtml/sashtml/sp.html.

11. FDR's Chicago speech to the American Legion, October 2, 1933, in which FDR said, "No person, because he wore a uniform must thereafter be placed in a special class of beneficiaries over and above all other citizens." See chapter 3 for details. Joe Heffernan to Steve Early, September 18, 1935, in "Veterans of Foreign Wars, 1935–1937," OF 84, FDRL.

12. Joe Heffernan to Stephen Early, telegram dated September 20, 1935, and Frank M. Kirwin to Stephen Early, telegram dated September 20, 1935, in "Veterans of Foreign Wars, 1935–1937," OF 84, FDRL.

13. Frank M. Kirwin to Stephen Early, telegram dated September 20, 1935, in "Veterans of Foreign Wars, 1935–1937," OF 84, FDRL. Heffernan nominating speech in *36th National Encampment of the VFW*, *1935*, 72–73.

14. Memorandum for Mr. McIntyre, May 27, 1935 in "American Legion, 1935," OF 64, Box 2, FDRL. "Pledge the Nation at Legion Service," *NYT*, June 17, 1935, 37.

15. Vilas H. Whaley, "Shall the Legion Remain Non-Political?" *The American Legion Monthly*, September 1935: 14–17, 42–44, on Legion invitations, see *NYT*, "President Talks Relief to Lehman," September 10, 1935, 7; "Colby Drops Talk at Legion Request," September 16, 1935, 14; Memorandum to the President from Stephen Early, September 16, 1935, in "Soldiers' Bonus, May–December, 1935," OF 95c, Box 3, FDRL; *NYT*, "Roosevelt Limits Speeches in the West; Drops Legion Talk," September 19, 1935, 1; "Talk By President Still Legion Hope," September 21, 1935, 5;; "Roosevelt Drops Legion Visit Plan," September 23, 1935, 8; Frank Belgrano, Jr. to the President, September 26, 1935 in "American Legion, 1935," OF 64, Box 2, FDRL.

16. William McAdoo to the President, September 12, 1935, with enclosure William H. Neblett to Hon. William G. McAdoo, September 9, 1935, and Memo for Mr. Early, September 17, 1935, in "American Legion, 1935," OF 64, Box 2, FDRL.

17. For American Legion resolutions, see *NYT*, "Legion Urges End of Link to Soviet," September 26, 1935, 1; "Legion for Bonus, But Boos Patman and Bars His Plan," September 27, 1935, 1; "Elmers in St. Louis," *Time*, October 7, 1935, 14–15.

18. On Patman-Legion feud, see "Bonus Loss Blame Fixed," *Los Angeles Times*, July 5, 1935, 2; John Thomas Taylor, "The Battle of Capitol Hill," *American Legion Monthly* (July 1935): 12–13, 54–58; Whaley, "Shall the Legion Remain Non-Political?" *American Legion Monthly* (September 1935): 14–17, 42–44; and "Patriotic Emotion Stirs the Legion," *NYT*, September 24, 1935, 6. On convention bedlam, see "Legion Picks Murphy for Bonus Fight," *Los Angeles Times*, September 27, 1935, 1; "Elmers in St. Louis," *Time*, October 7, 1935, 14–15; *NYT*, "Legion for Bonus, But Boos Patman and Bars His Plan," September 27, 1935, 1; "New Legion Head Predicts Bonus," *NYT*, September 28, 1935, 4.

19. *NYT*, "11 Are in the Race to Head Legion," September 22, 1935, 28; "Legion for Bonus, But Boos Patman and Bars His Plan," September 27, 1935, 1; "Legion Picks Murphy for Bonus Fight," *Los Angeles Times*, September 27, 1935, 1; and "Elmers in St. Louis," *Time*, October 7, 1935, 14–15.

20. William McAdoo to Colonel McIntyre, October, 7, 1935, and Confidential Memorandum to Senator McAdoo from Dean Warner, undated, in "American Legion, 1935," OF 64, Box 2, FDRL.

21. William McAdoo to Colonel McIntyre, October, 7, 1935; Confidential Memorandum to Senator McAdoo from Dean Warner, undated; and George Berry to Marvin McIntyre, October 24, 1935, in "American Legion, 1935," OF 64, Box 2, FDRL.

22. *Digest of Minutes, National Executive Committee Meeting, November 1 and 2, 1935*, ALNHL; *NYT*, "President to Make Armistice Speech," October 26, 1935, 3; "Roosevelt Puts World Peace First in National Aims," November 12, 1935, 1; "Bonus Demand Put Before Roosevelt," November 16, 1935, 2; "Roosevelt Hears Legion Bonus Plea," December 18, 1935, 3. On the Murphy-Van Zandt meeting, see *Foreign Service* (February 1936): 7, 42, and Mason, *VFW*, 95. DAV statement in "Urges Unity on One Bill," *NYT*, January 1, 1936, 3.

23. Van Zandt in "Bonus Bill Hope Aired," *Los Angeles Times*, October 23, 1935, 7. Murphy's comments in *NYT*, "Legion Head Warns of Bonus Fumble," November 24, 1935, 2; "Roosevelt Hears Legion Bonus Plea," December 18, 1935, 3. Poll results in "Veterans Bonus, Interviews Conducted Nov. 4–9, 1935," in *The Gallup Poll: Public Opinion, 1935–1971*, Vol. 1 (New York: Random House, 1975), 4; "Veterans Are People," *American Legion Monthly* (January 1936): 25; and Keene, *Doughboys*, 203. Byrnes in "Congress Leaders See Passage Early in Session," *NYT*, December 20, 1935, 1, and "Country and Cash," *Time*, December 30, 1935, 7.

24. Between November and January 6, 1936, Coughlin included lengthy discussions of the Patman plan in two of his addresses. "Our Sovereign Right and the Patman Plan" and "The Bonus and Neutrality" rehashed the arguments for the Patman bill given in 1934 and early 1935. Both are found in *A Series of Lectures on Social Justice* (Royal Oak, MI: Radio League of the Little Flower, 1936), 22–37, 111–115. Patman sent repeated telegrams to Coughlin on the renewed Bonus fight. For copies of telegrams and Coughlin-Patman correspondence, see the "Rev. Charles E. Coughlin" file, Box 122c in the Papers of Wright Patman (WPP), Lyndon B. Johnson Library (LBJL). Daniels, *Bonus March*, 240–241. House Bill preamble in "Marching Orders," *Time*, January 20, 1936, 16.

25. Daniels, *Bonus March*, 240; "Hat and Handkerchief," *Time*, January 27, 1936, 18; *NYT*, "Bonus Bill Passes in Senate, 74–16," January 21, 1936, 1; "Bonus Bond Bill Passed and Rushed to President," January 23, 1936, 1.

26. Ickes diary entries of January 17 and 24, 1936, *The Secret Diary of Harold L. Ickes*, 516, 525 and Farley, *Jim Farley's Story*, 58–59.

27. Ickes diary entry of January 24, 1936, *The Secret Diary of Harold L. Ickes*, 523–525, and "Politics and People," *Washington Post*, January 25, 1936, 2. Text of 1936 Bonus Veto Message in Roosevelt, "The President Vetoes for a Second Time the Soldiers' Bonus, January 24, 1936," in Samuel I. Rosenman, ed., *The Public Papers of Franklin D. Roosevelt, Vol. 5: The People Approve,1936* (New York: Random House, 1938), 67.

28. *Los Angeles Times*, "House Overrides Roosevelt's Veto of Soldiers' Bonus," January 25, 1936, 1; "Appeal Goes to Veterans," January 28, 1936, 2; and "Bonus Bill Swept Through Senate With Veto Upset," January 28, 1936, 1; "Neutrality Bill Given Approval of House Group,"*Washington Post*, January 28, 1936, 2; "Nearly 200,000 Veterans Get Federal Jobs," *National Tribune*, January 9, 1936; and "Bonus Bill Becomes Law," *NYT*, January 28, 1936, 1. Frank R. Kent, "That Great Game of Politics," reprinted in *Los Angeles Times*, January 31, 1936.

29. Veteran organizations' statement in "Neutrality Bill Given Approval of House Group," *Washington Post*, January 28, 1936, 2. See also "Legion Head Fixes Policy," *Los Angeles Times*, April 3, 1935, A1, and Ortiz, "Soldier Citizens," 193–221. On FDR's foreign policy and neutrality legislation, see Robert A. Divine, *The Reluctant Belligerent: American Entry Into World War II*, 2nd ed. (New York: McGraw-Hill, 1979); Wayne S. Cole, *America First: The Battle Against Intervention, 1940–41* (Madison: University of Wisconsin Press, 1953), *Roosevelt and the Isolationists, 1932–1945* (Lincoln: University of Nebraska Press, 1983), and *Gerald P. Nye and American Foreign Relations* (Minneapolis: University of Minnesota Press, 1962); Robert Dallek, *Franklin D. Roosevelt and American Foreign Policy, 1932–1945* (New York: Oxford University Press, 1979); and Justus D. Doenecke, *Anti-Intervention: A Bibliographic Introduction to Isolationism and Pacifism From World War I to the Early Cold War* (New York: Garland, 1987), and *Storm on the Horizon: The Challenge to American Intervention, 1939–1941* (Lanham, MD: Rowman and Littlefield, 2000).

30. Hines and Van Zandt in Dickson and Allen, *The Bonus Army*, 254, and Mason, *VFW*, 95. VFW charter in Mason, *VFW*, 92 and *Foreign Service* (July 1936): 9, 38–39.

31. Louis Johnson to Stephen Early, January 11, 1936, in "Louis A. Johnson," PPF 2822, FDRL.

32. "Two Records: Hoover vs. Roosevelt," in "American Legion, 1936," OF 64, Box 2, FDRL, and Louis Johnson to Monroe Johnson, January 31, 1936, in "American Legion, 1934–1938," PPF 350, FDRL.

33. *Foreign Service* issues from March through July 1936 contained instructions and stories on the VFW's efforts. Legion Post No. 8 in "Bonus Blank Data Given," *Los Angeles Times*, February 1, 1936, 4. VFW Post 768 in *Foreign Service* (July 1936): 38. Bonus application totals in *National Tribune*, May 14, 1936, and Veterans Administration Report, Frank T. Hines to the White House, November 14, 1936, in "Veterans Administration, 1936," OF 8, Box 1, FDRL. "Farley Sees Early Bonus Payments," *Los Angeles Times*, May 24, 1936, 1.

34. John Thomas Taylor, "Got a Housing Problem?," *American Legion Monthly* (May 1936): 20–21, 68–69; *Foreign Service* (March 1936): 4; (April 1936): 9; and (May 1936): 9; and "Veterans Will Urge Spending of the Bonds," *Los Angeles Times*, May 24, 1936, 10.

35. Percentages add to more than 100 because respondents to the poll could pick all that applied. American Legion News Service Press Release, January 6, 1936, in "American Legion, 1936," OF 64, Box 2, FDRL; "Bonus Payment Would Aid Many," *National Tribune*, January 9, 1936; and "Bonus Dreams Are Coming True," *Los Angeles Times*, February 23, 1936, I4.

36. Post Office figures in James Farley to Marvin McIntyre, June 30, 1936, in "Soldiers' Bonus, 1936, 1942," OF 95c, Box 3, FDRL, June through November figures in memo from

Frank T. Hines to Marvin McIntyre, November 14, 1936, in "Veterans' Administration, 1936," OF 8, Box 1, FDRL. Other figures from Lester G. Telser, "The Veterans' Bonus of 1936," *Journal of Post Keynesian Economics* 26.2 (2004): 227–243.

37. This and the preceding paragraph rely heavily on the analysis and data in Telser, "The Veterans' Bonus of 1936." On financial gains in the summer of 1936 and 1936 figures, see Daniels, *The Bonus March*, 240, and Thelma Liesner, ed., *Economic Statistics, 1900–1983 : United Kingdom, United States of America, France, Germany, Italy, Japan* (New York: Facts on File Books, 1985). Quarterly reports in "Black Ink," *Time*, November 2, 1936, 55.

38. See note 20 to the Introduction on the "second" New Deal.

39. Veteran Administration information in Keene, *Doughboys*, 201. WPA totals in *Foreign Service* (July 1936): 5.

40. Ray Murphy, "The National Commander's Column," *The National Legionnaire* (April 1936): 1, 4. Stephen Early to Jim Farley, April 22, 1936, and Farley to Early, April 24, 1936, in "American Legion, 1936," OF 64, Box 2, FDRL. Van Zandt statement to VFW posts in *National Tribune*, June 11, 1936.

41. For earlier veteran partisan mobilizations, see Pencak, *For God and Country*, 113–114. Louis Johnson Memorandum for Mr. Early, July 24, 1936, and list of members on Veterans' Advisory Committee stationary such as that found in Louis Johnson to Stephen Early, October 15, 1936, in Stephen Early Papers, "Johnson, Louis (1936–1940)," Box 8, FDRL.

42. "Veterans: 1932 versus 1936" in "Vertical File: Campaign Literature, 1936, Democratic Veterans Advisory Committee," in FDRL.

43. For Republican ticket, see Schlesinger, *Politics of Upheaval*, 561–644. Republican tactics in Memo from Louis Johnson and DNC veterans Advisory Committee to all veteran state chairman (copied to Steve Early), September 18, 1936, in Stephen Early Papers, "Johnson, Louis (1936–1940)," Box 8, FDRL.

44. "Their Service in War" and "Franklin D. Roosevelt as Soldier and Peacemaker" in "Vertical File: Campaign Literature, 1936, Democratic Veterans Advisory Committee," in FDRL. Memo from Louis Johnson and DNC veterans Advisory Committee to all veteran state chairman (copied to Steve Early) and text of speech for use, September 18, 1936, in Stephen Early Papers, "Johnson, Louis (1936–1940)," Box 8, FDRL. Pamphlet "Veterans Have Won *Full Recognition* Under the New Deal" in "Vertical File: Campaign Literature, 1936, Democratic Veterans Advisory Committee," in FDRL.

45. Louis Johnson to Stephen Early, August 19, 1936, and Early to Johnson, August 27, 1936, in "Louis Johnson," PPF 2022, FDRL. Louis Johnson to Stephen Early, September 16, 1936; Johnson to Early, September 25, 1936; and Early to Johnson, September 29, 1936; in the Stephen Early Papers, "Johnson, Louis (1936–1940)," Box 8, FDRL.

46. Reports in Louis Johnson to Stephen Early, October 15, 21, and 28, 1936, in Stephen Early Papers, "Johnson, Louis (1936–1940)," Box 8, FDRL.

47. For the best accounts of the New Deal Dissidents and the Union Party's bid for the presidency in 1936, see Brinkley, *Voices of Protest*, 242–268; Schlesinger, *The Politics of Upheaval*, 550–561; Bennett, *Demagogues in the Depression*, and David Horowitz, *Beyond Left and Right: Insurgency and the Establishment* (Urbana: University of Illinois Press, 1997). "No Man's Land," *Time*, June 29, 1936, 10–11.

48. Brinkley, *Voices of Protest*, 242–268. *Time*, "No Man's Land," June 29, 1936, 10–11, and "Hopper," November 2, 1936, 10–11. Brinkley quotations, *Voices of Protest*, 242.

49. For election results, see Kennedy, *Freedom From Fear*, 285–287, and Michael Parish, *The Anxious Decades*, 559–563. Krock and Farley statements in "Poll Sets Record," *NYT*, November 4, 1936, 1.

50. Detailed election results from Dave Leip's Atlas of U.S. Presidential Elections, http://uselectionatlas.org/, accessed August 23, 2008. For the fall of the New Deal Dissidents, see Brinkley, *Voices of Protest*, 242–268.

51. *National Tribune*, May 7, June 18, November 12, 1936. For Republican progressives' stances in the 1936 election, see Ronald L. Feinman, *Twilight of Progressivism: The Western Republican Senators and the New Deal* (Baltimore: Johns Hopkins University Press, 1981), 91–117.

52. For the best discussion of the 1936 campaign, see Schlesinger, *Politics of Upheaval*, 561–644.

53. Many historians and political scientists have pointed to the improved economic conditions as one of the causes of Roosevelt's victory, but new work by political scientists Christopher Achen and Larry Bartels contends that voters in 1936 made their decisions on the basis not of ideological criteria but of their short-term economic interests. Achen and Bartels explain their findings: "the voters made no judgment about the ideological appropriateness of New Deal policies . . . they cared about 1936 conditions." In other words, the substantial gains in real income throughout the United States in the summer and fall of 1936 translated into a Democratic rout and to long-term partisan identification with the party of Roosevelt. See Christopher H. Achen and Larry Bartels, "Myopic Retrospection and Party Alignment in the Great Depression," unpublished paper presented at the Annual Meeting of the American Political Science Association, August 26, 2008, cited with authors' approval and in my possession.

54. For the best discussion of FDR, his attitudes about spending, and the impact of the Roosevelt Recession on contemporary liberalism, see Alan Brinkley, *The End of Reform*.

CONCLUSION

1. On the GI Bill's origins, see Ross, *Preparing for Ulysses*; Bennett, *When Dreams Came True*; Keene, *Doughboys*, 205–214; Amenta and Skocpol, "Redefining the New Deal"; Olson, *The GI Bill, the Veterans, and the Colleges*, 3–24; Frydl, *The GI Bill*; and Mettler, "The Creation of the GI Bill of Rights of 1944," and *Soldiers to Citizens*.

2. FDR, Fireside Chat on the Progress of the War and the Plans for Peace, July 28, 1943," in Samuel I. Rosenman, ed., *The Public Papers and Addresses of Franklin D. Roosevelt, Vol. 12* (New York: Harper and Brothers, 1950), 333. Ross, *Preparing for Ulysses*, 52–69; Olson, *The GI Bill, the Veterans, and the Colleges*, 4–10, and Mettler, "The Creation of the GI Bill of Rights of 1944," 349–357.

3. Preliminary Report to the President of the United States from the Armed Forces Committee on Post War Educational Opportunities for Service Personnel, July 30, 1943, in "Armed Forces Committee on Post War Educational Opportunities," OF 5182, FDRL. Ross, *Preparing for Ulysses*, 89–94; Olson, *The GI Bill, the Veterans, and the Colleges*, 10–15; and Mettler, "The Creation of the GI Bill of Rights of 1944," 357–359.

4. Keene, *Doughboys*, 208; Dickson and Allen, *The Bonus Army*, 269; Olson, *The GI Bill, the Veterans, and the Colleges*, 14–15; and Mettler, "The Creation of the GI Bill of Rights of 1944," 359–360.

5. "Pensions Again," *Time*, December 8, 1941, 18–19.

6. Rumer, *The American Legion*, 277–282; "Bullets, also Ballots," *Time*, November 9, 1942, 19–20. Soldier poll in "What They Think," *Time*, February 7, 1944, 72–73.

7. *NYT*, "Legion Will Drive for New Veterans," May 5, 1943, 7; "Legion Roll Sets Record," July 24, 1943, 14.

8. "The Legion and New Blood," *Time*, October 4, 1943, 24–25; Mettler, "The Creation of the GI Bill of Rights of 1944," 361, 363; and Ross, *Preparing for Ulysses*, 77.

9. "V.F.W.'s 150,000," *Time*, October 11, 1943, 18.

10. *NYT*, "Veterans' Future Main Topic of VFW," September 25, 1943, 17; "VFW Convention Here to Meet Tomorrow," September 27, 1943, 22; "World Police Held Desire of Fighters," September 29, 1943, 42; and "VFW Would Draft War Plant Youth," October 1, 1943, 13. VFW Commander Carl J. Schoeninger to FDR, November 8, 1943, and "Ten Point Postwar Veteran Welfare Program Adopted by 44th National Encampment of the VFW" in "VFW, 1943–45," OF 84, FDRL. Mason, *The VFW*, 102–103. In early October, a joint federal/private approach to veterans' employment was announced by the Selective Service. Seven government agencies would work collaboratively with the Selective Service: the Veterans' Administration, the U.S. Employment Service, the Veterans' Employment Service (special group in USES), the Vocational Rehabilitation and Training Division (within the Federal Security Agency), the Civil Service Commission, Army Emergency Relief, and the U.S. Armed Forces Institute. Joining the federal agencies in the push for reemployment of veterans were the Red Cross and fifteen other labor and civic organizations, including the AFL and the CIO, the Legion, DAV, the VFW, the Kiwanis, the Lions, and the U.S. Chamber of Commerce. Returning veterans would return to their local draft boards, which would then utilize all of the agencies and organizations to get them their old jobs, when possible, or new ones, if necessary. See "Draft Heads Map Postwar Job Help," *NYT*, October 10, 1943, 7.

11. *NYT*, "Bonus of 15 Billion Is Proposed by VFW," December 21, 1943, 17; "Opposes High Pay on Mustering Out," January 13, 1944, 11; Ross, *Preparing for Ulysses*, 84–88.

12. Rumer, *The American Legion*, 244. Ross, *Preparing for Ulysses*, 98–102; Frydl, *The GI Bill*, 152–159; and Olson, *The GI Bill, the Veterans, and the Colleges*, 15–18.

13. Statement of Warren H. Atherton before the Senate Finance Committee, January 14, 1944 in "Veterans Welfare—Jim Boyle, GI Bill," ALNHL; Letter from Legion Commander Warren Atherton to all post commanders, February 12, 1944, and suggested radio interview in "Veterans Welfare—GI Bill—Servicemen's Readjustment Act," folder 3, ALNHL; and Memorandum to Department Adjutants, April 3, 1944, in "Veterans Welfare—GI Bill—Servicemen's Readjustment Act," folder 3, ALNHL. Ross, *Preparing for Ulysses*, 121–124; Olson, *The GI Bill, the Veterans, and the Colleges*, 18–19; Frydl, *The GI Bill*, 177–191 and Mettler, "The Creation of the GI Bill of Rights of 1944," 360–365. For full range of publicity efforts including backroom pressure on Congress, see David Camelon, "I Saw the GI Bill Written, parts 1–3," *The American Legion Magazine*, September, October, and November 1949, especially October, 55–56.

14. Letter from Omar Ketchum, Millard Rice, Frank Haley, and W. M. Floyd to Senator Bennett C. Clark, dated February 16, 1944, in "Veteran Welfare—GI Bill—Serviceman's Readjustment Act," folder 16, ALNHL, and copy of Semimonthly Report to National and Department Officers on Legislative Affairs, dated February 17, 1944, in "Veteran Welfare—GI Bill—Serviceman's Readjustment Act," folder 12, ALNHL.

15. "Trillions for Bonuses," *Time*, March 13, 1944, 12; *NYT*, "$4500 Bonus Asked for Armed Forces," March 7, 1944, 10. Ross, *Preparing for Ulysses*, 103–105, and Stelle in Bennett, *When Dreams Came True*, 147.

16. James E. MacMillan, "Father of the GI Bill: Ernest W. McFarland and Veterans' Legislation," *Journal of Arizona History* 35.4 (1994): 367; Bennett, *When Dreams Came True*, 145–148. Much later, a VFW official suggested in correspondence to the Legion that

Ketchum had been acting without the approval of the full legislative committee in early February 1944. Merle F. Hopper reminisced that "we gave Ketchum Hell for signing" the letter to Clark. Merle F. Hopper, VFW National Legislative Director, to Preston J. Moore, Legion National Commander, dated November 19, 1958, in "Veteran Welfare—GI Bill—Serviceman's Readjustment Act," folder 12, ALNHL.

17. National Publicity Division, America Legion press release of February 23, 1944, and amended draft of same, in "Veterans Welfare—GI Bill—Servicemen's Readjustment Act," folder 3, ALNHL.

18. Copy of letter from Millard W. Rice to Senator Walter F. George, February 22, 1944, in "Veterans Welfare—GI Bill—Servicemen's Readjustment Act," folder 3, ALNHL; "Disabled Group Fears Long Delay on Claims Under Centralized Service for Veterans," *NYT*, March 9, 1944, 34; and Mason, *The VFW*, 108.

19. "'GI Bill of Rights' Passed by Senate," *NYT*, March 25, 1944, 3; Ross, *Preparing for Ulysses*, 105–116; Frydl, *The GI Bill*, 180–188; and Mettler, "The Creation of the GI Bill of Rights of 1944," 366–367.

20. Atherton, Roosevelt, and Maverick in Olson, *The GI Bill, the Veterans, and the Colleges*, 20–21; McFarland in James E. MacMillan, "Father of the GI Bill," 359, 363. Weiss in *Congressional Record*, 78th Congress, 2nd Session, Vol. 90, pt. 10 (June 13, 1944, to September 8, 1944): A3008.

21. Lane in *Congressional Record*, 78th Congress, 2nd Session, Vol. 90, pt. 3 (March 22, 1944, to May 11, 1944): 3285; Kearney in *Congressional Record*, 78th Congress, 2nd Session, Vol. 90, pt.4 (May 11, 1944, to June 23, 1944): 4453; D'Alesandro in *Congressional Record*, 78th Congress, 2nd Session, Vol. 90, pt. 10 (June 13, 1944, to September 8, 1944): A3363; and Weiss, *Congressional Record*, 78th Congress, 2nd Session, Vol. 90, pt. 10 (June 13, 1944, to September 8, 1944): A3008.

22. Frydl, *The GI Bill*, 188–190; Ross, *Preparing for Ulysses*, 116–118; and Mettler, "The Creation of the GI Bill of Rights of 1944," 366. FDR, "The President Signs the GI Bill of Rights, June 22, 1944," in Samuel I. Rosenman, ed., *The Public Papers and Addresses of Franklin D. Roosevevlt, Vol. 13* (New York: Harper and Brothers, 1950), 180–182, and "Roosevelt Signs GI Bill of Rights," *NYT*, June 23, 1944, 1.

23. Olson, *The GI Bill, the Veterans, and the Colleges*, 44–56, and Mettler, *Soldiers to Citizens*, 6–8, 41–105.

24. Ibid.

25. On veterans' political participation, see Mettler, *Soldiers to Citizens*, 39–135. For the limitations of the GI Bill, see Onkst, "'First a Negro . . . Incidentally a Veteran'"; Canaday, "Building a Straight State"; Mettler (on women's exclusion), *Soldiers to Citizens*, 144–162; Katznelson, *When Affirmative Action Was White*, 113–142; and Cohen, *A Consumer's Republic*, 137–173.

26. *NYT*, "Roosevelt and Dewey Evenly Matched, Recent Elections Show, Gallup Poll Finds," May 21, 1944, 37; "Is It Time to Change? Seen as the Chief Issue," November 5, 1944, E3; "Soldier Vote Seen Key in 16 States," November 4, 1944, 12; "Factors Known and Unknown, in This Election," November 5, 1944, E4; "Election Key Sensed in 12 States," October 2, 1944, 11. For the best discussion of the election of 1944, see James MacGregor Burns, *Roosevelt: The Soldier of Freedom* (New York: Harcourt Brace Jovanovich, 1970), 497–531.

27. *NYT*, "Truman Puts Peace in Veterans Hands," August 24, 1944, 13; "Bricker, Truman Urge Veteran Aid," September 19, 1944, 14; and "Bricker Assails Roosevelt Vetoes," October 10, 1944, 16.

28. *NYT*, "Roosevelt Strong in War Vote Tally," November 8, 1944, 1; "War Vote Here 72% for Roosevelt, 12% Higher Than Among Civilians," November 9, 1944, 1; "Philadelphia GI's Voted 2 to 1," November 29, 1944, 11; "Service Ballots Put at 4,400,000 in Last Election," December 10, 1944, 1.

29. *NYT*, "Legion Will Debate War Enrollments," September 18, 1944, 6; "Legion Is Pictured Mighty in Politics," May 22, 1944, 13; *Time*, "The Next Forty Years," July 10, 1944, 60; "Peace Campaign," December 3, 1945, 23; *Foreign Service* (October 1945): 4 and Mason, *The VFW*, 115. Amy Porter, "The Legion Eats 'Em Alive," *Collier's* (October 5, 1946): 18–19, 52–53. The Legion archives hold a series of bitter correspondence between the VFW and the Legion over credit for the GI Bill. This correspondence is from 1949, 1959, 1969, and 1991–92! See GI Bill folders in ALNHL.

30. *NYT*, "New Veterans Organize," December 11, 1944, 12; "The Veteran," April 15, 1945, 7; *Time*, "The Next Forty Years," July 10, 1944, 60; "Peace Campaign," December 3, 1945, 23. Frydl, *The GI Bill*, 143. For good discussions of the AVC in particular and World War II veterans more generally, see Robert Francis Saxe, *Settling Down: World War II Veterans Challenge to the Postwar Consensus* (New York: Palgrave Macmillan, 2007).

POSTSCRIPT

1. *The New Republic*, "The Progressive and the Veteran," 113.17 (October 22, 1945): 515, 517.

2. *The New Republic*, "The Progressive and the Veteran," 517. For the postwar period, see Brinkley, *The End of Reform*; Cohen, *A Consumer's Republic*; and Meg Jacobs, *Pocketbook Politics: Economic Citizenship in Twentieth-Century America* (Princeton: Princeton University Press, 2007). For a good overview of conservatism, see Bruce Schulman and Julian Zelizer, eds., *Rightward Bound: Making America Conservative in the 1970s* (Cambridge, MA: Harvard University Press, 2008).

3. Anna Quindlen, "Because It's Right," *Newsweek*, March 31, 2008, 68; "What the GIs Deserve," *Washington Post*, June 29, 2008, B06.

4. *NYT*, "Clinton and McCain Differ on Iraq Strategy at Veterans' Meeting," August 21, 2007, 16; "Obama Sees a 'Complete Failure' in Iraq," August 22, 2007, 11; "In Bush's Words: Resist the Allure of Retreat,'" August 23, 2007, 8. For the full text of Obama speech, see Obama "Organizing For America" Web site, "Senator Obama Addresses VFW Conference, August 21, 2007," http://my.barackobama.com/page/community/post_group/ObamaHQ/CJ8s (accessed May 3, 2009).

5. David R. Francis, "The Economic Stimulus Package: How Does Spending Help?," *Christian Science Monitor*, February 4, 2008, 15.

Index

About the Author

STEPHEN R. ORTIZ is an assistant professor of history at Bowling Green State University in Ohio.